LATIN POETS AND ITALIAN GODS

THE ROBSON CLASSICAL LECTURES

ELAINE FANTHAM

Latin Poets and
Italian Gods

UNIVERSITY OF TORONTO PRESS
Toronto Buffalo London

© University of Toronto Press Incorporated 2009
Toronto Buffalo London
www.utppublishing.com
Printed in Canada

ISBN 978-1-4426-4059-7 (cloth)

Printed on acid-free, 100% post-consumer recycled paper with
vegetable-based inks.

Library and Archives Canada Cataloguing in Publication

Fantham, Elaine
  Latin poets and Italian gods / Elaine Fantham.

  (Robson classical lectures)
  Includes bibliographical references and index.
  ISBN 978-1-4426-4059-7

  1. Latin poetry – History and criticism.   2. Gods, Roman, in literature.
  3. Goddesses, Roman, in literature.   4. Rome – Religion.   I. Title.
  II. Series: Robson classical lectures

  PA6029.R4F36 2009   871'.01093820211   C2009-903769-6

University of Toronto Press acknowledges the financial assistance to its
publishing program of the Canada Council for the Arts and the Ontario
Arts Council.

  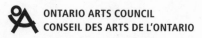

University of Toronto Press acknowledges the financial support for its
publishing activities of the Government of Canada through the Book
Publishing Industry Development Program (BPIDP).

Contents

Preface

The form of this book requires an explanation, if not an extenuation. I embarked on preparing the three Robson Lectures of 2003 intending to demonstrate how the deities inhabiting the Italian landscape and primitive rural Rome were represented in Augustan poetry; my hope was to ground discussion of some key passages in Virgil and in Ovid's *Fasti* in republican allusions to these originally rustic cults, and draw on the limited epigraphic evidence for individual worshippers and their attitudes. Thus the gods of place, including the nymphs of sacred waters and the gods identified with rivers, were my main focus, along with the freer and more mobile spirits of the open land beyond cultivation, the ancient Faunus and the gods Pan and Silvanus, who seem to have displaced him as early as our earliest literary evidence.

For Varro, for Virgil,[1] and for the Greek immigrant Dionysius of Halicarnassus, Italy was the best and most bountiful of all countries; Dionysius enumerates Italy's richness in trees, in grain, in cattle – the wheat of Campania, the olives of Messapia (modern Calabria), the vineyards of Tyrrhenia (Etruria), and the Alban and Falernian regions – its grazing for horses and cattle with rich, well-watered grasslands, and its glades; and returning to his first claim, the forests, most wonderful of all (Dionysius of Halicarnassus 1.37). Nor is that all. Dionysius moves on, as we shall do, to Italy's waters, especially her hot springs 'affording most pleasant baths and cures for chronic ailments.' And gods were always present and propitious: just as primitive Italy had been the peaceful kingdom of the exiled Saturn, conceived of as god of grain crops, so the site of Rome itself was once the hill of Saturn.[2]

Because Rome was already a semi-sophisticated urbanized community in the time of our first literary witnesses, Plautus and Ennius, at the turn of the second century BCE, there is a constant pressure to peer behind the written evidence, to second-guess the earlier Roman beliefs and attitudes which led to, for example, the creation of special priests (*flamines*) for Flora and Pomona, the rite of throwing the straw dummies called Argei into the sacred river Tiber, the naming of Rome's earliest priests as Bridge-builders (*Pontifices*), even the creation of a shrine and festival of Fons. The truth is that this layer of Roman thought cannot be discovered like historical facts, only made the subject of speculation, and I came sadly to the conclusion that I had no divinatory skills to improve on any of the existing theories. Instead I have tried to outline the evidence for the survival of these cults and contrast the patterns of Roman worship of country gods like Pan, or the nymphs of Italy's springs, with the fuller picture left to us by such cult in Greece. As Burkert puts it in *Greek Religion*, 'the idea that rivers are gods and springs divine nymphs is deeply rooted not only in poetry, but also in belief and ritual; the worship of these deities is limited only by the fact that they are inseparably identified with a specific locality. Each city worships its river or spring.' Greek poets represent nymphs from the time of Hesiod and Homer and the later *Homeric Hymn to Aphrodite*, which offers a vivid image of their idealized existence: 'The deep-breasted mountain nymphs who inhabit this great and holy mountain shall bring [Aeneas] up. They rank neither with mortals nor with immortals; long indeed do they live, eating heavenly food and treading the lovely dance among the immortals, and with them the Sileni and the sharp-eyed slayer of Argus [Hermes] mate in the depth of pleasant caves; but at their birth pines or high-topped oaks spring up with them upon the fruitful earth' (*Homeric Hymn to Aphrodite* 257–65). These nymphs are hamadryads, and this passage is the first evidence for their supposed death along with their trees; but the association of Greek nymphs with dancing and with the nursing of young children is common, and counts, along with their nubility and sexual freedom, among the defining aspects of nymphs listed by Jennifer Larson in *Greek Nymphs: Myth, Cult, Lore*.[3]

Neither in Greece nor in Italy were Satyrs and Sileni worshipped, but if Roman Mercury loses some of the associations of Hermes with the wilderness, Hermes' son Pan⁴ seems to be established early in Rome, combining with Silvanus (who has no Greek counterpart) to upstage the role of Faunus. Faunus too does not seem to have been the object of individual worship, and is met only in legend and historical record. With Janus, Jupiter, Mars, Picus, Tiberinus, and Hercules, Faunus is one of the seven gods whose worship Augustine (*De Civitate Dei* 4.23, relying on Varro) attributes to Romulus himself; and Faunus makes vignette appearances in Augustan poetry as a recognized alias of Pan. Tiberinus, the god of the Tiber, is similarly more honoured in poetry than by surviving epigraphic evidence. As a transition from this preliminary discussion of the gods of the land to the fuller study of their roles in Virgil and Ovid, I have included the divergent evidence of Tibullus and his friend or acquaintance Horace (cf. Horace *Epistles* 1.5), who outlived him.

For the book, I remodelled my original oral presentation of the Italian country gods in *Aeneid* 7–12 to include a brief discussion of how these divinities appear in the *Eclogues* and the *Georgics*. This reworking seemed to me necessary in order for us to understand where Virgil was coming from in making his imaginative reconstruction of prehistoric Latium and the legendary community of Evander's Rome in *Aeneid* 7 and 8 and more intermittently in *Aeneid* 9–12.⁵ But where the divinities mentioned in the *Eclogues* are strongly coloured by Virgil's desire to reflect Theocritus and his Hellenistic models, I believe Virgil consciously selected and shaped the religious references in the *Georgics* to stress the native Italian tradition.

The third of my Robson Lectures confined itself to Ovid's *Fasti*, so replete with echoes and reconstructions of primitive Roman worship that any treatment can only be selective. Like Ovid I have focused on the cults situated in Rome itself, and briefly traced echoes in lesser poets of Ovid's presentation of Tiber and Faunus.

What needs more justification may be the second half of this work, which I think of as the right-hand panel of a diptych based on the contrast between the devotion and will to believe common to the *Aeneid* and *Fasti* and the sense of detached fantasy with which Ovid treats non-Roman myths in the *Metamorphoses*. Only when the *Metamorphoses* reach Italy itself, as Hugh Parker has shown in *Greek Gods in Italy in Ovid's* Fasti: *A Greater Greece*, does Ovid allow himself to identify with a mythical figure – one he probably had to re-create for the purpose. Ovid's Vertumnus and Pomona, like his interview with Flora in *Fasti* 5, can be contrasted to the amoral, even turbulent behaviour of Greek rivers like Alpheius and Acheloüs and the lustful exotic nymphs of Mysia (the ravishers of Hylas first described by Propertius) and Caria (Salmacis in *Metamorphoses* 4).

The next two chapters each take their starting point from landscapes, but from cultivated landscapes rather than wild nature. In chapter 5, I consider a foreign god uniquely planted in the cultivated landscape of the Italian kitchen garden and orchard, the god Priapus. From Catullus, the first Latin poet who acknowledges him (and even offers some sort of dedication), all Latin poets and agricultural writers of the Augustan age and first century of our era spare a moment of attention to Priapus, and the god becomes the patron of his own genre, with the collection called *Priapea*. There can hardly be question of devout worship, but the god's essentially comic nature and his role as an intrusive figure in the garden seem to have appealed to every poet in all the genres, including the same Ovid in the same poem, the *Fasti*, which treated other cults with unalloyed respect. Priapus may have been the relentless pursuer of the bisexual and promiscuous Encolpius, but outside the *Satyricon* he seems to have served as the clown in Latin poetry, as he no doubt was in mime.

Statius, the subject of chapter 6, is harder to characterize. Here is a Latin poet of Greek family from Naples, bilingual and intensively schooled in sophisticated Hellenistic poetry: this poet introduces nymphs and river-gods into both his high heroic epic *Thebaid* and the elegant contemporary epideictic of his *Silvae*. The semi-divine inhabitants of the natural landscape of forest and stream in the *Thebaid* reappear in the *Silvae* as furnishings for the artificial landscapes of luxury. Within the increasingly doom-laden saga of Thebes, a case can be made for treating the laments of the Nemean nymphs for their woodland home, like the grief of Ismenus' family for their lost child Crenaeus and the river-god's furious vengeance, as a kind of light relief. But it also makes sense to credit the same function, that of a foil to human activity, to the divine supernumeraries who populate the villa grounds of Statius' wealthy patrons. This poet writes from a long and bicultural literary tradition, as a courtier ready to give colour to whatever figures will animate his scenery; and these nymphs and satyrs are decorative, contributing to the celebratory mood of these ecphrastic poems like an opera chorus or corps de ballet.

I hope, then, that together the book's two parts, each grouping three chapters, will provide a better sense of what was gained and lost when Rome's increasingly cosmopolitan culture moved beyond Augustus' renewal or re-creation of Italian religion to replace piety with fantasy and emotional detachment from Italy's countryside and its gods.

When I retired from Princeton to come home to my family in Toronto, it was a great pleasure to be welcomed back to my old department at the University of Toronto, and most of my acknowledgments are to my old and new friends there. Three successive chairpersons, Brad Inwood, John Magee, and Alison Keith, all took pains to make me feel at home (though the old location in the Rabbit Hutch next to the mini-observtaory in Hart House Circle had been demolished, and we would leave the comfortable Victorian 97 St George Street, for the marble halls and pseudo–Burne Jones stained glass of the former Faculty of Domestic Science). I owe to my colleagues the honour of giving the Robson Lectures at Victoria College in 2003, and to Alison Keith in particular excellent guidance in converting the lectures and exploring the themes of my three supplementary chapters. Through Alison I was able to benefit from the expert and tactful suggestions of K. Sara Myers, of the University of Virginia, and to draw on the very professional editing and checking of Dr Jonathan Tracy. It was a pleasure to discuss problems and points of view with all three scholars. But my debts to Toronto and its University are broader and deeper than I can formulate in words. In heartfelt thanks I would like to dedicate this study to the Department of Classics: long may it flourish!

Elaine Fantham

Notes

1 Cf. Varro *Res Rusticae* 1.2.3–10, and the so-called *Laudes Italiae* of Virgil, *Georgics* 2.136–76.
2 Cf. Dionysius of Halicarnassus 1.36 and again 38; *Aeneid* 8.319–25 and 357.
3 Especially chap. 1. On the second prevailing sense of *nymphe*, bride or girl ripe for marriage, see chap. 1.1, and for Nymphs in the landscape, 1.2.
4 The classic discussion of Pan is P. Borgeaud's *Recherches sur le dieu Pan*, translated by Atlass and Redfield as *The Cult of Pan in Ancient Greece*. See especially chap. 3.
5 I must mention here a book which has given emotional and imaginative depth to my perhaps sentimental response, the 2008 novel *Lavinia*, written as the princess's autobiography by the anthropologist and novelist Ursula K. Le Guin. Le Guin stresses how much she owes to Virgil (whose not-yet-born shade appears to Lavinia in the book). Her major change in narrative form is the omission of the homerically intrusive Olympians.

PART I

HONOURING THE ITALIAN GODS

CHAPTER ONE

Rustica Numina: The Country Gods of Italy and Their Reception in Roman Poetry

Early in Ovid's great history of the world, the *Metamorphoses*, Jupiter loses patience with the human race; but he still hesitates to consume the world in fire, because he wants to preserve it for a different and more innocent kind of creation. He explains to a dutiful and unquestioning divine senate, 'There are my demigods, those spirits of the countryside, Nymphs, Fauns and Satyrs, and the mountain-dwelling Silvani: since we don't yet think them ready for promotion to the sky, we should at least let them occupy the lands we assigned them!'

> sunt mihi semidei, sunt rustica numina, Nymphae
> Faunique Satyrique et monticolae Silvani
> quos quoniam caeli nondum dignamur honore
> quas dedimus, certe terras habitare sinamus.
>   (Ovid *Met*.1.192–5)

Instead Jupiter invokes Neptune's aid to drown the guilty human race. The flood comes and goes without any further account being taken of the demigods, but they do survive in Ovid's mythical history – witness the many identified nymphs who provide the only sexual relief for Apollo and Jupiter, and, collectively, for the fauns and satyrs. In fact Ovid reports the tale from an onlooker who had travelled to Lycia and was shown an altar. After the automatic invocation 'be well-disposed,' he asks whether this is an altar of the naiads or Faunus, or some local god (*indigenaeque dei, Met.* 6.329–30). It is actually an altar of Latona, and after telling the story of her transformation of the inhospitable peasants into frogs, the poet hears from another local of the cruel death of the satyr Marsyas, flayed by Apollo. Marsyas – whose statue near the Comitium in the Roman forum symbolized popular liberty[1] – is mourned by his own community: the country-dwelling Fauni, spirits of the woods, and his brother satyrs and nymphs all weep for him, along with the herdsmen who pastured their fleecy flocks and horned oxen in those mountains. Have the demigods been driven far away from Italy into the remote mountains of Asia Minor? No, for they reappear on Italian soil as the persistent suitors of the Latin nymph Pomona, during the almost historical reign of Proca: 'Was there any trick the Satyrs, those dancing lads, did not try, or the Pans, with their horns wreathed in pine, or Silenus, always younger than his years, or the god [Priapus] who scares away thieves with his sickle and erect member, did not try to get possession of her?'

> quid non et Satyri, saltatibus apta iuventus,
> fecere et pinu praecincti cornua Panes
> Silenusque suis semper iuvenilior annis,
> quique deus fures vel falce vel inguine terret,
> ut poterentur ea?
> (14.637–41)

But what have Ovid's fantasies, these *fabulae*, to do with the daily life of the Roman countryside or the cults practised by its peasants? We will see in due course that Fauni at least have a strong connection with *fari*, the root of *fa-bulae*, but I would like to argue that Ovid's clustering of nymphs and Fauni with satyrs and Pans and Silvani in these pastoral settings deliberately undermines the real-life standing of spirits honoured by Italic country-folk by applying two devices – the pluralization that trivializes and renders anonymous, and association with creatures taken over by pastoral and other genres from the Greek imaginary.

What I would like to do in these pages is to leave aside the great Olympians who were honoured in the countryside, passing over great Ceres and Bacchus, worshipped in temples in towns and cities; instead I want to focus on truly local spirits, whom the countryman could worship in his own fields or by his spring, and worship individually with humble offerings. Our freeborn countryman might not have the spare time to go into town for formal worship, because he was kept busy; others, like Virgil's Tityrus (a slave) or Moeris (*Ecl.* 1.26–35; 9.2–6), could go into town only when permitted or actually sent by the master.

I want first to go as far back as our surviving texts and inscriptions will let us; to reconstruct the natural and supernatural world of these countrymen in central Italy, and provide historical and epigraphic evidence of actual cult offered to the country spirits; and then to show the emotional importance of the same local Italian deities of land and water to the sophisticated poets of the Augustan age. For now it will be enough to evoke the world of the Italian smallholder and the conception of early Rome and Italy cherished as the city itself grew cosmopolitan. I will argue that in some ways this conception was actually enhanced in the high Augustan period, when the countryside was at last being restored to agricultural fertility after fifteen years of civil war. Then we will be ready to sample how our country gods feature in elegy and lyric. We will save for independent discussion (in chap. 2) Virgil's changing shift of emphasis from *Eclogues* to *Georgics* to the welcome given to Aeneas by the gods of Latium in *Aeneid* 7–12, and return to Ovid in chapter 3 for the Roman cults and aitia of the *Fasti*.

I am only too conscious that in focusing on these country gods I am reverting to an aspect of Roman religion that was an object of sentiment, if not wishful thinking, for nineteenth and early twentieth century scholars such as William Warde Fowler (1899, 1911) and Cyril Bailey (1907, 1932, 1935), just as I believe it was for the Augustans. Then and now the educated person might believe and regret that 'we are all too sophisticated to worship such gods, but in the past – or deep in the countryside – honest hardworking men and women had faith in their protection and made what offerings they could.' This is the version of early Rome which Denis Feeney has called with gentle irony 'an admirable piety, linked to an agricultural and communal life, with simple forms of worship directed towards pleasingly primitive *numina* or aniconic deities' (Feeney 1998, 3).

Feeney was anticipated, of course, in a less gentle spirit, by Lucretius, who argued that peasants superstitiously interpreted the echoes heard in the mountains as the music-making of spirits:

The local people imagined that such places were occupied by goat-footed satyrs and nymphs, and said there were Fauni whose night-wandering din and sportive play broke the silence: there were the sounds of stringed lyres and the sweet laments which the flute pours out when played by the fingers of musicians, and the tribe of farmers heard it far and wide when Pan, shaking the pine wreaths of his half-animal head ran his curved lip over the hollow reeds so that the pipe never flagged from pouring out the woodland muse.[2]

> haec loca capripedes satyros nymphasque tenere
> finitimi fingunt et faunos esse loquuntur
> quorum noctivago strepitu ludoque iocanti
> adfirmant vulgo taciturna silentia rumpi,
> chordarumque sonos fieri dulcisque querelas,
> tibia quas fundit digitis pulsata canentum,
> et genus agricolum late sentiscere, cum Pan
> pinea semiferi capitis velamina quassans
> unco saepe labro calamos percurrit hiantis,
> fistula silvestrem ne cesset fundere musam.
> (Lucr. 4.580–9)

Lucretius explained this as he did most religious beliefs. The peasants populated the world of nature with such fantastic and incredible spirits out of sheer terror, 'so as not to think they were left alone to occupy spaces deserted by the gods':

> cetera de genere hoc monstra et portenta loquuntur,
> ne loca deserta ab divis quoque forte putentur
> sola tenere.
> (4.590–2)

But it will be an inevitable corollary of my purpose to trace the gradual withdrawal of such trusting acceptance, and mark the phases in which these spirits protecting actual springs and woodland came to be thought of as quaint superstitions and represented as charming fictions, denaturalized by contamination with post-classical Greek storytelling and the decorative arts.

Let us start with the central Italian landscape. In the last fifty years archaeological land surveys and scientific analysis of strati-fied rock and soil cores have helped to create a different picture of Rome's hinterland in southern Etruria and Latium. A generation ago, in his epoch-making *Landscape and History in Central Italy*,[3] Brian Ward-Perkins (1964) demonstrated that southern Etruria was still so heavily forested in Rome's first few centuries that away from the coast and the course of the Tiber river the new pi-oneering settlements grew up in isolation from each other and continued to function as small units separated by surrounding forest. Only after the Hannibalic war, with the construction of the Via Cassia (around 154 BCE), does archaeological evidence show a spurt of agricultural development in this part of Etruria. The pollen of cultivated plants appears in the soil, and there is evidence of 'a sudden increase in mineral salts resulting from the cutting and burning of a wide strip of woodland on either side of the new road.' Ward-Perkins goes on to trace the effect of de-forestation in the erosion of the light volcanic soil of Etruria, whereby were created the hills and valleys which have made Tuscany beautiful, along with the building up of alluvial pla-teaus.[4] But what I would like us to bear in mind is the remoteness of those early settlers, and – something we have only recently come to realize – the extent to which even less fertile hillsides and woodlands of central Italy were used, if not occupied, by smallholders who eked out the produce of their notional two-*iugera* plots on more fertile land by pasturing sheep and pigs in the *saltus* on what was effectively common land. This mixture of agriculture and pasturage was the pattern for the hamlets of three or four farms that formed at intersections of the few roads, and even for the inhabitants of small towns, who would walk or ride out at dawn to their bit of land; for much of each day, such peas-ants would be alone with the landscape – and its gods.

When Dionysius of Halicarnassus immigrated to Augustan Rome and composed his sprawling account of Roman antiquities, his

focus was on depicting the growth of the early city, its ante-
cedents, foundation, and early kingship; but as a Greek newcomer
he was equally impressed by the sheer fertility of Italy, and follows his praise for the products of its various regions by introducing the roles of the local gods.[5]

It is no wonder therefore that the ancients looked upon this country as
sacred to Saturn, since they esteemed this god to be the giver and fulfiller
of all happiness to mankind ... and since they saw this country abound-
ing in every kind of plenty and every beauty craved by man, and judged
that those places which were congenial to them were most agreeable to
both divine and human beings, they assigned the hills and dales to Pan,
the meadows and flowering places to the nymphs, and the shores and
islands to the deities of the sea. (D.H. 1.38.1)

While Livy does not try to evoke the appearance of the republican city but is content to record only the new monuments and
public works, Dionysius aimed to represent the primitive community as still embedded in rustic landscape and activities, and
his account, however imaginative, is relevant to Augustan ideas of
Rome's landscape setting. Thus he reports the story of Ascanius'
younger brother Silvius, the posthumous child of Aeneas and
Lavinia, who was given his name because the royal swineherd
Tyrrhenus hid Lavinia and the baby in the forest until it was safe
for them to return to the city. Romulus and Remus too were left
to drown away from human settlement and rescued by a swineherd, Faustulus, after being suckled by the wolf in a cave sheltered
by a thick grove sacred to Pan, near the Circus Maximus (D.H.
1.32 and 79). The Augustan image of early Rome is the shepherd
community of the Palatine we know from Livy, with the Capitoline
still uninhabited.[6] When Romulus sets aside the Asylum to attract
new citizens, it is on the ridge between the two peaks of the citadel and future Capitol, known as Between Two Groves[7] because it
was surrounded by thick woods on both sides. While Asylum as
sanctuary was not the regular feature in Italy that it had been in
the Greek world, this must be imagined as a grove sacred to a
deity, most likely the old Italian Saturn. Accounts of the auspices
taken at the site of Rome spell out the clear division, established

by augurs who defined the *templum* or region of divination by using trees as its boundaries, from the untamed *tesca* or wild land outside these limits. Place names often outlive their original descriptive meaning, and the name 'Between Two Groves' survived into the days of Cicero.[8] Dionysius has reconstructed from such details his idea of a primitive settlement, one in which the Latin and Sabine communities must first cut down the forest and drain the marshes before they can pave the forum. And Rome's first Sabine king, Numa, claims to consult a nymph, Egeria, who advises him on his religious institutions.

Given our understanding of Rome's development by the period of the Hannibalic war, it is surprising to learn that Rome erected a shrine to Faunus[9] – the god of the wild and uncultivated land – as late as 196 BCE, when the curule aediles Domitius Ahenobarbus and Scribonius Curio vowed to use the fines they had collected from trespassing ranchers (*pecuarii*) to put up a temple to Faunus on the Tiber island (Livy 33.42.10).[10] The decade after the Hannibalic war seems to have been a time of renewed prosperity, marked, for example, by ritual excuses to repeat the games – in the same year, 196, the Ludi Romani were repeated three times, the Plebeii seven times – and the same aediles had already used surplus funds to erect three bronze statues, of Ceres, Liber, and Libera (33.25.3).

Three years later more fines imposed on the grazers (*pecuarii*, 35.10.11) financed further religious expenditure on a gilded quadriga of Jupiter and a set of twelve gilded shields, and Domitius, now urban praetor, dedicated the temple to Faunus that he had vowed in 196. Is there a reason why it was erected on the island? We would expect Faunus to be worshipped outside the pomerium, perhaps on the Aventine, where the plebeian trinity of Ceres, Liber, and Libera had had their temple. Aesculapius had been given a temple on the island, but he was a foreign god, and that was a century earlier.

The strange thing is that nothing more is heard of this temple of Faunus after its dedication, except for the record of sacrifices to FAUNUS IN INSULA marked for 13 February on the inscribed republican calendar of Antium. The offering is still being made in late Augustan times, as reported by Ovid in his calendar-poem:

'On the Ides the altars of rustic Faunus smoke, there where the island breaks the parted waters,' *Idibus agrestis fumant altaria Fauni / hic, ubi discretas insula rumpit aquas* (*Fasti* 2.193–4, ed. Frazer). Centuries later, Macrobius (or rather his earlier source) refers to the temple of 'Jupiter and Faunus.' Did Jupiter take over the shrine from its old-fashioned dedicatee? Or did it continue to moulder away quietly, with aging custodians? The answer may be suggested when we come to the inscriptional evidence.

By the time the temple of Faunus had been erected on the island, Rome already had a literature, starting from the Tarentine Greek Livius Andronicus, who opens his *Odyssea* with an appeal not to a Greek muse but to one of the Camenae (*virum mihi, Camena, insece versutum*), local nymphs with a grove and spring in the Vallis Egeriae, whose name is derived by Varro and others from their connection with song or poetry, *Carmen/casmen*.[11] In the forum itself was the pool of Juturna, called after another Italian nymph whose name was derived by our Roman sources from the verb *iuvare*, to help;[12] she was associated with Castor and Pollux (whose temple stood near her pool) and like them was a helper who would come to the aid of the Romans.

In philosophical mode Cicero has his friend the sceptic Pontifex Cotta formulate a challenge to the existence of nymphs and other country spirits, despite their public recognition:

Are *even* Nymphs gods? If so, then so are Panisci and Satyrs: but they are not gods, so neither can Nymphs be divine. Yet they have temples vowed and dedicated to them.

Si di sunt, suntne etiam Nymphae deae? Si Nymphae, Panisci etiam et Satyri: hi autem non sunt, ne Nymphae [deae] quidem igitur. et earum templa sunt publica vota et dedicata. (Cic. *ND* 3.43)[13]

And the Nymphs had their own public – that is, state-sanctioned – temple in the very heart of Rome: the Aedes Nympharum, seat of the public records in the forum, which was burned down, like the nearby senate-house, in the rioting over the death of Clodius. As for satyrs, although the mimicking of satyrs was a popular theme of entertainment and featured in state processions,[14] there was no reason to worship them, and they will not reappear in this discussion.

In her valuable study of Greek nymphs, Jennifer Larson (2001)[15] has isolated the most important aspects of these deities in Greek cult and poetry: their birth, from divinities, chiefly river-gods like Asopus, and human women; their form – that of nubile young women; the length of their lives (they were *makraiones*, far outliving humans but not immortal); and their local nature, both in their supposed existence and in their cult. Naiads were inseparable from, and even equated with, their streams, but the ubiquity of local nymph cults in the Greek world meant that no regions were without their nymphs of mountain, woodland, meadow, and stream. Larson adds their festivities in choral dancing and their useful activities as nurses of young gods or beekeepers. We shall see that on Italian soil nymphs were more limited in their functions, and predominantly associated with water (*lymphae*).[16]

So if Rome had public cults and shrines of the Nymphs and of Faunus, were the Nymphs, was Faunus, the object of private cult? Did ordinary Italians untroubled by philosophical scepticism actually believe in nymphs? That is, in the existence of deities protective of natural springs and responsive to prayer and vows? We know so little about private religion in the middle and even the late republic, because hardly any inscriptions survive from that period, in contrast to the increasing number of votive inscriptions from the early empire.

But the sheer utilitarianism of Roman thinking, concerned primarily with personal ambitions and gods who could favour them, may have done as much to hamper belief as to foster it. When wealthy Romans built ornamental fountains and adorned them with images of naked and attractive water nymphs, did they still feel respect and gratitude to the nymphs of natural springs? However devout, a man can hardly treat as supernatural a fountain statue which he himself has commissioned, like the court-yard fountain of Martial's rich poetic friend Stella (Martial 6.43). But halfway between religion and aestheticism was a stage of sentimental interest, when Augustans like Propertius' Cynthia or Ovid himself seem to have visited local shrines and festivals as a form of sightseeing, or in hope of a cure. This was particularly common with medicinal waters, such as the various sulphurous springs in Latium and Etruria, and by the late first century of our era visits to the spa waters are so common that Martial praises the new indoor baths of his patron Claudius Etruscus by means of a hyperbolic comparison with all the fashionable waters – Fontes Aponi, the waters at Sinuessa and the hot springs of Passer and Anxur, the springs of Apollo (unlocated), and the leading resort of Baiae (6.42). His next epigram apologizes to his friend Castricus for staying home at suburban Nomentum instead of joining him at the waters, as he used to do.

While fertile Baiae indulges you, Castricus, and you swim in the white wave with its sulphurous waters, the leisure of my country place at Nomentum gives me strength ... Once I too delighted to visit the much praised waters, and did not fear long journeys, but now the neighbourhood of Rome and an easy retreat please me, and it is enough if I may be lazy there.

> Dum tibi felices indulgent Castrice, Baiae
>   canaque sulpureis unda natatur aquis,
> me Nomentani confirmant otia ruris ...
>
> quondam laudatas quocumque libebat ad undas
>   currere nec longas pertimuisse vias;
> nunc urbis vicina iuvant, facilesque recessus,
>   et satis est, pigro si licet esse mihi.
>   (Martial 6.43.1–3, 7–10)

Another epigram, ostensibly addressed to the nymphs of Sinuessa (11.82), claims that a certain Philostratus, who went to take the cure, fell to his death after imbibing too deeply at dinner – which would never have happened if he had limited himself to their waters. Such visits are confirmed by the evidence of inscriptions. An early inscription from the Appian way reports, 'The freedman Satyrus set up this shrine to the nymphs, and did so gladly from his heart,' SATYR[US] LIBER[TUS] / NYMPHABUS / SACRUM / INSTITUIT / L[IBENS] A[NIMO] D[E] S[UO] F[ECIT] (*ILS* #3860);

and compare this dedication from Sutrium, 'Q. Hortensius Hymnus gladly offered this to the divine nymphs, having been granted his vow, together with Cascellia Arethusa, by authorization of Ti. Latinus' (*ILS* #3864).

We can expect the nymphs presiding over healing springs to receive many such vows. But we cannot gauge the frequency of the vows by the surviving inscriptions. First, just as a worshipper could make a sacrifice or post a dedication without making a formal vow, so he might offer and fulfil his vow without posting an inscription. And if he recorded his vow with a wooden picture (like Horace's imaginary *votiva tabella, Odes* 1.5.13–14) because he could not afford bronze or marble, it would not survive to join the corpus of inscriptions assembled in the last two centuries.

Even so, nymphs were often honoured with dedications when their waters achieved a cure. Thus a set of dedications to Apollo and the Nymphs of the Aquae Apollinares at Lake Sabatinus are included in Dessau's selection as *ILS* #3876–6a–7: one to Apollo and the Nymphs of Domitius; another specifying that the donor had given a silver cup to holy Apollo and the Nymphs; and a third, which combines Apollo and the Nymphs with Silvanus. To carve an inscription was costly, and the abbreviated form often listed only the deities honoured; yet in this one find-spot three dedicators refer to the divine patrons of the springs in different ways. And some donors were not afraid of costly inscriptions; during or after the reign of Hadrian, a dedicator called Samis, who was wealthy enough to go boar hunting, composed or commissioned a highly literary inscription honouring the nymphs of Aquae Albulae, near Tibur (*CIL* XIV.3911). This epigram reports that the nymphs cured Samis when he had been gored by an Etruscan boar and his wound was inflamed; to reward them, once he was restored to health he presented a marble statue of himself (SEMET DE MARMORE DONUM) at the point where the water flows 'under the road midway, where the lord of Tibur (Hercules) looks down on your shrine as you face him and the painted facade of Hadrian's villa gleams' (Courtney 1995, #38). Another verse inscription to the nymph of Albula once accompanied the dedication of a metal portrait of the donor's wife in return for the deity's help in his vow.[17] Perhaps she had been sick and then recovered after taking the waters. Whoever stole the portrait for its precious (if unspecified) metal would have had no use for the inscription and left it *in situ*. Unfortunately, the artwork accompanying such inscriptions, with its representation of the divinities, is not reproduced in the epigraphic sources: for example, the decorative relief of Marcus Aurelius' freedman chamberlain Epitynchanis (*ILS* #3862) apparently shows three nymphs arranged like the Graces in alternating position; the outer nymphs carry corn-ears, and a bearded river-god reclines at their feet, while Hylas is ravished and Hercules and Mercury stand by.

Finally, although we think of nymphs as benevolent, even nurturing, they could also be asked by petitioners to execute a curse: compare the *defixio* of Q. Latinius Lupus consigning a rival to the *Aquae Ferventes*:

I commit, vow and offer in sacrifice this man, so that you, O seething waters, whether you wish to be called Nymphs or by any other name, may destroy and slay him within the year.

HUNC EGO APUT VESTRUM NUMEN DEMANDO DEVOVEO DESACRIFICO, UTI VOS AQUAE FERVENTES, SIVE VOS NIMFAS SIVE QUO ALIO NOMINE VOLTIS ADPELLARI, UTI VOS EUM INTERIMATIS INTERFICIATIS INTRA ANNUM ISTUM. (Audollent 1904, #129)

Gods might not answer prayers if they were addressed under the wrong name or epithet, so in order to make sure the nymphs acknowledge his curse the petitioner adds the rider 'whether you wish to be called Nymphs or by any other name.'[18] Admittedly the nymphs had a less girlish rival, the deity Fons, celebrated at the Fontanalia on the Ides of October by throwing garlands into springs or placing them on well-covers.[19] Inscriptions honour Fons as 'divine,' 'ever-flowing,' or 'most holy' (*divinus, perennis, sanctissimus*). Horace's offering to his spring at Bandusia (*Odes* 3.13) is not to a protecting nymph but to the Fons itself, which he honours with the slaughter of a young kid. Fons survived even in cities: Cicero cites an Altar of Fons on the slopes of the Janiculum as a landmark by means of which to find Numa's tomb; but if this altar is dedicated to the generic god 'Spring,' Rome also contained a number of wells or springs with local names – the city was full of such small shrines and monuments, of which we hear only by accident.[20]

In fact it would seem from Varro's notice of the Fontanalia that this one day was an occasion for offerings to many gods of springs and rivers and other famous waters, like Velinia the deity of the Lacus Velinus; even so, Varro gives pride of place to Tiberinus, Rome's own river-god. Now the Tiber crossing, provided by what Romans called the *insula Tiberina*, was the raison d'être of Rome, and the river dominates many of the early legends.[21] Like Faunus, the river-god had a shrine on the island, but he may have seemed too grand to be the natural object of private cult; in contrast to the many poetic texts we shall meet, Dessau's selection includes only one bare dedication, TIBERINO / SACR(UM) (*ILS* #3902, from Ameria). When the Tiber god appears to Aeneas, the hero offers prayers without erecting an altar, still less an inscription. However, Terence Eden's extensive commentary on the scene in his edition of *Aeneid* 8 illustrates this kind of ritual homage with the inscription of the veteran Atusius, who proudly records dedicating the altar he had vowed when on active service (*caligatus*): SEXTUS ATUSIUS PRIMUS OMNIUM ARAM TIBERINO POSUIT QUAM CALIGATUS VOVERAT (*CIL* XI.1.3057). It is not clear why Atusius claims to be first of all (*primus omnium*), unless the emphasis is on this particular location.

Our antiquarian sources are full of information about ritual address to the river-god. Cicero quotes *Tiberinus* as the form used in Augur's prayers (*in augurum precatione, ND* 3.51); and when Virgil introduces the river as *Tiberinus* in *Aen.* 8.31, Servius praises the poet for using the correct address and knowing that this was the river's cult name, as opposed to prosaic Tiberis and the exotic literary version, Thybris. At *Aen.* 8.72, Servius actually quotes a prayer summoning the god: *Adesto, Tiberine, cum tuis undis*, 'Attend me, Tiber, with your waters,' and we can compare the appeal from book 1 of Ennius' *Annales* quoted by Macrobius: *teque pater Tiberine, tuo cum flumine sancto*, 'and I appeal to you too, Father Tiber, with your sacred stream' (Macr. *Sat.* 6.1.12, quoting Enn. *Ann.* 54V).[22] Rivers were both sacred and inclined to be more anthropomorphic than most Italian *numina*. There was an old legend that when Ilia was thrown into the river by her wicked uncle, the Tiber – or, in other versions, his tributary, the Anio – saved her and made her his bride; so this Ennian appeal is most likely Ilia's, but the poet may have given a similar appeal to Horatius Cocles, if Ennius was the model for Livy's narrative of Horatius' defence of the Tiber bridge against the Etruscans. As the Romans cut down the bridge behind him and he was forced to leap into the river, he prayed to the river-god for rescue: 'Father Tiber, I beg you, holy one, to receive these weapons and this warrior with favouring stream,' *Tiberine pater, te sancte precor, haec arma et hunc militem propitio flumine accipias* (Livy 2.10.11). ·

The divine *numen* of the great river was still an issue early in the reign of Tiberius, when there was opposition on religious grounds to a Roman plan to combat the Tiber floods by diverting some of its tributaries (Tac. *Ann.* 1.79).[23] One speaker, who warned that the senate must respect the religious scruples of the local communities having rites and groves and altars dedicated to their rivers, also claimed that the Tiber himself would resent the loss of dignity from the subtraction of his tributaries: *ipsum Tiberim nolle prorsus accolis fluviis orbatum minore gloria fluere.*

Just as the Tiber was revered by the Romans and those living on its banks, so lesser streams and springs throughout Italy were revered and even became objects of pilgrimage. Pliny the Younger offers a fine description of the marvellous springs of the Clitumnus, which are still a favourite tourist site in Umbria:

Nearby is the ancient and revered temple; there stands the god himself, dressed and fitted out in a *toga praetexta*. Lots stacked for predictions indicate that the god is accessible to men and even prophetic. Scattered around him are many little shrines and as many gods, each with his own cult, his name, and even his own spring. Besides Clitumnus, acting as Father of the others, are lesser gods distinguished by their sources, but they flow into the main stream of the river, which is crossed by a bridge. This is the boundary between the sacred and the profane.

Adiacet templum priscum et religiosum; stat Clitumnus ipse amictus ornatusque praetexta; praesens numen atque etiam fatidicum indicant

sortes. Sparsa sunt circa sacella complura totidemque di. Sua cuique ven-
eratio, suum nomen, quibusdam vero etiam fontes. nam praeter illum
quasi parentem ceterorum sunt minores capite discreti; sed flumini mis-
centur, quod ponte transmittitur. Is terminus sacri profanique. (Pliny
Letters 8.8.5–6)

One senses Pliny's ironic detachment from the statue of the river-
god, which worshippers have dressed up in the special toga of
magistrates and priesthoods. When he mentions the crowds of
grateful inscriptions honouring the spring and the god (*fons ille
deusque*), he adds that his reader, Voconius, would find some of
them comic if he were not so humane. On another occasion Pliny
is taken to visit Lake Vadimon, near Ameria.

The lake is shaped liked a wheel on its side, hemmed in and even all
around; there is no bay or irregularity, everything is proportionate and
matching as if hollowed and excavated by a craftsman's hand. Its colour
is more white than blue, and more dense and shadowy than green, smell-
ing of sulphur and tasting of medication, with the power to fuse broken
objects. There are no boats on its waters, since it is sacred, but islands
float on its surface, all green with reed and rushes and other such plants
as the fertile marsh and tail end of the lake produces.

lacus est in similitudinem iacentis rotae, circumscriptus et undique
aequalis: nullus sinus, obliquitas nulla, omnia dimensa, paria et quasi arti-
ficis manu cavata et excisa. Color caerulo albidior, viridi lividior et pressior,
sulpuris odor saporque medicatus, vis qua fracta solidantur … nulla in hoc
navis (sacer enim) sed innatant insulae, herbidae omnes harundine et iunco
quaeque alia fecundior palus ipsaque illa extremitas lacus effert. (8.20.4–5)

No doubt the lake was held sacred because of its sulphurous waters; both Ovid and Pliny's uncle[24] write extensively about both
the healing and the more harmful powers of lakes and rivers. In
every locality there must have been springs and pools cherished
for their beauty or alleged healing powers.

In contrast, when we return to look for evidence of personal devotion to Faunus, the god of the uncultivated land, we find a sudden

void. As Dumézil points out, the Italian smallholder looked to the Lares to protect what lay within his own small property, but as soon as he stepped out into the bush, he was in the territory of Faunus (Dumézil 1966, I, 340–50; Faunus 344). So Faunus should have been an important, if potentially dangerous, spirit. The bare fact is that by the time literacy came to Rome, Faunus was overwhelmed by competition:[25] in poetry and the visual arts he was put in the shadow by the Greek god Pan; in personal cult his role was usurped by Silvanus. Did Faunus fall from grace because of his own nature, or from a change in the farmer's thinking and perhaps his farming methods? In the poetry which will be our focus, Faunus appears as often as, or slightly more often than, his rival Pan. Why then does the only inscription to him in Dessau's selection (*ILS* #3580) come from Thabraca in Africa? Why can even Dorcey (1992), in his careful study of Silvanus, offer only four atypical dedications to Faunus?[26]

As I see it, one problem or deterrent to Faunus attracting cult lay in his invisibility, and yet another in his unsolicited and arbitrary manifestations: the prophetic Faunus was a disembodied voice, and not only the visual arts but poetry prefers a god with a visible reality. Romans sometimes talk as though there was only the one god Faunus, but just as often of plural Fauni. The name was variously derived from *fari* and *favere*, from his function as either a speaker or a favourer of men, one who addressed them with prophecy or warning when they were alone, either in the wilderness or at dead of night. Thus in Cicero's *De Natura Deorum* the stoic Balbus, a believer in divination, is set up by his author. Very early in his plea for the existence of the gods, Balbus argues that the voices of *fauni* have been heard and shapes of the gods seen, so that any man who was not either brutish or impious would be forced to admit that gods came among us and came to our aid (*deos praesentes esse*, *ND* 2.6). This puts the sceptic Cotta in a position so strong he can afford to veil his disbelief in courtesy: 'I myself have never heard the voice of Faunus; if you tell me you have heard it, I will believe you, even though I have no idea what sort of creature Faunus is,' *nam Fauni vocem equidem numquam audivi. tibi, si audivisse dicis, credam, etsi Faunus omnino quid sit nescio* (3.15).

If we leave aside for the next, Virgilian, chapter the euhemeristic King Faunus of the Latins, what remains is an elusive and some-what scary spirit. For Ennius at least, *Fauni* are not yet contamin-ated with Satyrs; they are the utterers of primitive verse, imitated by the Saturnians of his predecessor Naevius, which Ennius rejects as old-fashioned and unsophisticated. When Varro quotes this com-ment, he notes that 'Fauni were gods of the Latins, so that there were both Faunus and Fauna. The tradition is that they were ac-customed to utter [*fari*] what was to come in verses called Saturnians, and so were called Fauni from *fando*,' *Fauni dei Latinorum, ita ut et Faunus et Fauna sit: hos versibus quos vocant Saturnios in silvestribus locis traditum est solitos fari <futura, a> quo fando Faunos dictos* (*LL* 7.36). It looks, then, as though for Varro *Fauni* meant a specific pair of male and female spirits. But Varro does not include either Faunus or Fauna among the gods in the opening prayer to his book on agriculture, *Res Rusticae* (1.1), or mention him in his discussion of sheep-breeding in book 2. Nor does he mention Faunus (or any other god) in connection with the Lupercalia (*LL* 6.13). We have seen earlier that Dionysius of Halicarnassus, writing in the age of Augustus, saw the mountains and woods of Italy as the territory of Pan (D.H. 1.38), and Wiseman (1995a) argues in his study of the Lupercalia[27] that Romans assimi-lated the Lupercal cave, at the foot of the Palatine beneath the tem-ple of Victory, to the grotto of Pan at the foot of the Acropolis. The cult of Pan had come early to Rome, very soon, it would seem, after it spread beyond Arcadia in fifth century Greece (though not as early as tradition would have it, brought by the pre-Homeric Arcadian founder-king Evander). Pan would have been welcomed to Rome along with other Greek cults introduced in this period (such as those of Demeter/Ceres and the Dioscuri). Once the highly recognizable goat-faced and goat-footed Pan was known, the Lupercal became his cave, and the Lupercalia his cult.

Although there is no established iconography of Faunus, known for being heard but not seen, Wiseman has persuasively identified him in the wild man of Etruscan fourth and third century mir-rors.[28] It is difficult to worship a god who manifests himself only in unpredictable places and at unforeseen times. Yet Faunus was important to the countryman, in fostering the fertility of flocks, and was treated by Augustan poets even before Ovid as Inuus, the Italian patron of animal breeding matching the same aspect of Pan. It looks as though the festival, in which young members of the Luperci fraternities stripped naked to run to and fro all around the base of the Palatine, lashing whomever they met with strips of goat-hide, became too raunchy, even before it was the occasion of Antonius' embarrassing offer of a crown to Julius Caesar; and for this reason or another, Augustus did his best to emasculate the festival, but it persisted until the fourth century. So was Faunus perhaps discredited by the open preoccupation of his cult with animal fertility?

There is a second problem. If the festival was taken over by Pan, how is it that yet another god of the wild, Silvanus, seems to have displaced Faunus in private worship and dedications? Like Pan, Silvanus will have been worshipped informally long before his cult is attested by durable inscriptions and reliefs. If we imagine displaced peasants flocking to the cities for employment, we can understand that they must have felt an attachment to the recognizable old country god dressed in skins and accompanied by his faithful sheepdog. Whatever the cause, the dedications we might have expected to this god of uncultivated land are directed neither to Faunus nor to Pan but to Silvanus. Silvanus even steals from Faunus' record of service to Rome. The story told by Dionysius (5.16.2–3) of the mighty voice of Faunus coming from the Silva Arsia to foretell Roman victory over the Etruscans is transferred by Livy (2.7.2) and Valerius Maximus (1.8.5) to Silvanus. And the story in D.H. 1.56.3, where Aeneas is ordered by an unidentified voice coming from the wood to follow the escaped sacrificial sow, looks like a vestige of another utterance of Faunus.[29]

I would suggest two reasons for Silvanus' increasing popularity: his recognizable image, as a mature male carrying a sickle and an uprooted tree and often accompanied by a dog, and his association with Hercules. But long before the association with Hercules, Silvanus is honoured for the first time in the Roman historical record as early as the end of the fifth century, when a fig tree in front of the temple of Saturn had to be removed because it was upsetting a statue of Silvanus (cum Silvani simulacrum subverteret).[30] And Silvanus turns up practically at the beginning of

Roman literature, in an unexpected allusion in Plautus' *Aulularia*. When the old miser Euclio is trying to hide his gold, he thinks of the grove of Silvanus, out of the way outside the city walls and hidden by willow thickets (*Silvani lucus extra murumst avius / crebra salicto oppletus, Aul.* 674–5; cf. 766): that is where he will hide it. Given the role played by Pan in the *Dyskolos* of Menander, we can be sure this offstage grotto of Silvanus started its life in the Greek text as a grotto of Pan.[31]

If Silvanus drove out the cult of his rival, how early did this happen? Certainly Cato the Elder, writing only a generation after the temple of Faunus was erected on the Tiber island, makes Mars Silvanus the recipient of sacrifice on behalf of his cattle:

This is how you offer a vow for the health of your herd of cattle. Make a vow to Mars Silvanus in the woods by day for each head of cattle. Place three pounds of emmer meal and four and a half pounds of lard and the same amount of meat in a container, and three pints of wine in another. Either a slave or a freeman may do this. Once the sacrifice is made, eat it on the spot. Let no woman participate in the sacrifice, nor witness it.

Votum pro bubus, uti valeant, sic facito. Marti Silvano in silva interdius in capita singula boum votum facito. Farris L III et lardi P. IIII S et pulpae P.IIII S, vini S.III, id in unum vas liceto coicere, et vinum item in unum vas liceto coicere. Eam rem divinam vel servus vel liber licebit faciat. Ubi res divina facta erit, statim ibidem consumito. mulier ad eam rem divinam ne adsit neve videat quo modo fiat. (Cato *Agr.* 83)[32]

Dedications to Silvanus alone or in divine company are found all over the empire, but two examples from Rome itself show the wide social spectrum of his worshippers. One is from Ti. Flavius Sabinus (*ILS* #3531), almost certainly Vespasian's brother, the unlucky prefect of Rome in 69 CE. The other, dated by consular year to 90 CE, is erected and dedicated to Lord Silvanus (DOMINUM SILVANUM, *ILS* #3532) 'at his own expense' by Thallus the charioteer and slave of Avillius Planta. By this time there are colleges of Silvanus and the Lares, whose members make loyal dedications (*ILS* #3541, 3542, 3543, and 3546). When we come upon such urban organizations, which combine potential office for ambitious members with visible tributes to the emperor and imperial cult, we are no longer dealing with actual religious devotion, but with the ancient equivalent of Freemasonry and the Shriners.

The Country Gods in Augustan Elegy and Lyric

Although Varro invoked neither Faunus nor Silvanus for his work on agriculture, Virgil found room for both gods (along with Pan) in the dedicatory preface to his *Georgics*, as we shall see in the next chapter. A more ambiguous case is the elegist Tibullus. While Horace sees his country farm as a place of blissful escape from the duties of city life,[33] elegists choose their favourite places according to the presence of their beloved, and the most elegant objects of desire, like Tibullus' Delia (or Corydon's Alexis in *Eclogue* 2), stayed in town. On the face of it, Tibullus loves the country, and his elegies have sometimes been called 'bucolic' in their sympathies; but he wants to have Delia with him (1.5.21–30, and Messala too, 31–2); so does Sulpicia, who writes petulantly that she must celebrate her birthday without her beloved Cerinthus.[34] Tibullus' country-centred elegies (1.1; 1.3; 1.5; 1.10; and 2.1) seem to reflect the point of view of a relatively prosperous landowner, one who supervises the work and worship of the estate, but need not perform his own chores.[35] Thus his opening elegy speaks of acts of reverence for anonymous tree-trunks and stones, marked as cult objects by the garlands around them,[36] and of offerings of the new season's fruit to the unidentified 'farmer god' (*agricolae deo*, 1.1.14), to whom we will return.

> Nam veneror, seu stipes habet desertus in agris
>   seu vetus in trivio florida serta lapis:
> et quodcumque mihi pomum novus educat annus,
>   libatum agricolae ponitur ante deo.
>   (Tib. 1.1.11–14)

To Ceres, Tibullus promises a garland of wheat, 'a circlet of wheat-ears to hang before the doors of her temple,' and he sets up 'an image of Priapus painted with ruddle and equipped with a cruel sickle, to scare the birds from his vegetable garden.'[37]

flava Ceres, tibi sit nostro de rure corona
  spicea, quae templi pendeat ante fores;
pomosisque ruber custos ponatur in hortis
  terreat ut saeva falce Priapus aves.
vos quoque felicis quondam nunc pauperis agri
  custodes, fertis munera vestra, Lares.
    (1.15–20)

Tibullus is now a poor man, and can offer only a lamb to the Lares, seen as guardians of his now diminished estate, instead of the calf he used to offer them. But the poet seems to give actual livestock a low priority; he mentions them only as an afterthought. (It is known that arable farmers would keep a small flock of sheep simply for the fertilizing power of their manure.) He is prepared to search out the sick lamb or abandoned kid and bring it home, but begs thieves and wolves to spare his scanty flock (1.33–4). But he recognizes the need to pray to the appropriate deity; to purify his sheep and shepherds, Tibullus offers milk to gentle Pales (*placidam ... Palem*, 36) at her spring festival each year.

There were many yearly festivals, but in connection with Pales, Tibullus must have in mind the Parilia, celebrated on 21 April – a date that had become better known as the foundation-day of Rome itself. A nostalgic retrospect to early Rome is one of the main themes of Elegy 2.5. Later in that elegy Tibullus has the shepherds drunk with wine as they hymn Pales at this festival and leap across ritual bonfires (2.5.87–90). But he does not seem to know or care much about Pales.

In fact Augustan poets more often honour the Parilia than speak about its titular patron deity.[38] Only Virgil mentions Pales independently of the festival, in *Ecl.* 5.35 along with Apollo (as herd-god Nomios) and in the double invocation of the two parts of *Georgics* 3 dealing first with the major cattle and horses (cf. 3.1) and then with the small cattle. It was left to Dumézil (1969, 274–87; 1966/1970, I, 381–3) to clarify why later writers thought that Pales was masculine (they were referring to the homonymous Etruscan deity) and why the republican *Fasti Antiates* list an offering to the Two Pales (*Palibus II*) on 7 July. Just as Varro in his second book of *Res Rusticae* uses a reference to Pales to mark the division between the discussion of larger cattle (which were usually mated in July) and that of sheep and goats, so Virgil will follow his opening address to Pales with a renewed appeal at 3.294, when he comes to discuss the small flocks. Except for the youngest ewes, sheep were mated in late April, and it is on their behalf that Ovid, working from the *Fasti Praenestini*, presents his shepherds purifying their pens and making offerings and a prayer to the goddess. The prayer is imagined, not a quotation from liturgy (would any poet have incorporated a real prayer into his work?), but the ritual details are surely genuine. Pales did not receive blood sacrifice, but milk, unfermented grape juice, and millet cakes. And this god's function must have been in some way complementary to that of deities like Inuus and Faunus, who actually guaranteed the fertility of the rams and billy-goats. Perhaps Pales presided over lactation?

Like Faunus, Pales has no known visual representation, but Tibullus does not seem to know this; in his sentimental reconstruction of early pastoral life before Rome's foundation, cattle graze on the grassy Palatine, and Jove's future citadel has a hut village.

There was a statue of Pan wet with milk in the shade of an ilex, along with a wooden statue of Pales hacked with a country sickle. The shepherd has hung his pipe on a tree in fulfilment of a vow to the woodland god.

> lacte madens illic suberat Pan ilicis umbrae
>   et facta agresti lignea falce Pales,
> pendebatque vagi pastoris in arbore votum,
>   garrula silvestri fistula sacra deo.
>   (2.5.27–30)

We would expect the second god to be Silvanus,[39] but the indefinite *silvestri deo* recalls the even more indefinite[40] 'farmer [dative] or farmer's [genitive] god' (*agricolae deo*) of Tibullus' first elegy. To judge by the offering of fruit in 1.1.14 this ought to be Priapus – but Priapus is mentioned separately at 1.17–18. In his edition of the *Elegies*, Murgatroyd considers the possibility that *silvestris* means Pan or is some kind of collective for all woodland deities

(p. 187); perhaps in both passages Tibullus left the phrase deliberately vague, using the indefinite form so as to leave no rustic divinity offended at not being honoured. Tibullus repeats the same pattern when Delia offers to the farmer god (again *deo ... agricolae*, 1.5.27–8) grapes on behalf of the vines, corn-ears on behalf of the crops, and a feast on behalf of the flock. The last elegy of book 1 renews this motif when Tibullus follows his own tribute to his family Lares with the offering by an unidentified countryman whose vow has been granted (*voti compos*, 1.10.23) of grapes and grain and cakes to an unnamed 'wooden god' (*ligneus ... deus*, 1.10.20); this humble image must serve as a symbol for any or all country gods.

Is Tibullus as unspecific in his invocation at the purificatory ritual, probably the Ambarvalia, which opens the first elegy of book 2? He first calls on the chief gods of such rituals, Bacchus and Ceres, and then orders that everyone should be attentive to 'the god.' The *di patrii* addressed in 2.1.17 are most likely his Lares, but by line 36 he is giving thanks in song to *agricolis caelitibus*, 'the farming [or country-dwelling?] heavenly ones.' Thus when Tibullus follows with the formal declaration 'I sing of the countryside and country gods,' *rura cano rurisque deos*, we cannot say that he is honouring specific gods. Since he hymns them as teachers of arable farming, of the growing of fruit trees and vines, and of human housing,[41] Tibullus is most probably reverting to Ceres and Bacchus and is no longer concerned with lesser country gods. We can see that the poet wants a backcloth of 'authentic' country religion, but he is really more interested in praising the rustic origin of song and dance, and passing on to the love-making after the feast. Tibullus likes his country tame, with no hint of Faunus, and nary a nymph in sight – indeed he does not even mention springs or streams, either for the Naiads or for thirsty farm labourers.

It is no wonder that Horace gently reproaches his friend with creeping in anxious hypochondria around the healthy woods (*tacitum silvas inter reptare salubres*, *Ep.* 1.4.4.) and reminds him that the gods have given him good looks, wealth, and the art of enjoying it – good health and a decent livelihood, with a purse that does not run dry. But then Horace earned his country home after poverty and displacement: *O rus quando ego te aspiciam?* I doubt very much that he depended on the produce of his Sabine farm; rather it was his refuge from the smoke and wealth and noise of the city (*beatae / fumum et opes strepitumque Romae, Odes* 3.29.11–12). With Horace we come to a poet who loved the idea of country gods: in his very first ode he boasts that 'it is the cool grove and bands of nimble Nymphs and Satyrs which shelter me from the common crowd.'

> me gelidum nemus
> Nympharumque leves cum Satyris chori
> secernunt populo.
>   (Hor. *Odes* 1.1.30–2)

The nymphs and satyrs are not invoked just because they were part of Bacchus' retinue, as commentators rightly note.[42] Horace values their youth and the dance itself, as the physical embodiment of poetry and song (*Mousike*). Dance reappears in 1.4 with the onset of spring, as the poet shares the wanderlust of the cattle eager to leave their stable and populates the meadows with happy divinities: Venus leads the band of dancers (1.4.5), and the Graces join with the Nymphs in treading the earth. This is a picture that delights him again in the spring poem of book 4, as the grass returns to the field and foliage to the trees, with dancing Graces and Nymphs (4.7.5–6).

Tibullus' land is productive; Horace's landscape is a glad sight to the eyes. It certainly held five tenant farmers, but it nestled in the hills and was probably relatively large because it was on marginal and unprofitable soil, and it gave the poet a world of his own. And his invitation to Tyndaris (*Odes* 1.17) opens with the lively guardian spirit of Faunus, a Faunus who must also be partly Pan, for the poet describes him as exchanging Arcadian Mount Lycaeus for Horace's Lucretilis. Eduard Fraenkel (1957, 204–9) sees in this poem a fusion of two types: the cletic ode inviting the presence of a god (but this god comes spontaneously and often), and the poem of preparation for a party. The poem begins with two happy epithets – 'nimble Faunus often chooses lovely Lucretilis, protecting my goats from the fire of summer and windy rains [of winter],' *velox amoenum saepe Lucretilem / mutat*

Lycaeo Faunus et igneam / defendit aestatem capellis / usque meis pluviosque ventos (1.17.1–4). Faunus, swift like the goats and musical like Horace's guest, turns out to be a proof of the poet's own sense of being under the protection of the gods.

As the nanny goats, wives of the reeking husband, seek out lurking arbutus and fragrant thyme without risk in the safe woodland, and the kids need not fear green serpents nor the wolves of Mars, whenever the valleys and smooth rocks of low-lying Ustica echo with the sweet sound of pipes, so the gods protect me, and my piety and poetry please their hearts.

> impune tutum per nemus arbutos
> quaerunt latentis et thyma deviae
>   olentis uxores mariti,
>   nec virides metuunt colubras
> nec Martialis haediliae lupos,
> utcumque dulci, Tyndari, fistula
>   valles et Usticae cubantis
>   levia personuere saxa;
> di me tuentur, dis pietas mea
> et musa cordi est.
>   (1.17.5–14)

Who is playing the pipes? Not Tyndaris; she is a lyre player. Fraenkel (1957, 206) recognizes that the *dulcis fistula* is the pan pipe; in fact, although he speaks of this and *Odes* 3.18 as odes to Faunus, he repeatedly speaks of Horace invoking Pan. If Horace chooses to appropriate the musical talents of Pan for his rustic god, shouldn't we stop trying to distinguish between them? The whole poem delights in the idea of natural shelter (*hic in reducta valle*) and supernatural protection. But this is not the only time Horace will lay claim to the patronage of Faunus. He writes dramatically in 2.13, 3.4.27, and 3.8.7–8 of the falling tree that almost killed him; but it is in the heartfelt ode to Maecenas (2.17) that he matches Maecenas' lucky escape from maleficent stars to his own rescue by Faunus: the tree trunk would have carried me away, crushing my brain, if Faunus, the protector of mercurial men, had not eased the blow with his right hand.

>   me truncus illapsus cerebro
>   sustulerat, nisi Faunus ictum
>   dextra levasset, Mercurialium
>   custos virorum. reddere victimas
>   aedemque votivam memento;
>   nos humilem feriemus agnam.
>   (2.17.27–32)

While Maecenas will offer victims and a votive shrine to some dignified Olympian, Horace will honour Faunus by sacrificing a lamb. Among the odes with country themes in book 3, 3.18 is an open invitation to Faunus, lusty pursuer of nymphs, to 'come gently into my fields and sunny countryside' (this, after all, is not open land, where Faunus is lord, but ground protected by Horace's Lares) and 'depart well-disposed towards my young flock.'

>   Faune, Nympharum fugientum amator,
>   per meos fines et aprica rura
>   lenis incedas abeasque parvis
>   aequus alumnis.
>   (3.18.1–4)

This is Faunus' festival, the Nones of December, and there will be abundant wine to foster sexual desire while the altar smokes with the smell of roast meat. As in 1.17, this is a time for carefree play; all the flocks sport on the grassy turf, and the village itself is free, with the oxen at leisure in the meadows. Just as Horace's goats in 1.17 did not have to fear the wolf, so the wolf can wander harmlessly among fearless lambs, while the ditch-digger stomps gleefully on the hated ground. Other odes show the same appreciation of country gods – the promise of a present sacrifice and future glory to the spring Bandusia (3.13); the dedicatory epigram to Diana, *montium custos, nemorumque virgo*, in which the poet presents her with a pine tree and promises the annual offering of a wild boar (3.22); Phidyle's prayer to the Lares in 3.23, offering incense, wheat, and a pig in return for their protection of her vines and corn and flock. So, we might ask, where is Silvanus? He did not appear to rescue Horace from the wolf, *silva ... in Sabina* (1.22.9); instead it was the poet's love for Lalage that saved him. Horace includes Silvanus in his antiquarian version of the coming of drama to Rome, Silvanus receiving the ancient peasants' worship and, somewhat surprisingly, appeased with an offering of milk (*tellurem porco, Silvanum lacte piabant, Ep.* 2.1.135), but in the lyrics the god is mentioned only once, in a context that makes his territory seem a last resort. When Horace is urging Maecenas to leave the stifling summer heat of Rome, the parching noonday sun drives the shepherd and his flock away from the river bank into the shade, to seek a stream and the thickets of rough Silvanus (*iam pastor umbras cum grege languido / rivumque fessus quaerit et horridi / dumeta Silvani,* 3.29.21–3). Good enough for goats, perhaps, but the frisky and lusty Faunus was closer to the poet's fancy – or his heart.

As it happens, Faunus does have one more moment of limelight after the Augustan period, but we do not know how long after; his appearance comes in the bucolic poems of Calpurnius Siculus. These poems were previously assumed to be Neronian, but they have been reassessed by most recent experts either as poetry of the second century or as later (undatable) work pretending to be Neronian.[43] In his first eclogue Calpurnius introduces two brothers whose role it is to offer a divine prophecy of the new emperor's coming golden age. Ornytus invites his brother to seek the shade in the grotto of father Faunus, and Corydon happily agrees, for his girlfriend's refusal to gratify him has left him pure for religious purposes, and he can enter Faunus' *sacraria* (1.15). There they find a long prophecy (*sacra pagina*) inscribed on a beech tree, so fresh that the letters cut into the bark show green. Ornytus, who can read it because he is taller, reports that this is no traveller's or herdsman's message but sacred verse composed by the god himself. The almost fifty lines which follow begin with the claim 'I, Faunus, begotten of Aether [Heaven], who inhabit the hillsides and woods, sing to the nations these things to come. It is my delight to inscribe glad songs on a sacred tree, revealing the fates.'

qui iuga qui silvas tueor, satus Aethere Faunus
haec populis ventura cano. iuvat arbore sacra
laeta patefactis incidere carmina fatis.
(Calp. Sic. 1.33–5)

What follows is a hymn to the forthcoming *aurea aetas*, when
happiness will follow a youth who will win the cause on behalf of
his maternal Iulii, and as god rule the nations. The content of the
prophecy need not concern us, but the misrepresentation of
Faunus is another matter. This ancient god had no traditional par-
entage (except in Virgil's Latin kingship dynasty, where he is child
of Picus and Circe), did not have formal cult sites, and did not
prophesy in writing. He is purely a literary convenience to lend
authority to Calpurnius' imperial flattery.

In the cult of Silvanus, too, poetic amateurs aroused to composition by the examples of the Augustan poets exercised themselves
in a new, if artificial, genre of verse inscription, and two of the
most interesting such poems are offered to Silvanus. First, the appeal of T. Pomponius Victor, imperial procurator in the Graian
Alps (probably to Marcus Aurelius and Verus), is set in lyric iambic trimeters:

SILVANUS, HALF-IMPRISONED IN THIS SACRED ASH,
GREAT GUARDIAN OF THIS LOFTY LITTLE GARDEN,
WE OFFER YOU THESE THANKS IN POETIC FORM
FOR BRINGING US THROUGH THE FIELDS AND ALPINE PEAKS
TO BE THE GUESTS OF THIS YOUR FRAGRANT GROVE.
WHILE I DIRECT THE LAW DOING THE CAESARS' WILL,
PRESERVE ME WITH YOUR BENEFICIAL FAVOUR.
ONLY RESTORE ME AND MY KIN TO ROME
TO TILL ITALIAN SOIL BENEATH YOUR CARE,
THEN SHALL I GIVE YOU A THOUSAND MIGHTY TREES.[44]
(*CIL* XII.103)

Pomponius was not inspired, but we can be sure his vow was
heartfelt. A near contemporary, who used to be identified as
Athenaeus, director of the Lateran library, knew where to borrow
the inspiration and building blocks for his hexameters.[45]

Greatest of gods, mighty Silvanus, holiest shepherd,
who rule the Idaean grove and Roman camp,
since the skilful pipe was joined by you with honeyed wax[46]
(for surely from afar the river joins us nearby;
Tirinus glides with light water over the dewy meadows
silvery with gleaming waves but shallow bed),[47]
you Silvanus, bearing a young uprooted cypress[48]
attend me propitiously, holy one, and bring back your divine favour
for giving you an image and altar for your services.

These acts have I performed for the sake of my masters' well-being
and mine own, praying for my dear ones and a kindly life
and doing my duty as your worshipper: be at my right hand
while I pay you your due from my vow, gladly and as you deserve
these things, which I now repay and give back to your altars.[49]

MAGNE DEUM, SILVANE POTENS, SANCTISSIME PASTOR
QUI *NEMUS IDAEUM* ROMANAQUE CASTRA GUBERNAS,
MELLEA QUOD DOCILIS *IUNCTAST TIBI FISTULA CERA*
(NAMQUE PROCUL CERTE VICINUS IUNGITUR AMNIS
LABITUR UNDA LEVI PER ROSCIDA PRATA TIRINUS
GURGITE NON ALTO, *NITIDIS ARGENTEUS UNDIS*)
ET TENERAM AB RADICE FERENS, SILVANE, CUPRESSUM
ADSIS HUNC MIHI, SANCTE, *FAVENS* NUMENQUE REPORTES,
QUOD *TIBI PRO MERITIS* SIMULACRUM ARAMQUE DICAVI.

HAEC EGO QUAE FECI DOMINORUM CAUSA SALUTIS
ET MEA PROQUE MEIS ORANS VITAMQUE BENIGNAM
OFFICIUMQUE GERENS FAUTOR TIBI, DEXTER ADESTO
DUM TIBI QUAE REFERO QUAEQUE ARIS, INCLUTE, REDDO
EX VOTO MERITOQUE LIBENS MEA DICTA RESOLVO.
   (*CIL* IX.3375)

Readers will recognize that the poet has borrowed his second invocation to Silvanus from *Georgics* 1; it is less obvious, perhaps,
that the odd reference to his creation of the pan pipes borrows a
half-line from *Eclogues* 3, and the river 'silvery with gleaming
waves,' *nitidis argenteus undis*, is lifted from Narcissus' pool in

Ovid's *Metamorphoses* (3.407). I have used italic type to indicate these and other shorter 'tags.' After this rather clumsy statement of his actual prayer, the poet appropriates the pseudo-Virgilian *ille ego qui*[50] to bring his poem to a close with an awkwardly modified version of the pre-battle speech from *Aen.* 9.157–8:

> I it was who included my name on the altar.
> *Now men, be glad at due success: prepare*
> *to groom yourselves and hope for lasting good fortune.*[51]

This pastiche of largely Virgilian motifs makes us impatient for the real thing. We should find it all the more satisfying to return to Virgil himself in the next chapter, and see how he involves the land of Latium and its gods in Aeneas' struggle to forge a new home.

Appendix. Inscriptions Honouring Faunus or Mentioning Fauni

See Dorcey 1992, 34n4.

FROM ROME/ITALY

CIL VI.2302 (=*Fasti Esquilini, Inscr. Ital.* XIII.2) ID. FEBR. FAUNO I]N INSULA (cf. Ovid *Fasti* 2.193–4)

AE 1927, 106 P SEXTILIUS / THEPTUS V.S. SANCTISSIMI FAUNI (from Umbria)

AE 1930, 54 FAUNI AUGUSTI (Did Augustus really authorize giving his own name to the unruly Faunus? Or was it a later title, simply meaning 'imperial'?)

CIL VI.23083 (A second(?) century funerary inscription for the sculptor Novius Blesamus, found beneath an altar in the church of St Cecilia in Campus Martius)

BLESAMUS HOC NOVIUS REQUIEM SORTITUS IN AEVUM
   [erased]
CONTRA LOCUS SANCTUS, PLAUSU QUI EXCEPIT AGRESTI
   CUM PRIMUM FUNDO VENERAT HIC DOMINUS,
PAREBAT NEMO, FAUNI NYMPHAEQUE SONABANT,
   LAETITIAM DIVOM SENSIT ET IPSE LOCUS.
HIC OLIM STATUIS URBEM DECORAVIT ET ORBEM;
   NOMEN HABET POPULUS: CORPORIS HIC TUMULUS.

FROM SECOND CENTURY AFRICA

AE 1895, 10 (=*ILS* #3580) FAUNO AUGUSTO SACRUM /
EPITYNCHAN / US PHILOSTOR / GI AUG. ARKAR / IUS

CIL VIII, Suppl. IV.27764 (= Courtney 1995, #151) (starting at line 4)
(A verse dedication of grove and spring sacrifices to Silvanus, it rel-
egates the fauns to literary ornament, as in the Novius epitaph.)

QUARE CETTE DEO PATRIUM DEDAM[US HONOREM
SILVANO DE FONTE BOVANT CUI FRON[DEA CLAUSTRA
GIGNITUR E SAXO LUCUS INQUE ARB[ORE RAMI.
HUNC TIBI DE MORE DAMUS DIFFICIL[EM
HUNC TIBI DE VOCE PATRIS FALCITEN[ENTIS HAEDUM
[Falcitenens = silvanus]
HUNC TIBI DE MORE TUO PINIFERA ES[T CORONA.
SIC MIHI SENIOR MEMORAT SA[CERDOS:
LUDITE FAUNI DRYADES PUELL[AE
LUDITE, CANITE IAM MEO SACELL[O
NAIDES E NEMORE MEO COLON[AE
   CANTET ADSUETA DE FISTULA ...
   ADSIT ET LUDO DE MORE PA[
   CANTET ET ROSEA DE TIBIA
   PREMAT BIIUGES DEUS A [After this, three fragmentary lines
     are omitted.]

CHAPTER TWO

Virgil's Gods of the Land

We might expect that no Latin poet would pay more affectionate attention to the rustic gods than Virgil, the farmer's son from fertile Lombardy, who began his career with pastoral poems modelled on the idylls of Theocritus and continued with a poem truly devoted to farming the land of Italy, his unprecedented and inimitable *Georgics*. Certainly it was my reading of Virgil, above all of the 'Italian' books of the *Aeneid*, which prompted me to explore the role played by these country gods and demigods in Latin poetry during and after the principate of Augustus. Although Varro invoked neither Faunus nor Silvanus among his tutelary gods in the *Res Rusticae*, composed in the same decade as Virgil's *Georgics*, Virgil would go beyond his prosaic model in giving both deities places of honour in his poem of the land. Thus collective Fauni are grouped (as if satyrs) with Dryad nymphs immediately after the great patron gods Liber and Ceres, and honoured for their country gifts, *munera*, in *Georg.* 1.11: 'Fauns and Dryads step here together,' *ferte simul Faunique pedem Dryadesque puellae.* But it is Greek Pan, not Italian Faunus, whom Virgil invokes as god of the herds, Pan from Arcadian Tegea, with his cult place on Mount Maenalus. And Pan is introduced halfway between two Greek cultural heroes: first Aristaeus, the pastoral *cultor nemorum* (1.14),[1] then Triptolemus of Eleusis, who discovered arable farming, grouped with Athena, who won her status as patroness and protectress of Athens for her creation of the olive tree (1.18–19). But Attic Triptolemus is followed by the Italian god of the woodlands, Silvanus.

Pan, guardian of flocks, come in person leaving your ancestral woodland, if Maenala is dear to you, god of Tegea, be at hand, propitious, with Minerva, originator of the olive tree, and Triptolemus, inventor of the curved plough, and Silvanus, carrying a young uprooted cypress.

> ipse nemus linquens patrium, saltusque Lycaei
> Pan, ovium custos, tua si tibi Maenala curae
> adsis, O Tegeaee, favens, oleaeque Minerva
> inventrix uncique puer monstrator aratri
> et teneram ab radice ferens, Silvane, cupressum.
>   (Virgil *Georg.* 1.16–20)

I will return to this litany below, as it identifies these gods and cult heroes with the crops and creatures of Virgil's four books. But the poet approaches his account of Italian husbandry as much from his literary Greek inheritance as from the native cults of Italy.

I bypassed just now Virgil's first poetry book, the *Eclogues* or *Bucolica*, songs of and by shepherds. Surely we will find the rustic spirits of Italy at least in his early pastoral poetry? On the other hand, if we think of the *Bucolica* as Virgil's inspired reaction to Theocritus, we might expect any mention of gods and demigods to be of Greek rather than Italian ones. On balance, in fact, Italian and Greek cults are about equally represented in the *Eclogues*. But the general impression is that the gods and demigods of Italy are subordinate, and mentioned only within limits.

Some poems, notably the first and ninth, are far more Italian than their companions, but they are also more clouded by the contemporary sorrows of civil war and confiscation. In the first poem the shepherd Tityrus has no room in his heart for other, less present deities once the godlike youth at Rome has given his blessing; instead he promises monthly (not annual) sacrifices to his saviour, an honour which Alexandrians paid only to their divine rulers the Ptolemies (1.42–3).[2] In contrast, the ninth poem, with its sense of sad aftermath, offers no occasion for hope or faith or piety with respect to any higher power.

In other *Eclogues* too we can distinguish between the poet's language in his framing verses and in the songs he gives to his shepherds. These shepherds are at times Arcadian (7.4, and cf. 10.33), while the poet appeals at times to Sicilian deities, *Sicelides Musae* (4.1) or Arethusa (10.1) and *Nymphae Libethrides* (7.21); but in any case his singers bear Greek names. Even *Eclogues* 1 and 9, apparently set in Virgil's own region of Cispadana in Northern Italy, introduce Greek slave shepherds, Tityrus (from the verb to whisper) and Meliboeus (from roots recalling melody and oxen, hence ox-song).

The predominant gods and divinities in the *Eclogues* are Pan, as teacher of music and *nymphagetes* (leader – or trainer and conductor?) of the nymphs, Apollo as inspirer of poetry, and Bacchus (also called Liber and Iacchus). When Corydon (the Greek name for a song-bird, the lark) sings to the hills and woods of his love for Alexis in *Eclogue* 2, he praises Pan as patron of his art, and invites his beloved to join him in music modelled on Pan's melodies: 'with me in the woods you will imitate Pan in your playing: Pan was the first to join several reeds with wax; Pan cares for sheep and their herdsmen.'

> mecum una in silvis imitabere Pana canendo:
> Pan primum calamos cera coniungere pluris
> instituit, Pan curat oves oviumque magistros.
> (*Ecl.* 2.31–3)

Again the poet in person speaks of competing with Pan in song in *Eclogue* 4: even if Arcadia itself was judge, he is confident that Pan would acknowledge him as superior in the contest (4.58–9).

The nymphs appear in different guises in almost every poem. While Italian nymphs are invariably guardians of springs, Virgil makes them the shepherds' friends and audience both as *Nymphae* and as Dryads (5.59). Corydon speaks of the Nais who brings flowers for his beloved Alexis in *Eclogue* 2, and in 7.21 opens his first entry in the contest by appealing to *Nymphae Libethrides* (from Theocritus' Sicily, like Arethusa of Syracuse addressed in 10.1). In *Eclogue* 5, the singers promise honours to the newly deified Daphnis when they offer the customary vows to the nymphs and when they purify their lands.

> et cum sollemnia vota
> reddemus Nymphis, et cum lustrabimus agros.
> (5.74–5)

In the two amoebaic *Eclogues* (3 and 7), the contestants are paired and invoke a selection of gods in their songs. Some gods, such as *Delia* (Greek Artemis or Roman Diana, 3.67 and 7.29) and, surprisingly, Jupiter (3.60–1 and 7.60), appear only in these eclogues. The third poem is exceptional in two allusions: Virgil has transformed the cheerfully obscene abuse of Theocritus' yokels[3] in an interesting way: he veils the charge of sodomy by aposiopesis, but sets the sex-act in a little shrine, apparently a shrine of the nymphs: 'we know what happened to you and in what shrine – but the easy-going nymphs just laughed!' *novimus et qui te ... /et quo (sed faciles nymphae risere) sacello* (3.9). If these sexual activities actually violated the shrine of the nymphs, it seems the watching nymphs found amusement in his rival's sexual humiliation, unseen by human onlookers. The decades of Virgil's youth and prime seem to have been the heyday of sacro-idyllic wall-painters. But these country vignettes do not usually contain nymphs or other non-human figures. Instead they are crowded with wayfarers and fishermen and drovers and shepherds with their flocks, visiting remarkably exposed and open shrines. Did these domestic decorations provoke Virgil's humour?

The other, more down-to-earth reference is the only allusion to Priapus in the eclogue book. When Corydon addresses Delia, promising her a marble statue (7.31–2), his rival Thyrsis runs the gamut of offerings to Priapus. At first he tells the scarecrow god to be content with an annual birthday bowl of milk, since he watches over a poor little garden (*custos es pauperis horti*), but then he overreaches and contradicts himself: for now he has set up Priapus in marble, but if the flock has a successful lambing the god is to expect his statue in gold (33–6)! From here on the names of gods are bandied about fast. Corydon wins the prize by capping Thyrsis' allusions to Liber and Jupiter (58, 60): he crowds two lines with the favourite trees of four Olympians, Alcides (Hercules), Iacchus (here standing in for Bacchus), Venus, and Apollo (61–2), before capping himself with his beloved Phyllis' favourite tree.

Like Priapus, the other country gods Pales, Ceres, and Silvanus are named only once in the collection. *Eclogue* 5 is the first of two poems evoking Theocritus' lovelorn shepherd Daphnis, and was interpreted by ancient commentators as composed in posthumous honour of Julius Caesar.[4] It depicts first the mourning of Nature and the nymphs for Daphnis, then the joyful offerings of milk, oil, and wine[5] which the shepherds will make in thanks for his deification. The grief for Daphnis' passing is marked by the simultaneous departure from the land of Roman Pales and Greek Apollo. Pales is a surprise, because the deity is seldom mentioned. Indeed this spirit was so antique that scholars questioned whether Pales was male or female; there was never any suggestion of a visual representation, as we noted in connection with Tibullus' odd reference in 2.5.

To celebrate the apotheosis of Daphnis there will be a feast at which Alphesiboeus will perform a Satyr-dance, imitating the Satyrs.[6] This is in fact the only reference to the Satyrs in the Eclogue book, and they are not part of the action, but the model for a kind of dance. The honours promised to Daphnis, 'whenever we shepherds pay our customary vows to the nymphs and purify the land,' are perhaps as near as the *Eclogues* come to formal worship. Daphnis is now to become a god like Bacchus and Ceres; he too will be answerable to the farmers' annual prayers, *tibi sic vota quotannis / agricolae facient: damnabis tu quoque votis* (5.79–80). Whether Virgil had Caesar in mind or not, this language of human vows is the form of worship he will address to Caesar's heir in the proem to the *Georgics*: 'draw near and from now on accustom yourself to be invoked with vows,' *ingredere et votis iam nunc adsuesce vocari* (1.42).

The sixth *Eclogue* is unique in having a supernatural cast, though editors are divided as to whether the nymph Aegle's two young companions are satyrs or human shepherds. What matters is Silenus, the father-figure of the traditional satyr chorus, featured here as a teller of tales. So magical is his song that Virgil breaks the narrative illusion to assure the reader that he would have seen *(videres*, 27) the Fauni and wild creatures dancing to the rhythm and the stiff oaks shaking their topmost branches:

> tum vero in numerum Faunos ferasque videres
> ludere, tum rigidas motare cacumina quercus.
> (6.27–8)

This is the only reference to Fauni in the collection, a vivid vignette of beings closer to the animal than to the divine.

In the last of the *Eclogues* the poet begins by invoking the Sicilian nymph Arethusa for inspiration, then turns to the Naiads with apparent reproaches for their neglect of Gallus when the poet was stricken by love and lamenting in Arcadia (10.1–8). As the Greek country gods come to console the dying Daphnis in Theocritus' first *Idyll*, so sympathizers come to console Gallus, first a human groom (*upilio*), then Apollo, then Silvanus, wearing his woodland wreath of pine cones and brandishing a flowering fennel and tall lilies. Pan too, 'the god of Arcadia,' arrives with his face painted red (26–7), but in the end Gallus rejects the Arcadian world and company of Hamadryads to return (this is implied) to his own elegiac condition.

Taking into account the Olympians, at home in both cultures, this pastoral world is constantly painted in Greek terms, and must have appeared to Virgil's audience or readers as an imaginative Latin version of Greek Bucolic song. Its countryside is not the countryside of Virgil's next poetic enterprise, the *Georgics,* and its imaginary world of leisure among the herds does not overlap with the strenuous engagement of arable farmers or vintners or stock breeders with the fertility of the valleys and plains. Yet surely one factor in the blending of Italian and Greek country gods which we have glimpsed in the opening prayer of *Georgics* 1 must be Virgil's desire to bring his public with him from the musical *otium* of the *Eclogues*, and lead them gently into the annual cycle of work and prayer, *labor* and *vota,* of the tiller's world and the constant preoccupation (*cura*) with the vines and orchard trees.

Ceres and Bacchus are the great benefactors of Lucretius' fifth book, inventors of grain crops and wine (5.14–15), surpassed only by Epicurus, since man can live without bread and wine, but not without the peace of mind conferred by the father of Epicureanism. Ceres and Bacchus come early in Varro's invocation in *RR* 1.1 and are the models in *Eclogue* 5 for the annual worship proposed for Daphnis: 'As vows are offered each year to Ceres and Bacchus, so they will be to you; you too will be obliged to fulfil men's vows.'

> ut Baccho Cererique tibi sic vota quotannis
> agricolae facient: damnabis tu quoque votis.
>   (*Ecl.* 5.79–80)

Thus Ceres, invoked in *Georg.* 1.7–8, dominates the first of the *Georgics*, and Liber, named before and after Ceres (1.7 and 9), the second. In both books acts of worship and a festival in honour of the patron deity form a major climax (1.338–50 and 2.380–96). Let Virgil's complementary treatment of these festivals stand for the pattern of simpler offerings to less powerful and more local gods.

'First and foremost, worship the gods and render annual offerings to great Ceres,' ... *inprimis venerare deos atque annua magnae / sacra refer Cereri* (1.338–9). The sacrifice is timed for the end of winter, when spring is already calm and smiling, and the farmer is to offer honeycombs steeped in milk and *miti ... Baccho,* mild or ripe Bacchus;[7] the sacrificial animal (a sow, as we learn elsewhere) is to walk three times round the smallholding, as the whole band of young countrymen[8] pray to Ceres and invite her into the farmstead (*et Cererem clamore vocant in tecta*, 343, 346–7). Then Virgil moves on to the harvest festival: 'let no one set his sickle to the ripe crop before he has garlanded his head with oak leaves and performed clumsy dances and uttered hymns.'

> neque ante
> falcem maturis quisquam supponat aristis
> quam Cereri redimitus torta tempora quercu
> det motus incompositos et carmina dicat.
> (*Georg.* 1.347–50)

The offering to Bacchus has a different presentation in book 2, as historical narrative, whereas the feast of Ceres was future and imperative. Starting from the sacrifice of a goat by the Athenians (*Thesidae*) as punishment for its damage to the vines – the traditional origin of *Tragoedia* – Virgil passes to the Italians (*Ausonii, Troia gens missa*, 385), who again sport and joke in clumsy verse (*versibus incomptis*), putting on masks, calling on Bacchus in happy hymns, and hanging the masked discs (*oscilla*) on the trees.

'So we will duly utter his tribute to Bacchus with ancestral songs and present dishes and cakes as the consecrated he-goat, led by his horn, will stand at the altar, as we in turn roast his rich innards on spits of hazelwood.'

Ergo rite suum Baccho dicemus honorem
carminibus patriis lancesque et liba feremus
et ductus cornu stabit sacer hircus ad aram
pinguiaque in veribus torrebimus exta colurnis.
   (2.385–8, 393)

Ceres and Bacchus both had official festival days – Ceres in April, Bacchus originally at the Liberalia of March and Vinalia in April, and again the greater Vinalia in the vintage season in late August. But it was open to each peasant to make offerings to the local country gods according to his means, and they are not forgotten. The devout country-dweller comes second only to the man of passionate inquiry and insight into divine matters, whom Virgil blesses in Lucretian language ('Happy the man who could discover the origin of things,' *felix qui potuit rerum cognoscere causas*, 2.490).

Blessed too is the man who knows the country gods,
Pan[9] and old Silvanus and the sister Nymphs.

fortunatus et ille, deos qui novit agrestes,
Panaque Silvanumque senem Nymphasque sorores.
   (2.493–4)

These are, of course, the gods of the untended lands and woodland, whose trees and coppices become Virgil's theme after he has moved from extended treatment of the vine to the olive (420–5) and other trees – the bushes of willow and broom that provide food for the herds and shade for the herdsmen in 434–53. Looking back to the *Eclogues* (and forward to the stock-breeding protected by Pales in *Georg.* 3.1 and 294), Virgil welcomes the rustic Italian gods back into the world of his poetry – and they form the background to the innocently happy accounts of the farmer's life and the feast days sacred to Bacchus of early Romulean Rome (2.527–31) which bring this book of the *Georgics* to its cheerful conclusion.

Let me turn aside briefly to introduce a Virgilian poem with a bucolic setting – one not composed by Virgil, although it was old enough in Lucan's day for him to believe it was Virgil's work. The miniature 'genre' epic called *Culex* follows a shepherd to his noonday nap, where he is about to be bitten by a snake but is saved by the warning bite of a gnat, which he fatally swats. The following night it appears to him in a vision, describing Hades and begging for burial. The author has absorbed the country atmosphere of both the *Eclogues* and the *Georgics*, and makes great play with our lesser *di agrestes*, in invoking both the Naiads and holy Pales, 'to whom the future good lambing of countrymen returns,' *ad quam ventura recurrunt / agrestum bona fetura* (20–1), to show concern for him, as he occupies the lofty habitations of the woods and green forests. Having read the *Georgics*, this poet also invokes the revered Octavian, the holy boy (25–6 and 37), before beginning his tale. But he comes perhaps closest to the *Georgics* in his counterpart to the passage just quoted, Virgil's blessing on the man who knows the country gods (2.493–4), in offering an extended praise of the shepherd's 'blessings, unknown to the cares that torment greedy minds with hostile hearts,' *bona pastoris ... incognita curis / quae lacerant avidas inimico pectore mentes* (58, 60–1). Among these pastoral joys the poet lists others, rising to rhetorical anaphora: 'to him are dear the goats dripping with milk, the woodland and fertile Pales, and in the valleys grottoes ever shady and seeping new springs.'

> illi sunt gratae rorantes lacte capellae
> et nemus et fecunda Pales et vallibus intus
> semper opaca novis manantia fontibus antra.
>   (Pseudo-Virgil *Cul.* 76–8)

His is the worship of a god (Priapus) artlessly carved with a sickle (*falce, non arte politus*), he reveres the sacred groves (*colere* is both to tend and to worship), for him country plants mixed with many-coloured flowers are the equivalent of exotic incense: reverence and innocent rest are combined as the countryman's service and reward (86–90). The country and its gods are also the poet's own delight: 'O flocks, O Pans, and most lovely landscape ... springs of the Hamadryads, by whose worship without extravagance any

shepherd aspiring to imitate the Ascraean poet may lead a carefree
life with tranquil breast.'

> O pecudes, O Panes et O gratissima tempe[10]
> +fontis+ Hamadryadum, quarum non divite cultu
> aemulus Ascraeo pastor sibi quisque poetae
> securam placido traducit pectore vitam.
> (94–7)

It is a far cry from that idyllic if overloaded setting to the prehistoric Italy of Virgil's heroic times. So let us make this an excuse to begin again, and maximize the contrast with the country
setting of Virgil's early work, by approaching the *Aeneid* from the
heart of Rome – the Campidoglio. We see it first through Augustan
eyes, the *aurea tecta*, or gilded roofs, of the Capitoline temple,
and then as Evander saw it, as primal forest, shaggy with woodland scrub and bushes. It is the poet who tells his Roman readers
that religious dread for this place held the countryfolk terrified
even in this distant past – that is, before there was any shrine to
honour – and they shuddered to see the rock and its woods. To the
newcomer Aeneas, Evander explains that this wood and leafy
summit is the home of a god, but no one knows which god; then
he adds that his Arcadians believe they have seen Jupiter himself.
What is remarkable is Virgil's insistence on the holiness of this
uncultivated site.[11] By imagining the rock as already home of the
unknown Jupiter centuries before Tarquinius Priscus, the poet
has made the construction of the Capitoline temple into a fulfilment of prehistoric destiny.

Seneca seized on this paradox of the as-yet-unknown god and
the Italic reverence for natural places and transfers the reverence
to man himself, as theme for a sermon on god within us. 'In every
single good man,' he says, quoting this very passage,

'a god dwells, though we know not who he is.' If you come across a wood
with ancient trees that have outgrown their usual height, one that takes
away your view of the sky with the shade of branches sheltering other

branches, the tallness of the wood, the seclusion of the place, and the wonder at a shadow so deep and unbroken under the open sky convinces you of divine presence. And if a cliff is vaulted by a cave with rocks deeply eroded, not an artificial one, but one hollowed out into such spaciousness by natural causes, it will strike your spirit with a feeling of religious awe. We worship the sources of great rivers: the sudden escape of an immense stream from hiding is honoured with altars. Springs of hot waters are venerated and either the darkness or immeasurable depth has made some pools sacred; so if you see a man undeterred by dangers ... who looks on mankind from above, and at the gods from their level, will you not feel reverence for him?[12]

Here, then, are the principal natural features in which the old Romans saw gods immanent. Held in awe because of their vast size, their mysterious and impenetrable darkness, these are the natural features we would associate with the sublime: woods, caves, springs, rivers, and pools. I say 'wood' rather than the conventional term 'grove' because 'grove' evokes a formal plantation, rather than the original sense of *lucus*, a glade or natural clearing. But the Latin word *lucus* (which Varro notoriously derived from *non lucendo*, not giving light) has a variety of applications, and purist attempts to define the word seem to me counterproductive. The many excellent papers published from the international conference Les Bois sacrés only bring out the diversity of the word's ancient usage and modern interpretations. The presiding geniuses, Cazenove and Scheid (1993), are purists, adhering to the distinction we meet, for example, in Servius on *Aen.* 1.310: a *lucus* is a quantity of trees enhanced by religious association, whereas a *nemus* is a group of trees organized and arranged; and a *silva* is primary woodland, straggling and unshaped by man: *lucus est enim arborum multitudo cum religione, nemus vero composita multitudo arborum, silva diffusa et inculta.* But as Coarelli shows in his paper, once the name *lucus* was applied to a sanctuary or holy place, it would remain the *Lucus* of Feronia or Diana however much the place was developed and formalized – like the plantation within the sanctuary of Gabii. Again, a famous sanctuary like that of Diana at Aricia contained a *lucus Dianae* as well as, or within, the *nemus Aricinum*, and the two areas are distinguished in one of our earliest references, the second-century *Origines* of Cato.[13] Other contributors to this symposium suggest that a *lucus* is inherently sacred, whereas a *nemus* is artificial, created and or- dained by human action. Certainly a *lucus* is outside the space taken for human use, whether as secular property or an augural *templum*. Once acknowledged as the dwelling of a god, it would be left unpruned and unthinned, or if any maintenance was advis- able, such action would require prior ritual procedure. Hence the poetic topos of the *silva incaedua* originating with Ovid.[14]

What I hope to do in this chapter is to take the woods, the caves, the springs, the rivers and pools of Virgil's Latium and Rome and see how he incorporates their holiness into his narrative. But first we need to raise several issues that affect equally any of the divin- ities of place.

Evander's reaction to the nearby Capitoline summit confronts one important issue. Virgil's Trojans have brought with them a load of Homeric baggage – the partisanship of Juno against them, which is offset by the support of Venus, Apollo, and (usually) Neptune. Particularly in the battle scenes, the *deorum ministeria* of these Homeric deities seem incompatible with the presence or partici- pation of the old Italic gods, and (with rare exceptions) we shall not find the Italic deities in the battle narratives of books 9–12. But divine action or divine attendance on a favoured mortal has to be a unique personal vision, so it is equally true that Venus will appear to her son only when he is isolated in nature. Scenes that involve the indwelling spirits of the land will contrast sharply with scenes of human encounter.

Another consideration is that of local loyalty, and this has two aspects. The first is not really a problem. Virgil insists that Aeneas and his men are destined to settle in Italy; he hears this first from Creusa, whose ghost tells him of the western land and the Tiber river, where he will find a settled home (2.781–4),[15] then from Helenus (3.377–83), and again from Mercury (4.265–76) and the Sibyl (6.87–94). Virgil has also made this Trojan landing a home- coming, a *nostos*, by spelling out that Dardanus came from Coruthos (Caere) and his descendants are now returning there. So there is no reason why Italian gods should act against the apparent invaders. And being pious, Aeneas takes every opportunity to do reverence to these local gods. But what about the Italians?

How can Italic gods let their own people suffer? Clearly this is to frame the problem incorrectly, for the peoples of Latium and Etruria have already suffered invasions and inflicted warfare; there has even been civil war in Mezentius' city, and the exile of Metabus springs from another such revolution among the Volscians. To reframe this problem we need to take into account how Virgil himself has worked to eliminate strictly tribal or local apartheid: early in book 7 he marries Latinus to Marica, a nymph from the region of the Liris (7:47);[16] in the parade of Italian leaders Halaesus does not command the people of Falerii, but those of northern Campania (724);[17] and Messapus (691) and Oebalus (734) are similarly assigned as leaders away from their normal geographical associations. Describing Rome's prehistory, Evander includes invasions of Ausonii and Sicani,[18] which have to be explained through the transference or modification of names. What Virgil does is to show his Italic gods of the land as supporting, not attacking, although support for one man or group entails attack on their enemy. As for piety, Turnus too, as we shall see, is pious, and receives favour from the local divinities.

An exception who deserves separate treatment is Faunus. As god of any uncultivated land, he cannot be associated with a single natural feature or region, but the Faunus we meet in *Aeneid* 7 has been transformed, following a tradition that euhemerized him as an ancient king and father of Latinus. In book 7, Virgil offers a genealogy for Latinus which he himself has combined and created. Earlier traditions had made him son of Ulysses, or even Telemachus, and Circe; and in Cato's *Origines* Latinus was still in his prime as a commander when he allied with Aeneas against Turnus. But when Virgil introduces Latinus to the story he makes him great-grandson of Saturn; Saturn, we are told, was father to Picus and Picus to Faunus, who married the nymph Marica and fathered Latinus. So he represents the generation of transition from deity to mortality. Later, indeed not much later, we hear of other ancestors, Italus and Sabinus, whose kinship to Latinus goes unspecified; and Circe will be identified as wife of Picus (an embodiment of Mars), just as the sun will be called *avus* of Latinus. But a recent article by Moorton (1988, 253–9)[19] shows that this account of Latinus' descent is consistent with accepting Circe as wife of Picus, and therefore mother of Faunus, provided we accept *avus* in the wider sense of great-grandfather, not grandfather.

There is a considerable slippage between this short genealogy and the time span implied by Evander in book 8, for whom the coming of Saturn to Latium was followed by a long period (8.319–32) – one sufficiently extended for the people to whom he had taught laws and agriculture to degenerate and then suffer successive invasions, before Evander himself came to Latium as a boy in the time of Hercules, a generation before the Trojan War.

What has this to do with Faunus? The foreshortened family tree means that this grandson of Saturn is also the divine father of the living Latinus. Shocked by the portents affecting Lavinia and the sacred laurel tree around which he built the innermost shrine of his palace when he founded the city, Latinus is driven to consult first everyday *vates* and then the oracle of Faunus, his divine father. He goes at dead of night to sacrifice at Albunea (*Aen.* 7.81–106).[20] Virgil sets the scene in groves beneath the great forest of Albunea with its sacred spring, a dark place that breathes out savage sulphurous gases (7.82–4). We saw that in earlier tradition Faunus was associated with a prophetic voice, and as Latinus' father, the god remains an unseen voice. Latinus performs incubation, sleeping on the skins of his victims, and sees a vision and hears *variae voces*, experiencing intercourse with the gods (*deorum conloquio*), speaking with Acheron in the depths of Avernus. In creating this incubation rite – for we have no reason to think that before Virgil this was a regular practice associated with Faunus or any other god – Virgil has made Latinus have communion with the underworld, appropriately enough if Faunus was mortal and now belongs with the human Manes. Although Seneca did not say so, the caves he mentions are associated in Virgil not with Olympian but with chthonic powers – it is through such depths, through the *specus* of Amsanctus, that Allecto returns to the underworld (*Aen.* 7.563, 565–71).[21]

Virgil gives in full the oracular words of Faunus which Latinus hears coming from the lofty grove. They warned the king to marry his daughter to a foreign newcomer, and Latinus had spread this oracle even before he knew of Aeneas' coming (7.95–106). We shall hear more of Faunus in book 12, when the story is almost played out. As the final confrontation of Aeneas and Turnus begins, Virgil introduces a wild olive tree sacred to Faunus (12.766, *forte sacer Fauno foliis oleaster amaris / hic steterat*) once held in reverence by shipwrecked sailors, who would set gifts in its branches in thanks for their survival, to Faunus as 'Laurentine deity'; we are told that like Horace[22] they hung up their wet garments as a dedication in fulfilment of their vows. But the foreign Trojans commit (unwitting?) sacrilege: with no respect for its sanctity (*nullo discrimine*), they have felled the tree in order to clear the battlefield.[23] Now Faunus has at least a temporary revenge: he holds Aeneas' spear fast in the tree's clinging root-system. As Aeneas tries to uproot it, Turnus in terror prays to Faunus and Terra, the earth goddess, also violated by this blow, for salvation in return for his pious devotion, and Faunus holds fast the spear until Juturna restores his father's honoured sword to Turnus. But both Faunus and Juturna are outsmarted by Venus' superior status, as she pulls out and returns Aeneas' spear. Strange as it may seem that sailors are venerating a god of the wild lands, Virgil here testifies in this brief episode to belief in an ancient practice, to the double status of Faunus as deceased king and surviving god, and to Italic reverence for sacred trees.

But it seems that the country cult of Faunus is already past (cf. *steterat* and *solebant*, 767–8), and this practice may be confirmed as past in Evander's guided tour of Rome. He speaks of the original inhabitants of Pallanteum as Fauns and Nymphs, and of subhuman mankind sprung from rocks and oaks. But the Lupercal (343–5) is nothing to do with Faunus or *Fauni*; Evander had named it after Lycaean Pan, the god of his homeland, Arcadia (*Aen.* 8.343–4).[24] It is natural enough for Evander to present the Lupercal in terms of his native religion, but Virgil seems to have hesitated at this point to treat Faunus as both an ancestor and a woodland spirit.

Along with the *Fauni*, Evander has mentioned nymphs, and the combination is a familiar one to us. Not only were nymphs and fauns the original native inhabitants (*indigenae*, 8.314), Virgil even invents a warrior, Tarquitus (10.550), son of Faunus and the nymph Dryope, to be one of Aeneas' victims when he rages after the death of Pallas. In doing so Virgil raises an ontological question, since this man is child of divine or at least semi-divine parents and should surely not be mortal. But nymphs actually take on a more important role in both cult and genealogy than was possible for the anonymous Fauns.

We saw in chapter 1 that nymphs were the object of personal cult, especially by those who hoped for a cure from sacred waters. Among modern scholars, however, there is a tendency to disregard Nymphs – not surprising in view of the ancient habit of treating them like an opera chorus, or a decorative element of wall-painting. Nor is it surprising that we must make an effort to take seriously what seems to be a frivolous form of deity, mere fun-loving teenaged girls (teaching in a girls' school did not encourage me to look favourably upon them). But nymphs have roles to play, both collectively and individually, in epic, which reflect their real-life significance as objects of cult in Greece no less than in Italy. In fact we must turn to Greek evidence for any helpful discussion of Nymphs. I owe much to the valuable introductory chapter of Jennifer Larson's recent *Greek Nymphs: Myth, Cult, Lore* (2001).[25]

Mythology in its literary form does not always identify nubile women as human or semi-divine nymphs, but it is possible to distinguish such young women as nymphs if, for example, they have a divine father (a river, for instance, like Inachus or Peneus). If not actually immortal they outlive many generations of men (nine times the life cycle of the phoenix), and this is one reason for Thetis or Juturna to lament their apparent privilege.

Collectively nymphs serve as the nurses of the infant Zeus or Dionysus, and provide escort and entertainment for Diana or Apollo or Bacchus. They have skills, such as beekeeping and song and dance, and they also confer benefits on chosen humans. Thus in Apollonius we find the Nereids helping Thetis by bouncing Argo through the air over the Planctae (Apoll. 4.930–67), and other groups of nymphs come to the heroes' aid: when they are stranded amid the Syrtes, the guardian nymphs of Libya (Apoll. 4.1308–29)[26] advise them to pay recompense to their mother (the ship) by carrying her for twelve days and nights until they reach Lake Tritonis. There the Hesperides appear but crumble into dust, only to rematerialize as three different trees, a poplar, an elm, and a willow, and inform the Argonauts that Hercules has preceded them[27] and produced a new spring by striking a rock with his club. This Greek legend has a Roman counterpart in the story reported by Servius that Hercules created Lake Ciminus in southern Etruria by striking the ground.[28]

Virgil uses Homeric-style traditions while Aeneas is not yet in Italy; thus the four references to nymphs in the Carthaginian books all have a Homeric or epic precedent. Juno bribes Aeolus with the offer of a choice of nymph as his bride, as Hera bribed Hypnos in *Iliad* 14.267 with a choice of Graces as his bride. When the Trojans finally reach harbour, there is a cave of the Nymphs, with fresh water and seats carved from living rock – *intus aquae dulces vivoque sedilia saxo, / Nympharum domus* (*Aen.* 1.167–8). As Richard Jenkyns (1998, 515) has said so perceptively, the description might well remind readers of the Cave of the Nymphs on Ithaca on which it is modelled; but Virgil mentions the Nymphs only fleetingly, as an allusion to his model at the end of his description, before he leaves the scene. When Aeneas himself makes reconnaissance on land and meets his disguised mother, he adopts the same approach as his father Anchises had done in the Homeric hymn,[29] diplomatically asking her if she is Diana or one of the Nymphs (1.329–30). And Dido, in a simile much discussed by ancient critics, is compared with Diana for the way her beauty outshines her chorus of Oreads (1.499–500), an image borrowed from Nausicaa's first appearance to Odysseus among her attendants in *Odyssey* 6. We might add to these the fateful moment of Aeneas' union with Dido in the cave (4.166–8), when Tellus and Juno preside over the nuptials, and the Nymphs (who in Apollonius celebrated the true marriage of Medea and Jason) utter cries of lament from the mountain peak.

These allusions all seem a reflection of Greek tradition, and others, even in the Italian narrative, may seem more literary and Greek than religious and Roman. But at the very beginning of Aeneas' narrative to Dido, when he describes the first landfall in Thrace and blood spurts from the bushes where the murdered Polydorus was buried, Aeneas addresses a real act of religious expiation to the Nymphs for laying violent hands on this desecrated tree: 'I offered prayer to the Nymphs of the lands (*Nymphas venerabar agrestis*, 3.34) and father Mars (the local god of Thrace), that they would turn to good what I had seen and ease the omen.'

So at Aeneas' last landfall, when he reaches Latium, other nymphs receive his prayers. In books 7 and 8 we can share with Aeneas two joyous moments. He first hails his new land in book 7, at the meagre feast of pita bread and local fruit, when Ascanius cries out auspiciously that they have been reduced to eating their tables. Recognizing the omen, Aeneas formally greets Italy, his destined new-found-land, and introduces it to the Penates of his old home: 'I salute you too, loyal Penates of Troy: this is my home, this my country,' *Salve fatis mihi debita tellus / vosque ... O fidi Troiae salvete Penates: / hic domus, haec patria est* (7.120–2). Covering his head ritually with leafy branches, Aeneas solemnly invokes in prayer the *genius* of the place, and Tellus, first of the gods.

Now the word *genius* occurs only twice in the *Aeneid*, and not in connection with the *genius* of any man (or the emperor, whose genius was not yet an object of cult when Virgil died). The other passage occurs when Aeneas revisits the tomb of Anchises with *inferiae*, which attract a sacred serpent; Aeneas is unsure, and so are we, whether this was the *genius* of the place, or an attendant on his father (5.95–6). It seems, then, that for Virgil *genius* is a local spirit.

Nor should we pass over the presence of Tellus. Tellus was a deity at Rome, and may be the beautiful mother depicted as suckling twins on the end-relief of the Ara Pacis (rival contenders are Italia, and Venus herself). The earliest known temple of Tellus, on the Carinae, probably goes back to the scandal of Spurius Cassius, whose house on the site was destroyed in 486 in condemnation of his attempt to win tyrannical power by bribing the people with grain. As in *Aeneid* 7, so Tellus is given priority (*prima*, 4.166) when she officiates at the fatal union with Dido – or was that the wrong Tellus, Africa?[30] In Lucretius and the *Georgics*, Tellus is repeatedly seen as a personified divinity who nourishes vegetable, animal, and even human life,[31] and this closeness to divinity is particularly clear in the poignant comparison of the dead Pallas to a plucked hyacinth between life and death, 'whom Mother Tellus no longer nourishes and supplies with strength,' *cui neque fulgor adhuc nec dum sua forma recessit / non iam Mater alit Tellus viresque ministrat* (11.70–1). Tellus can be identified with a specific land, as in Virgil's salute to Italy, 'Hail, Land of Saturn, mighty mother of crops,' *salve, magna parens frugum, Saturnia Tellus* (*Georg.* 2.173), but she is above all the embodiment of the land as mother and nourisher of all life.

Then (*Aen.* 7.135–40) Aeneas turns his prayer to the Nymphs and rivers still unknown, to night and the stars arising at that time, to Jupiter of Mount Ida and Cybele, and to his parents in Olympus and Elysium. A strange combination, we may think, but Jupiter and Cybele are both directly involved in a miracle we shall consider very shortly, and it is Jupiter who responds by sending Aeneas three well-omened thunderclaps and a golden cloud.

The next morning the Trojans set out to explore the rivers upstream from the shore, where they identify the pools of the Numicus, the Tiber itself, and the region of the Latins. These are the regions we will find Turnus commanding, both as prince of the Rutuli and as delegate for Latinus, in the parade of Italian forces (7.797–8).[32] It seems the Trojans have left the coast to sail up the estuary and camp on the banks of the Tiber. Whereas earlier tradition had Aeneas land along the coast near modern Pratica di Mare, Virgil deliberately brought the Trojans into the Tiber to honour the great river, and in so doing implicitly moved the Numicus, the city of Latinus, and even Ardea some fifteen to twenty miles nearer Rome.[33]

After all the disturbances generated by Allecto, the inflaming of Amata and Turnus, and the shepherd uprising against the Trojans, after the declaration of war imposed by Juno against Latinus' will and the parade of contingents from all known Italy, we return to Aeneas and his men at the Tiber mouth as book 8 opens. The Tiber-god himself appears to the sleeping Aeneas, and confirms the prophetic validity of his vision by describing the portent he will see on awakening, of the wild boar sow and thirty piglets. After offering Aeneas guidance to find Evander, the river-god identifies himself: 'I am Tiber, whom you behold in full spate,' *ego sum pleno quem flumine cernis* (8.62). The Tiber is immensely important to Virgil's Italy and will receive our attention very soon, but Aeneas does not forget to include the Nymphs in his

morning prayers. Turning towards the rising sun, he washes ritually in the running stream, raises his arms, and addresses the
river-nymphs first of all: *Nymphae, Laurentes nymphae,*

Nymphs of Laurentum, from whom comes the race of rivers, and you,
father Tiber with your sacred stream, welcome Aeneas and protect him
from danger; at whatever source the lakes possess you, who take pity on
our hardships, from whatever ground you emerge most splendid in your
beauty, you will always be celebrated by my worship, and by my gifts,
horned river and ruler of the western waters: only be at hand for me and
confirm your divine intent more nearly.

> Nymphae, Laurentes Nymphae, genus amnibus unde est,
> tuque, O Thybri tuo genitor cum flumine sancto
> accipite Aenean et tandem arcete periclis,
> quo te cumque lacus miserantem incommoda nostri
> fonte tenent, quocumque solo pulcherrimus exis,
> semper honore meo, semper celebrabere donis
> corniger Hesperidum fluvius regnator aquarum.
> adsis O tantum et propius tua numina firmes.
>   (8.71–8)

I have quoted this prayer in full because it is full of implications:
that Nymphs control the origin of rivers because they preside
over their source, and that the source of the river is its most truly
sacred part. In addressing the river at its mouth, Aeneas may feel
that he has started on the wrong foot, but he knows that Tiber is
the lord of all Italian (or even Western) rivers, and although the
river-god has appeared plainly before him in his vision, he now
wants waking confirmation that the god is propitious.

Something more should be said, before we return to father
Tiber, about Virgil's nymphs: they are mothers. Named Italian
nymphs provide the older generation of our heroes, Marica as
mother of Latinus, Venilia as mother of Turnus (whose grandfather seems to be the god Pilumnus), Carmentis as mother of
Evander, the prophetic mother who was called Themis or
Nicostrate in Greek legend. Others, like Egeria, serve as protectors of Virbius, the reborn Hippolytus, in Diana's grove at Aricia.

Juturna, Turnus' divine sister, is unique in being the recipient of cult at Rome, where her pool stood by the temple of Castor in the forum, and a full speaking and suffering character exploited by Juno to prolong the agony of book 12. While Roman tradition already derived her name from *iuvare* in the time of Cicero and Varro (*LL* 5.71), Virgil derives her name from both *iuvare* and *Turnus*: first mentioned as Turnus' unnamed sister and associated with *succedere*, coming to his aid (10.439) and then with the synonym *succurrere* (12.813–14), she despairs of her role in 12.872, as no longer able to help him (*iuvare*).[34]

But before this Virgil has brought his readers to witness the birth of a most unusual set of nymphs, when Turnus fires Aeneas' ships and Cybele intervenes (9.77–122). Awkward and unconventional as the miracle is, Virgil provides the explanation of the metamorphosis through his narrative of Jupiter's earlier appeal to his mother, and twice the poet identifies the new sea-nymphs not as man-made ships but by their original nature, as sacred trees (9.116–17, 10.230–1, *sacrae pinus* and *maris deas*), sacred in fact to Cybele, who has now transformed them. Their manufacture into ships had not annulled their natural origin and status. The poet is unambiguous that Cybele made them into gods, and gave them the privilege of living their (unlimited) lives beneath the waters (*aevumque agitare sub undis*, 10.235). When the Nymphs swim to meet Aeneas on his return journey and warn him of Ascanius' urgent need for help against Turnus, their spokeswoman Cymodoce identifies them as the band of his companions, to whom Cybele gave divine power over the sea (*numen habere maris*). This fantasy, of Virgil's invention,[35] brings back a more Hellenistic conception of nymphs. So too does the story of the human infant Camilla, another retrospective tale of Virgil's own creation involving a nymph of Diana (*Aen.* 11.535–94).

Although the warrior maid Camilla is only the human child of a mortal Volscian ruler, she was dedicated by her father to Diana, and has lived as the goddess's votary. As Camilla enters battle for the last time, Diana knows that she cannot save her, and so she sends Opis ('helper'?), not to protect the mortal girl but to avenge her inevitable death. Now Opis is not immediately identified as a nymph, but as one of Diana's virgin companions, the sacred band (*una ex virginibus sociis, sacraque caterva*, 11.532–3). Virgil's readers probably assumed she was a nymph, and this character is confirmed when Diana addresses her as *nympha* at the end of her narrative in line 588. When Camilla dies, Opis climbs a hill and, unseen by the fighting armies, shoots her killer Arruns, then flies away. Yes, she flies, on wings.[36] This is the first time I have found a winged nymph in Virgil, and I do not know of any elsewhere. But Opis conforms to one recognized function of nymphs, who attend to the dead, either by burying them (as they do for Phaethon in Ovid) or, in this case, by avenging them and protecting their bodies from defilement.[37]

In my haste to introduce the Tiber, I jumped ahead of one of the most glorious moments, as Aeneas' *Odyssey* is transformed into his *Iliad*. Before he breaks off to herald the second and greater part of his epic, Virgil offers only a glimpse of Aeneas' final landfall. The Trojans have travelled through the night, and at dawn the winds drop and the sailors must resort to rowing. Suddenly (7.29) Aeneas sees a vast wooded area – we can hardly call an *ingens lucus* a mere grove; indeed, this woodland straddles the estuary of the river, which Virgil identifies. The Tiber breaks into the sea, yellow with swift eddies and carrying a great deal of sand. There is a glorious assortment of sea- and shorebirds sweetening the air with their song and flying around the wood. So we have colour, movement, and sound. Aeneas orders his men to turn the ships to shore and happily draws near to the shady stream (*laetus fluvio succedit opaco*). Even so, he does not know that he has reached his destination until the evening, when Ascanius fulfils the oracle of the tables. It is the next day when they send different groups to explore the city, the territory, and the shoreline, and discover the shallow waters of the Numicus, the river Thybris, and where the warrior Latins are living. Their discoveries enable Aeneas to send out his hundred envoys to the city of Latinus, and to disappear from Virgil's narrative until the opening of book 8. The narrative follows his envoys, permitting an expanding portrait of the local geography seen from the central site, the camp and nascent city of the new Troia – the palace of Latinus and Turnus' home at Ardea, and then the woodland setting where Ascanius hunts and tragically kills the pet stag of the shepherd's daughter, provoking a rebellion of the countryfolk. The portrait is further extended by the survey of central Italy generated by the parade of allied contingents mostly characterized by the landscapes of their regions.

Aeneas does not yet know the multiple ferment that Allecto has stirred up, but he is tormented by anxiety. When night comes on, in a beautiful line designed to recall the night when he had his vision of the Penates in Crete,[38] he lies down in the open on the river bank and takes delayed rest. It is now that the Tiber, *deus ipse loci,* god of the place, seems to rise up with his pleasant streams among the poplar branches, clothed in a fine grey robe with shady reeds to cover his hair. Like the Penates, he will first address Aeneas by his function, before confirming that he has arrived: 'Child of divine race, who bring the Trojan city back to us from its enemies, and keep it everlasting, long awaited by Laurentian soil and Latin lands, this is your home; this the place of your gods.'

> O sate gente deum, Troianam ex hostibus urbem
> qui revehis nobis, aeternaque Pergama servas,
> exspectate solo Laurenti arvisque Latinis,
> hic tibi certa domus, certi (ne absiste) Penates.
>   (8.36–9)

As we saw just now, the river gives Aeneas his instructions and promises to guide him upstream to Evander's settlement. Last of all Tiber identifies himself: 'I am the river you see sweeping the banks with full stream and cutting through the rich cultivated land, the blue-grey Tiber, dear to heaven; here is my mighty home, but my source springs from lofty citadels.'

> Ego sum, pleno quem flumine cernis
> stringentem ripas et pinguia culta secantem,
> caeruleus Thybris, caelo gratissimus amnis.
> hic mihi magna domus, celsis caput urbibus exit.
>   (8.62–5)

Scholars have noted the ritual language with which Virgil enhances the river.[39] Its everyday name was Tiberis, which Virgil uses only once, during the catalogue of Italian warriors. But according to Cicero its ritual name was Tiberinus, and an ancient prayer always associated the name with a reference to its waters; so Virgil too adds *fluvio ... amoeno, pleno ... flumine* (8.31, 62). But Virgil is also the first Roman, as far as our evidence has survived, to use the form Thybris, which was thought to be Etruscan,[40] and this is the name he prefers. At its first mention, back in book 2, Creusa called it *Lydius ... Thybris* (2.781–2) because the Etruscans had supposedly come from Lydia, itself fairly near to Troy, and the Romans knew the river as the boundary between Latium and Etruria. It had one other name, Albula, believed to be the river's ancient name, from its sulphurous white waters; indeed, many local waters were called *aquae Albulae* or Albunea.

The river-god plunges into the deep pool, and Aeneas awakes at sunrise, prays to the nymphs and the river, finds the farrow sow, and sacrifices her and her litter to Juno. (Wild boars still root in the forest of Tuscany, and their flesh is delicious; it was no sacrifice if the Trojans could follow their offering to Juno with a meal of the farrow and her sucklings.) He has readied two light ships for the journey upstream, and now a natural miracle happens. The Tiber god quietens his stream, swollen as it was through the long night, and, reversing his flow, lies still with silent water, flattening the surface like some smooth pool or calm swamp so as to offer no challenge to the oars. Now at last we understand why Creusa spoke in her last farewell to Aeneas of the often fierce Tiber as flowing *leni ... agmine* (with gentle course, 2.782): the river's withholding of its adverse current (*luctamen*) recalls and cancels the Trojan's heavy rowing (*in lento luctantur marmore*) in the estuarial swell of their approach to land at 7.28.

Virgil's description of the journey is one of the most marvellous landscapes in Latin poetry, equal to Catullus' stunning description of the amazement of the Nereids at the first ship that carried Peleus and the Argonauts. But both Virgil and Catullus owe two elements in the beauty of this scene to Apollonius. The Trojans speed on with joyful shouting while the greased timber glides through the waters; but instead of describing the very real amazement of the sailors at the new landscape, Virgil inverts the relationship and speaks of the wonder felt by the river and the

inexperienced forest at the shields of men and painted keels float-
ing on the stream (8.91–3). So did Apollonius at the Argo's first
launching, when the nymphs of Pelion (Catullus' Nereids) mar-
velled at the sunlight glittering on the shields and the new creature gliding through the sea (Apoll. 1.544–52).[41] And so, before
Catullus, the Roman dramatist Accius created a messenger speech
for a shepherd reporting the sight of this marvellous new sea-
monster.[42] The journey upstream was only about fifteen miles,
but Virgil extends it in both time and distance, making it seem a
voyage into the depths of the unknown. Jenkyns (1998) in a most
perceptive account of this passage compares its impact with that
of Conrad's voyage into the heart of darkness along the Congo
river. The Trojans tire themselves at the oar night and day and
cover the long river bends, sheltered by changing trees, and cut
through green woods on its calm surface – that is, surely, the reflections mirrored by the calm stream. Were these the first ships
that ever travelled Tiber? Did not Evander come by ship? Certainly
Ovid depicts Evander and Carmenta arriving on shipboard, and
Saturn also traditionally came to Rome by water.[43]

From the river the Trojans see the walls and citadel and scattered houses of the settlement, and turn their prows towards the
city of Pallanteum. As in the previous book, the nearest place is a
wood, a grove in which Evander and his people are sacrificing to
Hercules. It is in fact the site of the Forum Boarium and newly
dedicated Ara Maxima (8.271), one of the most crowded and com-
mercial urban scenes of republican and Augustan Rome. But
Evander's Rome is full of the primeval woodlands: they send back
the echo in Evander's narrative when Hercules' cattle low to their
companions (216), just as the Tiber banks resound and the river
reverses its flow with the reverberations of the falling rock that
opens up Cacus' hell-hole (239–40). On either side of Evander's
settlement on the Pallanteum-Palatine are uninhabited hills: the
Aventine wilderness with its chthonic cave of Cacus, and the
dread and sacred Capitoline, stripped of its gilded temples to
metamorphose back into the numinous space hidden by thick
woods, where Romulus would declare his asylum 'between two
groves,' and, facing it, the cave of the Lupercal underneath the
Palatine (which Virgil revisits as the first scene of the great shield

of Aeneas, 8.630–4) – even the fashionable and busy Argiletum is still a wooded glade (345).

It is time to pay more attention to the many *luci* of our narrative. From early reading we think of Romulus' Asylum as unique. But both the concept and the context were established. Greek cities could declare an asylum, and under the empire were given right to offer asylum to offenders, but in essence every sacred grove was in some sense an asylum. Recent scholarship by Thomas (1988) and Bodel (1986/1994) has made us very much aware of the taboos and formal inscribed regulations associated with sacred groves, such as that of the Arval Brethren outside Rome and the famous grove of Spoleto. We know that even cutting back branches of a tree to allow light or human passage required an act of expiation; how much more any act of human violence. This is why Hippolytus Virbius is safe 'in the groves of Egeria, around the moist shores, where stands the wealthy and propitious altar of Diana,' *eductum Egeriae lucis umentia circum / litora pinguis ubi et placabilis ara Dianae* (7.763–4),[44] and other warriors too have grown up sheltered in *luci*. So in *Aeneid* 9.583–5 Arcens sent his son to be reared in his mother's grove near the pools of the river Simaethus by the altar of Palicus, and we may compare the similar upbringing of the Trojan gatekeepers Pandarus and Bitias, reared by woodland Iaira in the grove of Jupiter.[45]

A sacred grove is also the climax of Aeneas' journey, when he leaves Pallanteum for Caere and pauses outside the town at a vast cool grove (*ingens gelidum lucus*, 8.597) enclosed by hills and surrounded by black pine woods. Its origin is already lost in antiquity: 'according to legend the first inhabitants of the Latin lands, the ancient Pelasgi, had dedicated it to Silvanus, god of fields and herds, giving him a grove and a holy day.'

> est ingens gelidum lucus prope Caeritis amnem,
> religione patrum late sacer; undique colles
> inclusere cavi et nigra nemus abiete cingunt.
> Silvano fama est veteres sacrasse Pelasgos,
> arvorum pecorisque deo, lucumque diemque,
> qui primi finis aliquando habuere Latinos.
> (8.597–602)

This is how Virgil evokes cult, as offering the god a sacred space and a sacred time. Although the passage contains the only reference to Silvanus in the *Aeneid*, his importance is implied by the account of the grove as 'held sacred far and wide by the reverence of ancestors,' *religione patrum late sacer*. It is here that Aeneas will receive from his goddess mother the shield containing the engraved future of Rome. So within the two books of Latium and Rome, Silvanus' grove at Caere/Corythus towards the end of the narrative of book 8 corresponds in function to the prophetic shrine of Faunus, from which 'the tribes of Italy and all Oenotria sought oracles,' in the first phase of the narrative of book 7 (85–6). This correspondence argues against the notion that Virgil's age saw Silvanus as displacing Faunus. Far from being represented here as a new god, Silvanus with his cult has always existed, as old as, or older than, his rival.

Now it is time to leave Aeneas and consider the relationship of his rival Turnus to the gods of Italy. Until book 9 we have seen little of Turnus, but just as book 8 opened at dawn with Aeneas addressed by a god and responding with prayer and sacrifice, so book 9 finds Turnus sitting in the grove and sacred valley of his father Pilumnus.[46] Juno has sent Iris to him with an unauthorized message urging him to attack the Trojan camp. Like Aeneas the prince is pious, and washes in the running stream (Tiber? Numicus?) for ritual purity before uttering fervent prayers and weighing down the heavens with vows:

> ad undam
> processit summoque hausit de gurgite lymphas
> multa deos orans, oneravitque aethera votis.
> (9.22–4)

In their turn the old gods care for Turnus. When he is isolated fighting inside the Trojan camp and has performed an amazing *aristeia*, he escapes by leaping fully armed into the Tiber. The river welcomes him with its yellow eddies (*suo cum gurgite flavo*, 9.816) and bears him up on gentle waters, returning him joyful to his comrades, *abluta caede*, washed clean of the slaughter. This river is generous to the men who dwell around it, and Virgil's language, recalling Turnus' pious act at the opening of the book, makes clear that Tiber is offering Turnus both safety and ritual purgation.[47]

There is one last demonstration that Turnus has the Italian gods on his side, and it brings Faunus back into the narrative; this is not the king, but the old wilderness god of the countrymen. During the deadly duel, Turnus' sword shatters, leaving him potentially at Aeneas' mercy. But Aeneas' spear is caught in the wild olive stump sacred to Faunus, on which shipwrecked sailors used to hang offerings.[48]

> forte sacer Fauno foliis oleaster amaris
> hic steterat, nautis olim venerabile lignum,
> servati ex undis ubi figere dona solebant
> Laurenti divo et votas suspendere vestis;
> sed stirpem Teucri nullo discrimine sacrum
> sustulerant, puro ut possent concurrere campo.
>   (12.766–71)

Wild olives were not well regarded by farmers, as the second book of the *Georgics* shows: compare with the 'wild olive of bitter foliage' (*foliis oleaster amaris*, 766) the description of the wild but infertile tree at *Georg.* 2.314, *infelix ... foliis oleaster amaris*. Virgil defers the outcome of the combat in order to give the history of this particular tree. Not just the farmers of Laurentum but sailors brought safely back to the land hung grateful dedications on its branches. The Trojans, instead, have destroyed it 'so that they can fight on a clear field,' *puro ut possent concurrere campo*. We need to consider more carefully how Virgil used *purus*, which is a religious term, as in *manibus puris*, and ask whether the poet has constructed irony into the Trojan purpose. They have violated a sacred tree, and when Turnus prays not just to Faunus but also to earth (*optima ... Terra*, 777–8), the god ensures that his vows do not go in vain, and helps him (*opemque ... non cassa in vota*) by holding the spear fast, while Turnus' sister, the nymph Juturna, darts in to restore his sword to him. Crying 'unfair' at this intervention, Venus has her excuse and in turn dislodges the spear for Aeneas.

As Thomas (1988, 270n30) has expressed it, this act is the final instance of replacing the Saturnian order by the Jovian. As with the grove of Silvanus, we can read the episode as proof that not only are the free Italians doomed to absorption into empire, but their gods too are displaced. While Thomas goes too far, I believe, in reading the funeral of Misenus in book 6 as tree-violation, Virgil has left no doubt as to how we should read the Trojan action here, and we can see in the suppression of the old country gods (*di agrestes*) the spiritual loss which must come with the onset of the new order. It is not only the world-weary modern city-dweller who feels sentimental grief at the expulsion of the old Italian gods; we shall see in the next chapter that as Virgil celebrated Aeneas, a great poet was already reaching manhood who would cherish and celebrate the gods Aeneas had expelled.

CHAPTER THREE

Ovid's *Fasti* and the Local Gods of the City

The influence of the *Aeneid* seems to have spread even before Virgil's death and its posthumous publication. And Virgil's portrayal of the communities of early Latium and Rome is reflected not only in Tibullus, especially the fifth elegy in his second book, but in Propertius, who heralded the coming to birth of 'something greater than the Iliad' as early as the mid-twenties BCE (Prop. 2.34.61–6).[1] It is significant that in the poet's tribute to Virgil the *Eclogues* are privileged over the *Georgics*, earning ten lines (2.34.67–76) by their erotic content, while the *Aeneid* is identified not by narrative elements from the three books 2, 4, and 6, which we are told Virgil read to Augustus in 23 BCE, but by the victory of Actium depicted on the shield of Aeneas in book 8 (2.34.61–6). As Tibullus had celebrated the cults of the countryside, focusing on human devotion rather than naming specific gods, so Propertius' Cynthia makes a simple sacrifice in a rustic chapel: 'there you [Cynthia] will bring incense seldom offered in an untended chapel, where a country kid will be slain before the hearth,'

> atque ibi rara feres inculto tura sacello
> haedus ubi agrestis corruet ante focos.
> (Prop. 2.19.13–14)

If we suspect this (and the following reference to hunting as the rites of Diana) as a kind of formal cliché, readers will find Propertius more reverent towards Rome's great river and seven walled hills in his third book (3.11.42, 57, 65). His fourth book, the predecessor of Ovid's *Fasti*, which is our focus in this chapter, is formally announced as concerned with 'rites and anniversaries and the ancient names of places,' *sacra diesque canam et cognomina prisca locorum* (4.1.69). Five of its elegies honour the early city or its site, and ancient forms of religion (six if we include the contemporary anniversary of Actium celebrated in 4.6): 4.1., 4.2 (Vertumnus), 4.4, 4.9, and 4.10. Rome's original pastoral landscape and her oldest gods are honoured particularly in the opening elegy and the legends of Tarpeia (who betrayed the citadel to the Sabines early in Romulus' kingship, 4.4) and Hercules' foundation of the Ara Maxima, 4.9.[2]

Propertius' early Rome is full of groves and springs, and the Palatine is rich in grazing cattle (*pecorosa Palatia*, 4.9.3). In 4.4, Tarpeia, portrayed as a Vestal, comes down from the citadel to fetch water for Vesta's ritual: 'there was a fertile grove, hidden in an ivy-clad grotto, and abundant trees echoed with fresh sprung waters, the home of Silvanus thick with branches ...'

> lucus erat felix hederoso conditus antro,
>> multaque nativis obstrepit arbor aquis
>
> Silvani ramosa domus.
>> (4.4.3–5; cf. 4.8.31, *Tarpeios ... lucos*)

Again in 4.9, Hercules, victorious over Cacus and ranging over the Palatine in desperate thirst, comes upon a grove but finds it closed to him.

From a distance he hears the laughter of girls within, where the woodland formed a grove with its shady vault: these were the cloistered spaces of the women's goddess, springs protected by sanctity, and rites not revealed to any men without punishment. Scarlet headbands covered the secluded entrance and the crumbling cottage was lit by fragrant fire. The poplar adorned the shrine with its trailing branches, and abundant shade concealed singing birds.

> sed procul inclusas audit ridere puellas
>> lucus ubi umbroso fecerat orbe nemus,
>
>> femineae loca clausa deae fontisque piandos

> impune et nullis sacra retecta viris.
> devia puniceae velabant limina vittae,
>   putris odorato luxerat igne casa.
> populus et longis ornabat frondibus aedem,
>   multaque cantantis umbra tegebat avis.
>   (4.9.23–30)

The exciting new glorification of Augustus' Palatine precinct (shared with Apollo and Vesta, as Ovid will remind us) will have annihilated this beautiful natural wilderness during Propertius' adult years, but the poet evokes not only the lost landscape but the old pastoral world; not just the cult of Silvanus, and the Nymphs, honoured along with Vesta by Tarpeia (4.4.25; 4.4.36), but the earliest festivals of Parilia (4.1.19; 4.4.73) and Lupercalia (4.1.26). Propertius may speak of singing about rites and anniversaries; the real focus of his poetry in this last book is the *loca,* and the myths or legends that gave them their ancient names (*cognomina prisca*). Propertius, as much as Virgil, gave to Ovid in the next generation a sense of Rome's picturesque and romantic past. It is beyond the scope of these lectures to do justice to this fourth book of Propertius, which deserves and has received separate study in its own right.[3] Ovid was always a poet of multiple inspiration and allusion, and while readers can find reminiscences in the *Fasti* of all his predecessors – of Livy's prose narrative (books 1–5 were available from 25 BCE) and of both Tibullus and Propertius – it is Virgil's model which inspires and dominates Ovid's palette.

When James O'Hara called Ovid 'Vergil's best reader' in an important recent paper (O'Hara 1996), he was concentrating on etymological wordplay, but his wider focus was on the careful attention shown by the younger poet to his great predecessor. One of the most conspicuous features of Ovid's re-creation of the local gods of the Roman and Latin landscape is his adherence to the framework that Virgil constructed for his prehistory of Latium and Pallanteum in books 7 and 8 of the *Aeneid.*

It is an incidental result that the narrative of the anonymous 'Origin of the Roman Nation' (*Origo gentis Romanae*), converting

these books of the *Aeneid* into a continuous (if brief) prose chron-
icle, is as compatible in spirit and content with Ovid's *Fasti* as
with the *Aeneid* itself. And yet this text, which clearly has an
Augustan base and mentions many scholars and historians of and
before the age of Augustus, makes no mention of Ovid and contains no material that must have derived from him. But then this
prehistorian nails the names of Varro and Verrius Flaccus to the
mast, and Verrius' antiquarian work preceded Ovid; indeed, his
Fasti Praenestini were Ovid's most important source.[4] Affinities
with the *Fasti* derive from these common sources.

Ovid began his *Metamorphoses* with Chaos and took the work
up to his own time, *ad mea tempora* (*Met*.1.4).[5] His *Fasti*, too,
take history – in this case the history of Rome from before its human occupancy – back to Chaos, but not immediately. We do not
know how Ovid originally began his calendar poem. The first
book of the *Fasti* as it has come down to us was revised in exile,
indeed after the death of Augustus in 14 CE. Thus the poem has a
new beginning, with a new dedication to Tiberius' heir, Prince
Germanicus, as both a poet and a lover of astronomy. Once Ovid
has reviewed the recurring pattern of days common to all the calendar months, he reports his first interview; and in Callimachean
fashion this is an epiphany of the god Janus, who identifies himself with this same original Chaos. The god explains that from the
moment when the earth took shape from the original mass of all
four elements and claimed its position in the firmament, he,
Janus, was transformed 'from a shapeless mass into my own [two-
faced] appearance with a body worthy of a god,' *tunc ego, qui
fueram globus et sine imagine moles, / in faciem redii dignaque
membra deo* (*Fasti* 1.111–12).

Now although Janus is not one of the *di agrestes* who are my
main theme, he is a peculiarly Italian god, treated by Ovid as su-
premely autochthonous, local to Rome itself, so he will be a useful example from the beginning of Ovid's poem to illustrate some
special features of Italic gods isolated and discussed most recently
in John Scheid's *Introduction to Roman Religion* (1998/2003).[6]
Italic gods were identified by their function, and this was not just
a feature of the single-task *Indigitamenta* like Vervactor, the god
for ploughing fallow. Thus Ovid's Janus explains that he presides

over the doors of heaven, and derives his name *I-anus* from *i-re*, to go, because Jupiter comes and goes through his *officium* (1.125–6). Hence Janus identifies himself as Opener and Shutter (his titles in Latin prayer are *Patulcius* and *Clusius*, *Fasti* 1.129–30). However, although in Roman polytheism each god had or had acquired several functions, he or she did not have exclusive control of them, as in a modern trade union. In fact, as Scheid (2003, 158) notes, 'Roman deities are never on their own,' and prayers are usually addressed to several gods, whether these are sublime poetic prayers like Virgil's appeal at the end of the first *Georgic*, *di patrii, indigetes et Romule Vestaque mater* (1.498), or the quasi-comic appeal of a youth in Plautus, 'so may the gods great and small and even the gods of little libations help me,' *ita di me omnes magni minutique et etiam patellarii / faxint* (*Cist.* 522). The humorous ranking of gods and godlings in this relatively early text also suggests that there was a recognized hierarchy for gods as well as for mortals, that gods could be assimilated to different levels of authority and subordination in community and household. So, for example, when the temple of Jupiter Optimus Maximus is being constructed, the whole crowd of divine small fry gives way (*deorum / cuncta Iovi cessit turba locumque dedit, Fasti* 2.667–8). Terminus alone stays put, in keeping with his function as a landmark.[7] Again, as we shall see, minor *numina* like Picus and Faunus will not attempt intervention for which they are not authorized.

For Ovid, however, Janus is most valuable for his comprehensive memory of Rome's history. He is the god on the spot, expert by virtue of his autopsy, and as Ovid makes clear, Janus has seniority over Jupiter himself.[8] As the poet seeks the inside story of the form and function of the New Year, his question about the gifts of dates and figs, and the cash contribution, or *stips*, paid in Janus' name (*Fasti* 1.189), brings Janus to mention the reign of Saturn;[9] but he does not linger at this point. Instead he will perform two major feats of time travel before returning to Saturn and Rome's prehistory. First, Janus moves forward in time to evoke and praise the simple poverty of Romulus (1.197–208), and then he follows the theme of contrast with a tactful if inconsistent acceptance of the present gilded roofs of Augustus's Capitol (221–6).

Only after he has paid proper homage to this golden temple worthy of the supreme god's majesty[10] does the poet exploit the imagery of Rome's oldest coinage, the heavy bronze *as* which showed Janus on the obverse and a ship on its reverse, to describe Saturn's arrival at the site of Rome (235–8). Ovid's version has slightly shifted Virgil's account: Saturn certainly takes refuge in Latium, as he was said to do in *Aen.* 8.319–25, but he arrives by ship, and, after wandering worldwide, reaches the Tuscan Tiber (*Tuscum rate venit ad amnem, Fasti* 233) to make this land his home.

For Ovid's calendar poem is as much a poem of place as of time, and, in celebrating the places of Rome, Ovid will give continuing prominence to the Tiber both as river and, in due course, as god. Janus himself, even before Saturn came, tilled the soil on the calm Tiber's left bank (the Etruscan bank; we should think of the river as we travel like Saturn upstream from the coast).[11] He named and farmed the Janiculum (246) when the opposite, the Latin, river bank and site of the future Rome was still primary woodland fit only for pasture: 'I myself tilled the ground which the most peaceful water of the sandy Thybris brushes on the left bank. Here where Rome now stands, an unfelled wood flourished, and so great a city was pasture for a few oxen.'

> Ipse solum colui, cuius placidissima laevum
> > radit harenosi Thybridis unda latus.
> hic, ubi nunc Roma est, incaedua silva virebat,
> > tantaque res paucis pascua bubus erat.
> > (Ovid *Fasti* 1.241–4)

Indeed, unlike Virgil (*Aen.* 8.357), Ovid's Janus does not mention a Saturnian citadel,[12] perhaps because he has already explained that Saturn gave his name to the people, *gens Saturnia* (235–7). Apart from the studies of Schiebe (1986) and Parker (1997), there has been too little interest in the mysterious figure of Saturn, an Italic god of agriculture[13] very different from the Hesiodic Kronos, with whom he was gradually equated. The problem is that apart from Macrobius' (secondary) account in *Saturnalia* (1.7) we scarcely have any raw material, whether archaeological or linguistic, to reconstruct his role. Clearly Varro or Verrius had been prompted into speculating about the origin of this god by the Roman custom of sacrificing to Saturn with head uncovered, for Plutarch raises this anomaly in his *Roman Questions* (*Qu.* 14) and treats both Saturn and Janus as newcomers to Italy from the Greek world. As Virgil's Evander had explained to Aeneas, so in Ovid the pre-Jovian reign of Saturn was a golden age, a time of peace when the people needed neither intimidation nor force but were disciplined by their own sense of decency (*proque metu populum sine vi pudor ipse regebat,* 1.251), and gods were still happy to live among men.

Evander's turn comes a little later in this remodelled first book, when Ovid takes the Carmentalia, or feast of Carmentis,[14] as an opportunity to retell the coming of the prophetic Arcadian nymph and her son to the site of Rome. The focus is on the nymph as mother and counsellor to her son when they are driven by political dissension from their native land, and she counsels in terms pointedly appropriate to Ovid's own condition of exile. Like Saturn, Evander is brought to Rome by travel westwards over the Ionian and Tyrrhenian seas from Greece to 'Hesperia' (*Fasti* 1.498). With his mother's encouragement he reaches the Tiber mouth, then steers his ship upstream against the Tuscan waters. When Carmentis sees the river bank near the shallows called Tarentum, with some scattered cottages (Ovid is echoing Aeneas' first sight of Pallanteum, in *Aeneid* 8),[15] her hair stands on end with inspiration, and she stays Evander's hand at the helm, as she greets the land in words we can take as our guide to its divine landscape:

Hail, gods of the places we have been seeking, hail, land that will give new gods to the heavens! Hail, rivers and springs enjoyed by this welcoming land, and nymphs of the woods and bands of Naiads! May it be with good omen that I and my son behold you, and may we tread your bank with lucky foot.

> Di ... petitorum ... salvete locorum,
>   tuque novos caelo Terra datura deos.
> fluminaque et fontes, quibus utitur hospita tellus,
>   et nemorum nymphae[16] Naiadumque chori!
> Este bonis avibus visi natoque mihique
>   ripaque felici tacta sit ista pede.
>   (1.509–14)

Carmentis' prayer, with its appeal to local gods, rivers, and nymphs, may be shaped by two prayers of Aeneas, one reported at *Aen.* 7.136–8, the other quoted in full at 8.71–3. But Ovid has updated her script to incorporate the prophecy of Aeneas' coming, and then to honour first Augustus (*ipso ... deo*, the god himself, 1.530), then, in the rewriting after Augustus' death, his widow Livia and stepson and heir Tiberius (1.531–6). Let us bypass these courtly gestures and follow Carmentis and Evander onto the Latin river bank and their Arcadian settlement on the Palatine. As in Virgil but in faster mode, Hercules appears (543–6), has some cattle rustled by Cacus (547–8 and 559–60), and tracks down the thief and clubs him to death (561–78), before founding the Ara Maxima (579–82).

Ovid has opened his calendar poem by setting up the foundation of the Palatine community which Aeneas will visit a generation later. But Aeneas is not yet his focus; instead, Evander himself is the stranger and immigrant (*hospes ... advena*), first guest, then host to the other divinely born guest, Hercules. Both are welcomed by the land (I would give *Terra* in 510 the capital letter due to a deity) and, above all, by the great river, which has already been named or described four times (233, 242, 500, 511).

Throughout Ovid's chain of calendar elegies we will find emphasis on a recurring theme. What was in the *Aeneid* one cardinal migration, of the hero Aeneas and his people, is replaced in the *Fasti* by the repeated travel westwards of both gods and men, and the river Tiber will again and again be the medium of their arrival. The long voyage of the goddess Cybele from Pergamum in Asia Minor in book 4 is not the most extraordinary of these instances, but Ovid assigns forty-five lines to the brief final portion of her journey up the Tiber from Ostia to Rome (4.291–336).[17] The prize for such voyaging must go to the last overseas traveller in the *Fasti*, Ino, who leaps off a crag near Corinth and is divinely conveyed to the Tiber mouth and upstream to Evander's settlement (6.495–506). Now Ovid knows, and reminds us, that Leucothea, the sea-goddess who rescued the shipwrecked Odysseus from Poseidon's storm in *Odyssey* 5, had once been the human queen Ino.[18] But when he tells the charter legend of the Matralia, in which Ino is transformed into Mater Matuta / Leucothea, and her infant Melicertes into Palaemon, he has the mortal mother and child borne through the Ionian sea and up the Tyrrhenian coast to the Tiber by the nymph Panope and her hundred sisters; as he puts it, she was not yet Leucothea, nor was her boy the god Palaemon when they reached 'the mouth of the eddying Tiber' (*verticibus densi Thybridis ora*, 6.501–2). Ino comes to the grove of Stimula or Semele (to which we shall return), where she is attacked by Maenads and rescued by Hercules, who takes her to be welcomed by Carmentis, whose second prophecy (6.541–8) incorporates the deification of both Ino and Hercules.

But supernatural transportation is only one category of allusion to the great river. The Tiber is constantly used as a marker for the site of Rome,[19] from the first example in our text (*Tuscum in amnem*, 1.233) to the grove of Helernus at the Tiber mouth, which is honoured with cult on the first day of February (2.67–8), to the rite of the Argei in May (5.621–60), and to the last complex of references constructed around the Vestalia in June (6.249–460). The Vestalia saw the cleansing of the temple of Vesta by the virgins, and for some nine days during this cleansing there was a prohibition on marriages; it was the Tiber which cleansed the city, as Ovid illustrates through the informed advice of the Flaminica Dialis, who reports the ban on 6 June: 'until the gentle Tiber shall have carried to the sea on his yellow waters the dirt cleaned from the abode of Trojan Vesta,' *donec ab Iliaca placidus* purgamina Vesta / *detulerit flavis in mare Thybris aquis* (6.227–8). Ovid himself will address the Tiber directly to mark this moment some hundred lines before his poem ends, at 713–14 on 15 June, and mark it with a variation on the conspicuous line ending 'This is that day, O Tiber, when you discharge the dirt cleaned from Vesta's temple into the sea on your Etruscan current,' *haec est illa dies qua tu* purgamina Vestae, / *Thybri, per Etruscas in mare mittis aquas*.

The river-god, whether we call him *Tiberinus*, his acknowledged ritual name, or the more learned *Volturnus*, had a temple on the Insula Tiberina, and even games in his honour, though they seem to have been modest in scale. On 7 June, Ovid turns to the river to record these *ludi Tiberini* on the Campus Martius; these were not a national festival but a guild celebration, as it were, for the fishermen with net or with hook and rod (6.237–40).[20]

Twice in the last few references Ovid has apostrophized the river with a vocative – a metrically convenient device, as we notice when the pentameter ending *Thybris aquas* in 6.228 is followed by *Thybri tuos* ten lines later (6.238). But by June, Ovid has already proved that he is actually on speaking terms with the river. We saw how the river-god appeared miraculously to Aeneas and guaranteed his safe voyage from the river mouth to Pallanteum. In *Fasti* 5, Tiberinus appears to the poet himself in an epiphany as carefully reported as that of Janus. There was a strange ritual on 14 May, in which the Vestal Virgins threw straw dummies in human form from the wooden bridge; it is explained by a tradition that in the old days of Saturn, prophetic Jupiter uttered these words: *falcifero libata seni duo corpora, gentes, / mittite, quae Tuscis excipiantur aquis*, 'clans, offer to the scythe-bearing old god two bodies to be taken up by the Tuscan waters' (5.627–8). So this was once a human sacrifice, worthy perhaps of the cannibal Kronos, father of Zeus, but somewhat incongruous for the benevolent Saturn, just as there is a moral discrepancy between the Greek legend in which Jupiter (Zeus) drove his old father Kronos into exile, and the Italic cult prescribing offerings to Saturn.[21] The drowning of these Argei is one of several forms of human sacrifice which Romans believed had been observed until Hercules came to the rescue, and converted the old rite to a new and more clement offering by substituting *stramineos ... Quirites* ('citizens made of straw,' 5.631).

All this Ovid has explained in person, without claiming any expert source or consultant. He even offers an alternative and more discreditable explanation for the rite, quasi-political and in keeping with the role given to *maiores* in naming the month of May: the young men established the practice of throwing frail old men from bridges in order to monopolize the vote (5.633–4). It is ostensibly to avoid this slur that he appeals to the river: 'tell me the real reason!' (5.635, *Thybri, doce verum*). Tiber, like Janus, is aboriginal, since its banks were there before the city, and so would have witnessed the origin of the practice. Like Virgil's Tiber, the river-god rears up his reed-covered head from his channel, and opens his hoarse mouth[22] with a speech Ovid repeats for his readers: 'Yes, I saw this area when it was grass without a city wall,

when either bank gave pasture to scattered oxen. I, whom nations
know and hold in awe, was held in contempt even by cattle.'

> haec loca desertas vidi sine moenibus herbas;
>> pascebat sparsas utraque ripa boves,
> et quem nunc gentes Tiberim noruntque timentque
>> tunc etiam pecori despiciendus eram.
>> (5.639–42)

This is more than characterization; Ovid is making the river an
object of the same reverence given by Rome's empire to the city
and its gods. Tiber repeats for us what we learned in book 1, but
with a difference (continuing with 643–6): 'The name of Arcadian
Evander is often repeated to you: Evander was the first comer to
stir my waters with the oar, then Hercules came with an Argive
band of warriors. In those days my name was Albula, if I remember rightly.'

> Arcadis Evandri nomen tibi saepe refertur:
>> ille meas remis advena torsit aquas.
> venit et Alcides, turba comitatus Achiva;
>> Albula, si memini, tunc mihi nomen erat.

The story of Hercules as leader of a military expedition can be
found in Dionysius, as a quasi-historical alternative to the mythic
version, in which the hero brings back the cattle of Geryon single-
handed. But this other version is essential to the *aition* of the
men of straw. As in Dionysius's account, Hercules kills Cacus
and moves on with Geryon's herd, but his Argive veterans do not
want to leave, preferring to settle their Lares in the hills around
Pallanteum. As they grow old they are moved by homesickness,
and one or other of them makes a last request, that he be thrown
into the Tiber so that his ashes can be carried downstream and
back to Argos – another supernatural voyage no more credible
than Ino's westward journey. Ovid's Tiber quotes verbatim the
old veteran's *mandata morituri* (cf. 5.654, *hoc breve mandat
opus*), which should have been respected, but reveals that instead
his heir buried the old immigrant in Roman soil and tossed a

substitute straw dummy into the river to make the journey back across the long seas. And in case Ovid's readers should miss their poet's august model, he has the river dive down to the dripping rocks of his natural grotto,[23] while his waters suspend their current – an unnecessary trick, since Ovid, unlike Aeneas, is not planning to navigate the river.

I have left aside the most famous legend of the Tiber, which Ovid ingeniously retells in reverse order by narrating the exposure of Rome's founding twins before their actual conception. Now neither Ennius, in the wonderful passage of *Annales* 1 where the newly impregnated Ilia reports her dream, nor Ovid names the waters which the Vestal was seeking when Mars overcame her – and with good reason. In the legend, Ilia, whom Ovid calls Rhea Silvia, was a Vestal at Alba, and it was only the exposure of her babies which occurred by the Tiber bank on the site of Rome. This is the episode vividly imagined in *Fasti* 2.385–412 and briefly recalled at the beginning of the next book (3.51–2). The wicked Amulius orders the babies to be drowned in the river, and the servants carry them to an uninhabited place (*loca sola*, 2.388). But they are brought to a halt by the river in spate. Ovid introduces the river not as the Tiber, but by its former name of Albula, now renamed Tiberis after the drowned Alban king Tiberinus.[24] The servants abandon the babes in their little container near the Velabrum, the river's overflow at the site of the present-day forum and the valley of the Circus Maximus. But instead of sinking, the little ark containing the babes settles on the mudbanks under the shady wood, beneath a fig tree, where the she-wolf comes and feeds them. For Ovid's calendar this familiar tale of the *lupa* is part of his celebration of the February Lupercalia – the *aition* of the grotto called Lupercal[25] (2.381) – and is followed by tales basing the origin of the festival on Arcadian Mount Lycaeus and its god, Lycaean Faunus (2.423–4).

But our focus is on the Tiber, which is represented in book 3, with its usual benevolent and moral persona, as deliberately saving the children: 'he ordered the twins to be drowned in the river, but the water shunned this crime, and the babies are left on the dry ground,' *amne iubet mergi geminos: scelus unda refugit, / in sicca pueri destituuntur humo* (3.51–2).

The Tiber also has a role in some versions of the fate of their mother, Ilia. Dionysius reports that she was imprisoned, but a variant legend told that she too was intended for drowning, but was rescued by the river-god, who made her his bride; thus Horace makes her the bride of Tiber. Ovid omits Ilia's fate in the *Fasti*, perhaps because an earlier poem, *Amores* 3.6, had already told the myth of her rescue from suicide by the river Anio, a tributary of the Tiber. The contrast offered by this tale reflects the difference of genre between the poet's national, aetiological elegy and his earlier romanticizing love elegy. Anio treats Ilia with more respect than we will observe in the Greek gods and river-gods who populate the *Metamorphoses*: spying her wandering on his banks, he raises his head from his waters and addresses her by her heroic royal descent from Trojan Laomedon (*Ilia, ab Idaeo Laomedonte genus*) as he offers her what sounds like marriage:

Put aside your fears; my palace will welcome you as your home and rivers will honour you; you will be mistress of a hundred nymphs or more (for our streams possess a hundred or more nymphs): do not reject me, Trojan princess: you will win gifts more lavish than those I have promised.

> Ilia, pone metus! tibi regia nostra patebit,
>   teque colent amnes. Ilia, pone metus.
> tu centum aut plures inter dominabere nymphas,
>   nam centum aut plures flumina nostra tenent.
> ne me sperne, precor, tantum, Troiana propago:
>   munera promissis uberiora feres.
>   (*Amores* 3.6.61–6)

Like any Greek nymph, Ilia attempts three times to flee, but it is in Roman fashion that she laments her loss of virgin honour and condemns herself to die, hurling herself into the water. This is one of the elegiac *Amores*, so Ovid feels no inhibitions in cutting her scruples short, for the *lubricus amnis* to embrace her and make her his bride – or bedmate?

We saw in the previous chapter that Tiber was not the only sacred river in Latium. Virgil, who moved the sacred river Numicius (or Numicus) from its probable site near Lavinium to an imagined position near the Tiber mouth,[26] twice calls it sacred, and Ovid treats it with respect in *Metamorphoses* 14. There he continues history beyond the end of the *Aeneid*, and must describe the apotheosis of Aeneas. Much of this episode takes place on Olympus, where Venus canvasses the gods on behalf of her son, but she also stage-manages his fate on earth, by going to the shore where the Numicius joins the estuary (*Met.* 14.598–9).[27] and ordering the river to wash away all that is mortal in Aeneas and sweep it into the sea. The horned river-god carries out her orders, 'washing away Aeneas' mortal dross in his waters,' *suisque / quicquid in Aenea fuerat mortale repurgat / et respersit aquis* (*Met.* 14.602–4). The power of running river water to purify is a religious commonplace; the corollary seems to be that when a sacred river like Tiber or Numicius has to carry away impurities, such as the *purgamina Vestae*, this is not seen as harming the river, but as subjecting the impurities to the power of running water to remove all dross. That is no doubt why the newly arrived image of Cybele was ritually washed by a priestess in the waters of the river Almo at its junction with the mighty Tiber (*Fasti* 4.337–40).

We notice that even concentration on Rome's rivers has brought both groves and nymphs into our picture. There are of course many nymphs of Greek origin in *Fasti*. In the first book, Ovid develops a whole episode around a party given by Cybele and attended by nymphs and satyrs and Bacchic companions such as Pan and Silenus (1.395–400), at which the uninvited Priapus attempts to rape the nymph Lotis. In book 2, Ovid exploits star-lore to introduce another raped nymph, Callisto.[28] Another local nymph, Juturna, was commemorated by her pool, *lacus Juturnae*, in the forum, and Ovid honours the anniversary of her shrine on the Campus Martius on 11 January at *Fasti* 1.463–4.[29] But what other evidence does Ovid provide for the actual cult of an Italic nymph or nymphs, a ritual defined either by a calendar date or a specific place?

Juturna is certainly the best example of a spring nymph honoured at Rome who has a known genealogy (as daughter of Venilia and *Turni soror*, sister of Turnus, *Fasti* 1.463; cf. *Aen.* 12.138). Her name was explained as denoting her helpfulness (*iuvare*) to mortals, and she was associated with the Dioscuri, patron gods of

Rome's cavalry, to mark her status. But Ovid exploits the literary tradition of her seduction by Jupiter, reported in *Aeneid* 12 (139–41 and 877–8), as trigger to a tale about a quite different nymph, relating the origin of the mysterious Latin goddess Tacita, or *dea muta*, the object of an obscure rite practised during the Parentalia between 18 and 21 February (2.571–616). He supposes that when Jupiter was still trying to seduce Juturna, the god bound the nymphs of Latium by an oath to prevent Juturna from escaping him by plunging under the water. All the nymphs of Tiber obeyed (including those who worshipped Ilia and her marriage, 598) except for Lara, daughter of the river Almo, a notoriously indiscreet gossip, who in sisterly solidarity alerted both Juturna and Juno. Jupiter was enraged, tore out her tongue, and sent her down to Hades with Mercury to escort her. The next detail has surely been borrowed from Tereus and Philomela. The mutilated Lara was unable to cry for help when Mercury raped her, and so became the mother of the *Lares compitales*.

Ovid's other truly Italic nymph is Crane or Carna, who seems to have had no special shrine but was honoured with cult on the Kalends of June (6.101–69). This land-nymph and huntress was wooed by Apollo, and was raped by Janus, apparently without issue; to compensate (as often happens when a divine rape does not produce a child),[30] Janus conferred on her part of his function as a door-god by giving her power over hinges, which she exercises protectively, using her magic whitethorn to drive witches away from newborn children.[31]

Janus himself exemplifies Ovid's inventive powers in a rare instance where the poet tells the same cult-legend in both *Fasti* (1.259–76) and *Metamorphoses* (14.775–804), a story that illustrates how he could shape the details of a legend to highlight or exclude the role of demigods – in this case of Roman nymphs. As almost the last tale told by the god in his interview in *Fasti* 1, Janus explains the origin of his original temple, Janus Geminus, the arched double gateway which in Ovid's day stood between the republican forum and the forum of Julius Caesar.[32] When the Sabines, led by Titus Tatius, came to avenge and reclaim their womenfolk, and Tarpeia showed them the way up to the Capitol, Juno maliciously unbolted the gate which would give them access to the valley of the Forum. Janus himself was afraid to oppose her, so instead he used his powers over opening to unseal the mouth of a spring (*oraque qua pollens ope sum, fontana reclusi*, 1.269). The poet's language is ambiguous but suggests that no spring had previously existed in this place. Now the new spring spurted forth a geyser boiling with sulphur to bar Tatius' path. Once it had served its purpose, the site was restored to normal and an altar and shrine set up in honour of Janus (*ara mihi posita est, parvo coniuncta sacello*, 275), where Romans now make burnt offerings of cakes and suckling pig. This is Janus' answer to Ovid's question posed at 1.257.

But in Ovid's other account (*Met.* 14.775–804), Janus has plenty of divine help. When Juno acts, silently turning the door-pivots, Venus notices that the bolts have fallen away but, like Janus, obeys the rule that one god cannot cancel another's actions (*Met.* 14.784–5 = *Fasti* 1.267–8). All she can do is to ask the help of the Ausonian Naiads, who occupied a place next to Janus, dripping spray from their cool spring (*Met.* 14.785–6, *Iano loca iuncta tenebant / Naides Ausoniae gelido rorantia fonte*). It is the nymphs, then, who inject burning sulphur and bitumen into their spring, turning their waters 'that once competed with icy Alpine chill' into fiery streams. Ovid marks the miraculous change by addressing the waters directly: *Alpino modo quae certare rigori / audebatis aqua, non ceditis ignibus ipsis* (*Met.* 14.794–5, 'you who just now dared to compete with Alpine ice, now do not yield even to fire itself'). Both posts of the gate are wreathed in smoke, making access impossible, while the (Roman) soldiers of Mars find time to arm themselves and retaliate with a slaughter which finally ends in a mutually profitable treaty. This story is not told as an *aition*, nor does Ovid mention the subsidence of the fiery flow or any resulting cult honour. Did the legend already exist? Livy provides an alternative – Romulus' vow to Jupiter and consequent erection of a shrine to Jupiter Stator (Livy 12.3–7).[33]

From the Friendly Tiber to Rome's Urban Groves

A while back we left the infants Romulus and Remus in the grotto of the Lupercal. Roman tradition perhaps honoured this grove the most, of many woods and groves still remembered as existing in the ancient city. Thanks to an important international conference on *bois sacrés*, there is now available a great variety of expert discussions, by scholars of religion, archaeologists, and anthropologists, presenting the evidence of their disciplines for sacred groves of every kind, from the untouched natural groves credited with sanctity, to formalized and planted precincts used as places of assembly for the Latin federation. Despite the editors' careful attempts to articulate a distinction between *lucus* and *nemus*, it turns out to have been cheerfully ignored by our Latin poets, and both words are applied by the same poet at different times to the same sites. Indeed, the most famous Latin sanctuary at Aricia formally possessed both a *lucus Dianae* and a *nemus Aricinum*.[34] But nowhere do we meet so many *luci* as in Rome itself.

In his new study of Roman mythology, Peter Wiseman (2004, chap. 3) offers a marvellous picture of the wilderness valley that became the Circus Maximus, and the five sacred groves that lined its Aventine and Palatine slopes. First comes the grove of Stimula or Semele, where Juno incited the Bacchants to confront and attack the immigrant Ino (*Fasti* 6.503f.); a little further along the Aventine is the grove of Bona Dea Subsaxana, the setting of Propertius' aetiological *Elegy* 4.9, explaining why Hercules excluded women from his cult at the Ara Maxima.[35] (We saw earlier that Propertius offers an evocative picture of this secluded wilderness shrine, where women alone celebrated the mysterious goddess, and the priestess refused to admit Hercules.) The third grove mentioned by Wiseman is the one of which we know least, that of Venus Murcia, associated with myrtle but virtually unknown outside the glossaries. We are now at the far end of the Circus valley from the river, near the Capena Gate and the spring of the Camenae, Rome's Italic muses (whose name seems to imply their gifts of poetry and prophecy),[36] and near the grove to which Egeria had supposedly come from Aricia. But if we ask when Egeria came, we have only a marker impossibly distant for the coming of her cult. She is simultaneously the nymph who protected the pre-Homeric but resurrected Hippolytus/Virbius at Aricia, and who counselled Rome's second king, the seventh century Numa.[37] Around the Sabine Numa clustered the legendary origin of many of Rome's oldest cults and institutions, and we must return to him once we have enumerated our last *lucus*, back at the river end of the valley beneath the Palatine – this is of course the Lupercal itself, whether we call it, as does Wiseman, the grove of Pan, or of Italic Faunus.

It is, in fact, around the complex of the Lupercalia and the encounters of Numa with Faunus that Ovid creates his most elaborate evocation of ritual and cult. From the antiquarian point of view he has been ingenious in weaving a seemingly coherent narrative out of disparate material, stories that evolved separately to explain phenomena separate in the calendar and topography of Rome. Seen in literary terms, it is here that Ovid shows his most Callimachean powers of differentiating tone and genre in the separate elegiac entries of his calendar; because he is not composing a continuous epic, he can, for example, give us a quite different aspect of Faunus for the Lupercalia than he offers for the sacred shields of the Salii (3.259–398), or again for the Fordicidia of 15 April (4.649–66). In fact the poet begins in yet another grove – an exotic, foreign grove, which nonetheless provides one of the complex of legends offered around the theme of the Lupercalia. Note that Ovid has already told us, first, of the regular anniversary festival of Faunus on the Tiber island on the Ides of February .(2.193–4), and then of the Lupercalia, held two days thereafter (2.267–452). These games are introduced as 'the rites of horned Faunus' (*Fauni sacra bicornis*, 2.268), who is immediately equated with the Arcadian Pan, the god of cattle (*Pana deum pecoris veteres coluisse feruntur*, 2.271) and protector of sheep and mares, the woodland spirit (*silvestria numina*) whom Evander imported when there was not yet a city (2.277–80).

First of the self-contained narratives giving colour to the Lupercalia is a Lydian tale set near Mount Tmolus, in which the randy Faunus attempts the rape of Queen Omphale and mistakes the cross-dressed Hercules for his mistress, with disastrous consequences (303–58).[38] This story can be tied in with the Italian belief in *Fauni* or *Fauni ficarii* as incubuses, whether imagined in nightmare or suffered in actual nocturnal attacks. Another tale comes from the youth of Romulus and Remus and so dates before the foundation of the city (2.361–80); yet the twins preparing the sacrifice of a goat to Faunus on behalf of their shepherd community enjoy the formality of a priest to scrutinize the entrails, as they indulge in a primitive version of the public games (boxing, javelin and stone throwing) – when suddenly their lookout spies rustlers, and both brothers scatter with their bands. It is Remus and the Fabii (precursors of one of the two teams of Luperci) who are first to return successfully and eat up the sacrifice, apparently because they rode off without dressing or putting on armour, whereas Romulus and his merry men had slowed down to get dressed. The story is an alternative *aition* for the ritual nudity of the Luperci and serves not only to explain the nudity but to identify the teams of Fabii and Quintilii as the bands of each brother; it may also anticipate the bad relationship between the brothers demonstrated by Remus' fatal mockery of Rome's first walls in book 4 (841–3).

But apart from the shifts of tone between these component narratives, there is also – or seems to be – a shift of chronology, in the next narrative unit, which we might call 'The Voice from the Grove.' It is not the voice of Faunus; instead, after a reprise identifying Faunus with the Arcadian god (2.423–4), Ovid embarks on an explanation of the practice of young brides asking to be beaten by the Luperci (2.425–52). This is more recent, going back only to the year after Romulus had organized the games of Consus and the rape of the Sabine women in order to provide children for his city. In this story the new wives were failing to conceive, and Romulus began to deplore the useless seizure of the women at the cost of war with Rome's neighbours. Brides and grooms set out to the sacred grove of Juno at the foot of the Esquiline and bend their knees in prayer. It is now that the treetops quiver to indicate the coming of Juno, and her voice is heard proclaiming a strange message: 'let the sacred he-goat penetrate the Italian mothers,' '*Italidas matres,*' *inquit* '*sacer hircus inito!*' (2.441). Juno is not otherwise associated with riddling oracular utterance, but now an augur explains, and the sacred command is fulfilled by cutting the hide of a billy-goat into strips, with which the women's backs are beaten; and in due course the women give birth in the tenth month. Thus, according to Ovid, it is Juno's *Lucus* (instead of the Varronian etymology from *lux/lucere*, light, giving light) that gives the goddess the name of Lucina as protectress of childbirth.[39]

Riddles and sacred woods provide the link with two other narratives about Rome's second king, Numa, who is credited with many of its religious institutions. Twice in the *Fasti*, Numa is led to consult Faunus in order to devise a new ritual, and on both occasions the setting is a numinous grove. There is now an admirable study of Ovid's narrative by Joy Littlewood (2002) explaining the origin of the sacred shields called Ancilia, carried by the priestly Salii at the opening of the war season on 1 March. Littlewood notes how Ovid has doubled the associations by using as his spokesperson the nymph Egeria (Numa's consort), and setting her first in her original Arician grove, although it will not be the site of the episode. This gives the poet the opportunity to describe the grove and one of the nymph's functions. Here horses are banned so as to protect Hippolytus:

Here Hippolytus is sheltered, who was torn apart by his horses' reins; hence this glade is not approached by any horses. Ribbons hang down covering the long hedges, and many a votive tablet is posted to the deserving goddess. Often a woman who has achieved her vow comes from the city with garlanded brow and bearing glowing torches.

> Hic latet Hippolytus loris direptus equorum,
>   unde nemus nullis illud aditur equis.
> licia dependent longas velantia saepes,
>   et posita est meritae multa tabella deae.
> saepe potens voti, frontem redimita coronis
>   femina lucentes portat ab Urbe faces.
>   (3.265–70)

Despite the vivid picture of Egeria's grove and spring at Aricia, Ovid needs to bring the story back to Rome, and does so through Egeria's association with the Roman Camenae. He also, as Littlewood notes, borrows from Virgil's narrative of Aristaeus (*Georg.* 4.317–414), in which his mother, the nymph Cyrene, tells him how to capture the prophetic old man of the sea by trickery. Numa too is advised by a nymph, who tells him how to capture the prophetic demigods Picus and Faunus.

When Numa is confronted by prodigies of violent lightning sent by Jupiter, Egeria tells him to perform rites of expiation, which he will be able to learn from Picus and Faunus, both native deities of Roman soil – *Romani numen utrumque soli* (3.292). Why does Ovid add this? Because Numa is Sabine and not a native, so in some way out of the divinatory loop? Because Ovid wants us to think of them not as Latin kings but as Roman spirits? The two will later (315) identify themselves simply as '*di ... agrestes.*' On Egeria's instructions Numa goes to a grove beneath the Aventine, at whose spring Faunus and Picus come to drink (3.299–300). The resemblance to Aristaeus rests on a previous imitation, Virgil's borrowing from Menelaus' adventures when the nymph Eidothea tells him how to catch Proteus in *Odyssey* 4, which Virgil had already adapted for the capture of Silenus by Chromis and Mnasyllus (Fauns or human?) in *Eclogue* 6. Certainly Faunus and Picus now behave more like Satyrs than dignified Latin kings (and are virtually indistinguishable from each other). Numa sacrifices a sheep to the spirit of the spring (*fons*, 300) and sets out bowls of wine on which the spirits gorge, then fall asleep. This is his chance[40] to emerge from the cave and bind them. When they find they cannot break loose, he asks them to tell him how he can expiate the thunder. Now for the disappointment. Faunus explains that they are only country gods, who have power over the high hills, but Jupiter has sole control (*arbitrium*, 316) over his own weapons; somewhat inconsistently, however, although Numa cannot by himself bring Jupiter down from the sky, he will be able to entice Jupiter down with their help.

Ovid is again toying with his pleasure in hierarchy and classification of function; these gods are like court functionaries with limited powers. Picus confirms Faunus' promise, swearing by Styx; but to tease his readers, the poet withholds the key details of the magical procedure: 'it is not right for man to know, and we will report only what is permitted to them and to the lips of a devout poet,' *scire nefas homini: nobis concessa canentur / quaeque pio vatis ab ore licet* (3.325–6). In fact the demigods' role is ended once Jupiter makes himself manifest by the trembling of treetops and the shaking of the earth. There follows a contest of wits between god and king in which Jupiter demands the sacrifice of a *caput* (339), 'of an onion,' says Numa – 'no, of a man,' says Jupiter – 'yes, the hair of a man' – 'no, a living soul' (*anima*), says Jupiter, to which Numa replies by offering the living soul of a fish (342). When Jupiter accepts the compromise and agrees to provide a sure sign of authority (3.346), Numa repeats the guarantee to his people. At dawn the next day, with all his people gathered and with his head ritually covered (363, *niveo velatus amictu*, 'veiled with his white garment' – a detail passed over in Ennius' account of Romulus' auspicial procedure at the city's foundation)[41] – Numa receives from Jupiter three thunderclaps as the clear sky opens to let fall the celestial shield (3.369–74). For those who are trying to understand the nature of Faunus rather than the subsequent ritual, this episode seems to represent the way in which Faunus, as prophetic deity, was replaced by Jupiter (who came to share his temple on the Tiber island), no doubt because Jupiter, who was also *fatidicus*, could be consulted on demand, whereas Faunus' prophecies came only at his whim; nor is Faunus ever reported to have suggested any *piamina*, or means of expiating prodigies.

The other episode involving Numa with Faunus makes the god more central. Ovid traces the rite of the Fordicidia (4.641–72) to a year of famine, which drives the king to visit a grove left unfelled (*silva vetus nullaque diu violata secure*, 4.649) because it was sacred to Faunus – or to his Arcadian counterpart, the god of Maenalus. Like Virgil's Faunus, father of Latinus, the god gives responses to men by night, and Ovid's Numa replicates the ritual carried out by Latinus in *Aen.* 7.81–101, with added details: he sacrifices one sheep to Faunus but another to Somnus, and then lies on the fleeces to await the god's oracular advice. He observes ritual purity, sprinkling his head with water from the spring and covering his brow with beech leaves; he has shunned all sexual contact and wears no ring. First comes Sleep, then Faunus, who utters the mysterious command (4.665–6) *Morte boum tibi, rex, Tellus placanda duarum: / det sacris animas una iuvenca duas*, 'You must placate Earth with the death of two kine: let one heifer provide two living souls for the sacrifice.' Again Egeria is needed, this time to unravel the *ambages*, by advising Numa to offer a pregnant heifer. This, then, is the origin of the Fordicidia of 15 April, a preliminary to the other country festival, of Pales, six days later.

I have already paid some attention to Tellus, in the previous chapter, when considering Aeneas' first prayer on his landing in Italy (*Aen.* 7.135–40). The actual anniversary of her temple at Rome was not until 13 December, but the poet pays homage to her on three occasions between January and June: in the prayers to Tellus and Ceres at the *sementiva* in January (1.671), here and now at the Fordicidia, and again in *Fasti* 6, when he identifies the aniconic goddess Vesta with Tellus and finds the origin of her round temple in the spherical globe of Earth (6.267–70).[42]

Besides the association with groves and prophetic deities, another element that binds Lupercalia and Fordicidia together is the need for purification, for *piamina*, which Ovid has first introduced in *Fasti* 2 under their ancient name of *februa*. All the *februa* mentioned are natural country products; *lanae* (*Fasti* 2.21), the woollen loops used as headbands for women or officiating priests or sacrificial victims (cf. *taenia* and *vittae*),[43] a branch of a pure tree (pine or laurel), either dipped in the water of a running river (*fluminea* ... *aqua*, 2.46) or burned to fumigate. If we broaden our scope from specific ritual episodes in the calendar, it will be rewarding to see how Ovid reports the way in which groups or individuals offered appeasement to country gods in collective or personal worship, whether by purification, sacrifice, or prayer.

Ovid introduces three collective rituals, and even goes beyond the set calendar festivals in order to introduce the first of these: the sowing festival, or Sementiva, after the seed crop has been sowed in the earth (1.662). The farmers of each village or hamlet, the *coloni* of the *pagus*, are to make offerings to Ceres, who generates the crops, but also, most important, to Tellus, the soil where they grow: *haec praebet causam frugibus, illa locum* (1.674: does this correspond to the division of labour between father and mother?). Tellus can even displace Ceres, when Horace describes the early peasants celebrating their harvest festival by appeasing Tellus with a pig (or sow), Silvanus with milk: *agricolae prisci, fortes parvoque beati / ... Tellurem porco, Silvanum lacte piabant* (Hor. *Ep.* 2.1.139, 143). Varro too gives Tellus pride of place alongside Jupiter among his twelve gods of the country-side (*RR* 1.1.5), 'because these are our great parents; Jupiter is called Pater and Tellus *Terra Mater.*' In fact Varro deliberately sets the dialogue of his first book, on arable farming, in the temple of Tellus on the occasion of the Sementiva (1.2.1). But the prayer Ovid assigns to his farmers (*Fasti* 1.675–94), far from using ritual language, is a literary confection that draws on the agricultural details of Virgil's first *Georgic* to ask for protection against every kind of weed and pest that can harm the crops.[44] We need to keep this in mind as a contrast to the prayer Ovid will put into the shepherd's mouth at the Parilia.

There are two festivals to mark the end of February and the old year, which serve the Italian household in different ways. First the Caristia, or feast of kin, on 23 February, treats the *domus* as a descent group, offering a libatory prayer to the *di generis* (2.631). Immediately after, the Terminalia treats the household as a land-holding, and is celebrated by neighbours who share boundary stones, along with their families (2.639–82). Here a rustic altar is set up for offerings of grain, honey, and wine, and the boundary stone deliberately sprinkled with the sacrificial blood of a piglet or lamb. Instead of a prayer for favours, Ovid provides his own hymn (*laudes, Termine sancte, tuas,* 2.658) thanking the deity, who is simultaneously anthropomorphic and mineral, and begging him to stay on guard (674, *in statione mane*) even if he is wheedled by neighbours or beaten by farm implements. But although both Tellus and Terminus are gods of place, gods of the land itself, there is no hint at these festivals of the expiation or atonement which Horace implied by *Tellurem porco ... piabant.* Can it really be that the arable farmer never offends against the land, and never tries to overreach his boundaries? Richard Thomas has stressed in his commentary on the *Georgics* (pp. 195–6) Virgil's picture of the destruction caused when the vengeful farmer (*arator*) uproots the groves and evicts the birds in order to create new ploughland (2.207–11). Ovid has nothing similar.

We do have two instances of individual prayer in *Fasti*. First, the most frivolous. The Ides of May is the anniversary of the temple of Mercury *in Circo* – Mercury, the god of profit. Ovid takes his readers to a pool, the Aqua Mercuri, near the Porta Capena, where the trader comes with girt-up tunic and in ritual purity takes the waters in his fumigated jug: in this water he dips a laurel branch and sprinkles all the goods he has marked for sale, then sprinkles his own hair with the dripping laurel before uttering his wheedling prayers.

> Huc venit incinctus tunica mercator et urna
>   purus suffita, quam ferat, haurit aquam.
> Uda fit hinc laurus, lauro sparguntur ab unda
>   omnia, quae dominos sunt habitura novos.
> Spargit et ipse suos lauro rorante capillos
>   et peragit solita fallere voce preces.
>   (5.675–80)

And they are the prayers of a cheat. It is fair enough that he begins by asking to have his past false oaths washed away by the water of the sacred spring (681–6); we all ask that God forgive us our trespasses, but normally when we ask pardon for past offences we are not planning to commit more in the future, and we do not acknowledge full awareness of our deception (685, *sive deum prudens – fefelli*). Ovid's tricky trader cheerfully foresees future perjuries, in rounding off his prayer with a request for profit and its enjoyment (687–90).

This perverted prayer is designed to contrast with Ovid's longest personal prayer (4.747–76), offered at the Parilia, the double festival of Pales and of Rome's foundation. Here too the worshipper must be purified. First Ovid speaks for himself: he has often taken the ritual *februa*, compounded of bean stalks and the ashes of the October horse's tail and the heifer's embryo from the Fordicidia, and even performed the ritual leaping over the bonfires which added purification of the ground to that of its people (4.723–8). Next come the people: here, uniquely, Ovid addresses the Roman people and bids them go collect the purifying materials from the Vestals (731–4), before he returns to the original pastoral deity Pales, and to her shepherd worshippers. Before the shepherd can sacrifice and pray, he must purify his sheep at dusk, sprinkling the ground with water and sweeping the pen, which should be decorated with branches and garlanded across its doorway (735–8). Next he should burn sulphur to produce smoke to cleanse the sheep, and fragrant rosemary, Sabine herbs, and laurel to crackle in the centre of his hearth (739–42).

Only now can he offer the primitive food of millet cakes with warm milk and make his prayer to Pales (4.743–6). Before he looks to the future and asks for protection from wolves and disease and for fertility in his flock, the poet-shepherd reviews all the possible involuntary offences against the country gods, introducing the Nymphs or Dryads and Faunus.

Pales, take thought for the flock and the herdsmen of the flock; let all harm be driven away from my pens. If I have pastured my flock or seated myself beneath a sacred tree, or a ewe has unknowingly browsed on tombs; if I have entered a forbidden glade, or nymphs and the half-goat god have been put to flight by my eyes; if my sickle has stripped a grove of a shady branch to fill a basket with foliage for a sick sheep: pardon my offences.

> Consule ... pecori pecorisque magistris:
>   effugiat stabulis noxa repulsa meis.
> sive sacro pavi sedive sub arbore sacra,
>   pabulaque e bustis inscia carpsit ovis;
> si nemus intravi vetitum, nostrisve fugatae
>   sunt oculis nymphae semicaperque deus
> si mea falx ramo lucum spoliavit opaco,
>   unde data est aegrae fiscina frondis ovi:
> da veniam culpae.
>   (4.747–55)

The theme is so appealing to Ovid that he returns to it with variations.

Nor hold it against me that I sheltered my flock in a shrine until the hail should cease, nor let me suffer because I disturbed a pool. Nymphs, forgive me because the movement of a hoof clouded your waters. Goddess Pales, placate the springs and deities of the springs on my behalf, and all the gods scattered about the woodland. May we never see the Dryads nor bath of Diana, nor Faunus when he threatens the fields at noon. Drive away disease; let men and creatures thrive ...

Da veniam culpae, nec dum degrandinet obsit
    agresti fano supposuisse pecus,
nec noceat turbasse lacus. Ignoscite nymphae,
    mota quod obscuras ungula fecit aquas.
tu, dea, pro nobis fontes fontanaque placa
    numina, tu sparsos per nemus omne deos.
nec Dryadas nec nos videamus labra Dianae,
    nec Faunum, medio cum premit arva die.
Pelle procul morbos; valeant hominesque gregesque ...
    (4.755–63)

Here are the gods of the uncultivated land, not the gods who protect arable crops and farmers' property but the spirits that dwell
in groves, lakes, and pools. We can imagine the wilderness, or the
sacro-idyllic landscape familiar from Augustan wall-paintings,
dotted with tombs and country shrines. The nymphs and half-
goat god take on identities in the reprise (755–63), and slide into
the fantasies of pastoral and myth, with nymphs angered that
their pool has been muddied and cannot be used as a mirror.[45] But
alongside the more whimsical fantasy, the threat of Faunus (or
Pan infecting men with panic) brings the prayer closer to the awe
which was a very important ingredient in Italic *religio*. Ovid may
not have worshipped at either state or private religious ceremon-
ies, but he was a keen observer and a poet responsive to the supernatural surrounding us. We may suspect that he felt this most
strongly away from the city or the well-tilled estates with their
slave households and organized comfort. This is a poet who can
oscillate between the authenticity of antiquarian research and the
imaginative delight of sheer invention. It is our loss that we cannot always distinguish between them.

The *Fasti* almost certainly provoked an elegiac work whose nom-
inal dating must precede Ovid's calendar poem – the anonymous
Consolatio ad Liviam, composed to mourn the death of Livia's
younger son, the popular Drusus Caesar, fatally injured by a fall
from his horse in 9 BCE. One of the arguments for dating this
poem somewhat later than its actual occasion is precisely an episode which can be shown to derive from Ovid's *Fasti*.[46] Drusus

died in Germany, but his body was reverently escorted back to Rome by his brother Tiberius, for burial in Augustus' Mausoleum on the Campus Martius. The Campus was often flooded when the river was in spate; Horace in an early ode (1.2) speaks of the river overflowing its banks in anger at Roman offences. So the unknown poet dramatizes a scene where

the Tiber god shuddered amid his tawny waves and reared his misty head from the centre of the stream; with mighty arms he cleared from his eyes his blue-grey hair, interwoven with willow reeds and moss, and poured streams of tears from brimming eyes so that the deep bed scarcely contained the added waters. Next, in anger at the death of the beloved prince, he resolved to put out the funeral flames with his assault and carry off the body still unburnt.

> Ipse pater flavis Tiberinus adhorruit undis
>   sustulit et medio nubilus amne caput.
> tum salice implexum muscoque et harundine crinem
>   caeruleum magna legit ab ore manu.
> uberibusque oculis lacrimarum flumina misit,
>   vix capit adiectas alveus altus aquas.
> iamque rogi flammas extinguere fluminis ictu
>   corpus et intactum tollere certus erat.
>   (*Cons.* 221–8).

This river-god is described in terms similar to those for both Virgil's Tiber in *Aeneid* 8 and the river-god of *Fasti* 5; and just as Virgil's Tiber reversed his flow for Aeneas, so now Tiber tries to hold back his waters, but for a different purpose: 'the river was trying to hold back his waters and check his course towards the sea, in order to soak the pyre with his entire flow,' *sustentabat aquas cursusque inhibebat ad aequor, / ut posset toto proluere amne rogum* (229–30). But he is rebuked by Mars himself, speaking with moist cheeks from his temple beside the river. It is Mars' speech which echoes Ovid, or rather echoes Ovid's deliberate echo of Ennius. When the infant twins Romulus and Remus were about to drown in the Tiber's overflow, he approached the Fates asking for mercy. And just as Mars had obtained a guarantee from Jupiter in *Fasti* 2.483–90 that one of the two babies would live to become a god after his death, so now Mars is answered by one of the Fates granting part of his request: one of those twins shall live ('*partem accipe, quae datur,*' inquit, '*muneris; ex istis, quod petis, alter erit,*' 243–4); and presently the two great Caesars, Julius and Augustus (*Caesar promissus uterque*) will be the only gods Mars' city of Rome can claim (245–6). Thus rebuked, the Tiber releases his current and returns to his grotto, and Drusus' funeral is completed.

The imitation here is both a proof that the *Consolatio* must have been written after the publication of Ovid's *Fasti*, and a testimony to that poem's survival despite the imperial expulsion of the poet and the partial ban of his works. If we could only date this elegy it might well be the earliest testimony to a poem that is otherwise little used or quoted before the time of Statius.[47]

PART II

COUNTER-EXAMPLES, AND THE TRIUMPH OF ARTISTRY OVER FADING DEVOTION

One confirmation of the special sentiment, even reverence, with which Roman poets treated the country gods of Italy comes from studying deities treated with less respect. Ovid, for example, presents local nature gods from Greece and Asia Minor as more violent and undisciplined than Latin rivers and Roman nymphs. So I move in chapter 4 from his sympathetic representation of three Italian country deities, Flora in books 4 and 5 of the Fasti, and the lesser divinities Vertumnus and Pomona in the Metamorphoses, to his depiction of angry and lustful rivers and wanton nymphs in earlier books of the Metamorphoses. As we shall see, both Vertumnus and Hylas, drowned by the nymphs, were treated by earlier poets, but their stories bear out the pattern outlined in Hugh Parker's 1997 monograph Greek Gods in Italy in Ovid's Fasti: A Greater Greece.

In chapter 5, I treat another god who belongs in the country and is associated with horticultural fertility. Priapus was known from the time of Catullus to come from Lampsacus in Asia Minor, and was the theme of many Hellenistic epigrams. His enlarged membrum virile made him potentially comic, and we can trace a lack of respect (but not of affection?) in the whole generic range of Roman poetry, from actual Priapea in his peculiar metre to epigrams, elegy, didactic poetry, and epic.

Priapus was domesticated, and so, in a far more ornamental way, are the nymphs and satyrs who populate Statius' Silvae, providing a continuous chorus or year-long staff for the lavish villas of Statius' friends. And here, as in Ovid, we have a poet who featured nymphs and river-gods in epic – his epic Thebaid – and treated with sympathy both the collective anonymous nymphs of drought-plagued Nemea, and the loyal family of the divine river Ismenus, his nymph daughter (identified as Ismenis), and his aquatic but mortal grandson, Crenaeus. This family, which he may have created without a model, provides a foil for the more fully depicted Parthenopaeus and his mother, the nymph Atalanta, but the foil is one only of degree. Although neither boy and neither parent were objects of Italic cult, the poet treats them with a pathos and sympathy as delicate as if they were Trojan or local heroes, like the boys Nisus and Euryalus or the naturalized hero Virbius. With Statius we come to a new *fusion of Greek and Italian culture, since the Neapolitan poet was a man of Greek origin and education, whose sympathies no longer differentiate between Hellenistic and Italic deities.*

CHAPTER FOUR

Ovidian Variations: From Friendly Flora to Lewd Salmacis and Angry Acheloüs

Flora, Vertumnus, and Pomona: Agricultural Deities Revived

According to Ennius, King Numa, the traditional founder of Roman religion, created special priests called *Flamines* (kindlers of the fire?) for nine deities.[1] These are not the mainstream Olympians we might have expected. Ennius' text is reported by Varro (*LL* 7.45), who first cites Martialis and Quirinalis as being etymologically obvious priests of Mars and Quirinus, then adds that

> this same <king> created the *flamens* called:
> Volturnalem,
> Palatualem, Furrinalem Floralemque
> Falacrem<que> et Pomonalem.
> (Enn. *Ann.* 116–18, ed. Skutsch)

He explains that the original divinities were Volturnus (another name for the Tiber god), the goddesses Palatua, Furrina, and Flora, father Falacer, and Pomona.

But although two goddesses among these deities, Flora and Pomona, share a concern with the fertility of plants and trees, their cults seem to have evolved quite differently. First, Flora, who, again according to Varro *LL* 5.74, quoting Ennius, had already been vowed an altar by Titus Tatius, Romulus' Sabine co-regent. Varro himself honours Flora along with the ungendered deity Robigo in the prefatory prayer of his *Res Rusticae* (1.1.6), and Lucretius speaks of her allegorically accompanying Spring: 'Spring advances and Venus, and Venus' winged herald marches ahead close to the tracks of Zephyr; for them mother Flora sprinkling all their path saturates it with exceptional colours and fragrances.'

> It Ver et Venus et Veneris praenuntius ante
> pennatus graditur Zephyri vestigia propter,
> Flora quibus mater praespargens ante viai
> cuncta coloribus egregiis et odoribus opplet.
> (Lucr. 5.737–40)

What is more, games were held in honour of Flora before the first games of Ceres or Apollo or Cybele. When Ovid's calendar reaches Flora's games, which began on 28 April and continued with stage entertainments until 3 May, the final day of the Circus Games ('the circus races end on this day and the prize palm acclaimed in the theatre,' *Circus in hunc exit, clamataque palma theatris*, 5.189), the researches of Verrius Flaccus enabled Ovid to provide a precise history of the Games. In his fantasy the goddess Flora appears to him and gives an account of herself. Dating like a historian by specific consular years, Flora declares that her games were first vowed in 237 by the aediles and brothers Lucius and Manius Publicius Malleolus, with fines exacted from graziers who had trespassed on public land (*Fasti* 5.283–94), along with a new road, the Clivus Publicius, leading up from the Circus Maximus to the Aventine. But it seems that these games were intermittent. In a further instalment Flora explains that the theatre games were not yet annual (*annua ... spectacular*, 5.295). When the Senate neglected Flora's honours (5.312), she brought about a period of unseasonable weather to ruin the crops and fruit, until the Senate bowed to her anger and made the games annual in 173 BCE (*annua festa*, 327–30).

I have argued elsewhere (Fantham 1992) that in giving so much attention to Flora and the *Ludi Florales* Ovid was reacting against Augustan disapproval. Flora is not mentioned in the *Georgics,* and although Livy's book covering 237 BCE has not survived, his full account of 173 absolutely omits the new Floralia, in contrast to his detailed treatment of the games of Cybele. Again, Flora's temple erected by the Publicii near the temple of Ceres, Liber, and Libera was not restored until Tiberius completed the task in 17 CE (Tac. *Ann.* 2.49). It is not difficult to see why Ovid gives so much importance to this attractive goddess. He may begin his account of her festival with two Hellenistic myths, of her name Chloris and courtship by Zephyrus (from the same source as Lucr. 5.737–8?) and of the assistance she gave to Juno/Hera to help her conceive Mars/Ares, using a magic flower; but whatever their source, Mars himself provides the trigger to justify Flora's importance in the city founded by his son (5.259–60): 'Remembering that he had received his day of birth from me, Mars said, "You too are to have a place in Romulus' city," ' *habeto / tu quoque Romulea ... in urbe locum.*[2]

But most important to Ovid, after his antiquarian history of Flora's festival, was the sheer fun of the festival itself. As in Lucretius, the goddess comes 'twined in a thousand garlands of flowers,' *mille ... variis florum dea nexa coronis* (4.945), and her games are variously described as including greater naughtiness and more open play: *lascivia maior ... liberiorque iocus*, where *iocus* is not so much jesting as 'fun and games.' The poet celebrates her *deliciae* (again, 'fun,' 5.334 and 367) at the beginning and end of his account of the games, notorious for their popular licence, with mimes performed (unlike straight tragedy and comedy) by sexy actresses, who reputedly discarded their clothes at a signal of the trumpet. This moment was the single best-known aspect of the Ludi Florales, and it provoked a notorious protest by Cato of Utica, reported by Ovid's slightly younger contemporary Valerius Maximus[3] (2.10.8; cf. Seneca *Ep. Mor.* 97.8). Hence Martial used Cato's exit as a parallel for his outspoken epigrams in the preface to book 1:[4] 'Since you knew about the saucy rite of naughty Flora and the festive sport and licence of the crowd, why did you come to the theatre, severe Cato? Or did you just come in so that you could march out?'

> Nosses iocosae dulce cum sacrum Florae
> festosque lusus et licentiam volgi,
> cur in theatrum Cato severe, venisti?
> An ideo tantum veneras ut exires?

It seems, then, that while Flora had all the authenticity of her alleged early altar and priesthood, it was less her ritual standing than her appeal to the senses, to the street women (*turba ... meretricia*) and the common people, which delighted the poet. Among all the gods and goddesses 'interviewed,' Flora alone is addressed by the poet with a fervent prayer, a prayer echoing that of Callimachus (*Aitia* fr. 7 13–14) to the Muses: 'So that Naso's poem may thrive for all eternity, sprinkle, I pray, our breast with your gifts.'

> floreat ut toto carmen Nasonis in aevo
> sparge, precor donis pectora nostra tuis.
> (Ovid *Fasti* 5.377–8)

So Flora is treated by the poet with affection and admiration, but for her sex-appeal and sheer luxury of perfume and parties, not for her original agricultural powers to fix or set the fruit in the blossom.

With Pomona, for all that she had her own priest, a different pattern emerges. We do not know the location of any urban shrine[5] or of any feast in her name, and Ovid's readers would actually have been far more familiar with her aspiring lover Vertumnus, the Etruscan god from Volsinii whose (original Etruscan?) statue stood in the Vicus Tuscus and is impersonated by Propertius, as we noted in chapter 3, in the second aetiological elegy of his fourth book. There Propertius does not associate him with any favours done to passers-by, or with any mythical love affair; on the contrary Propertius celebrates Vertumnus' unlimited capacity to imitate man or girl ('put me in Coan silk and I become a far from ruthless girl,' *indue me Cois: fiam non dura puella*, 4.2.23) or indeed to use minimal stage properties to take on the role of any soldier or tradesman. It seems that Vertumnus was no more the object of formal cult at Rome than Marsyas, the satyr who symbolized popular liberty in the Forum; and being construed as god of the changing or turning year (*vertentis anni / ... VERTANNI rursus creditur esse sacrum*, Prop. 4.2.11–12), the god had no feast day or, as far as we know, temple anniversary.

With his powers as a shape-shifter or trickster, Vertumnus naturally appealed to Ovid. But he is also an Italian god from the good old days of good King Proca, only three generations before

Romulus (*Met.* 14.622–3), so the poet remodels his courtship of the ultra-chaste hamadryad, Pomona,[6] devoted to her orchards, to make him more respectful and sympathetic. He does not take her by storm, and finally wins her not by his persuasive arguments while disguised as an old procuress, nor even by his affecting story of the cruel death of Iphis (14.696–761), but when he abandons disguise and appears in his natural radiance. 'He plans to use force but there is no need: the nymph was taken by the god's beauty and felt responding wounds of love.'

> vimque parat sed vi non est opus, inque figura
> capta dei nymphe est et mutua vulnera sensit.
> (14.770–1)

River-Gods in Greek and Roman Poetry

We saw in the last chapter that Ovid's Italian river-god, the Anio, approaches the seduced and abandoned princess Ilia with tender and solicitous respect, and an offer which seems to be of lasting marriage. There is no doubt that, like the Tiber if to a lesser degree, other nearby rivers are mentioned with affection and gratitude by Roman poets, and in this respect Ovid does not diverge from Virgil's example. But to understand the poetry of the century after Virgil we must also give attention to foreign, even exotic rivers, which are treated as vivid and undisciplined personalities, often equipped with both supernatural powers and superhuman lusts. The chief responsibility for this portrayal lies with Ovid, and our focus in this chapter will be the Greek and Asiatic river-gods of his *Metamorphoses*, and their sexual adventures at the expense of equally lively nymphs. But first we need to understand how rivers came to be so prominent in Augustan poetry.

In the earliest Greek poetry we find rivers used by Homer to locate and identify communities and particularly barbarian tribes, a device that became a convention in both Greek and Latin poetry. It is the source of such Homeric identifications as 'the men that lived in Zeleia under the lowest spurs of Ida and drank the dark waters of Aesepus' (*Iliad* 2.824–5, Rieu 1950/1968), and the Paeonians who had come 'from far Amydon and the banks of the broad river Axios, the Axios whose waters are the most beautiful that flow over the earth,' and the Lycians 'from distant Lycia and the swirling streams of Xanthus' (*Iliad* 2.848–50, 876–7), and of Virgilian phrases like *qui Tiberim Fabarimque bibunt* ('those who drink the Tiber and Fabaris,' *Aen.*7.715). Rivers are important in the *Iliad*, but some are peculiar to the locality, as at 12.19–22, which catalogues the eight Trojan rivers that Apollo diverts and concentrates into one mouth so as to attack the Greek wall. And rivers are associated specifically with nymphs when Zeus summons the gods to council: 'excepting Ocean, not a single river stayed away, nor did any of the nymphs that haunt delightful woods, the sources of streams, and grassy water-meadows' (20.7–9, Rieu 1950/1968). But there was a hierarchy among gods and rivers, and in the next book, when Achilles fights Asteropaeus, descendant of the river Axius, he warns him that

a descendant of Zeus is greater than the scion of a river by as much as Zeus himself is greater than all the rivers that run murmuring to the sea. Look at the river that is flowing past you now. He is a mighty one and would help you if he could. But there is no fighting against Zeus the son of Cronos. Even Achelous, king of rivers, is not a match for Zeus, nor is the deep and potent stream of Ocean, the source of all rivers, every sea and all the springs and deep wells there are. (Homer *Iliad* 21.190–9, Rieu 1950/1968)

Rivers were no less important to Hesiod, whose *Theogony* has Earth mate with her sibling Cronos to give birth to Oceanus and Tethys; they in turn produce some twenty named rivers and more than forty nymphs, who nurse and rear men together with King Apollo, and with the rivers.[7] In subsequent poetry the nymphs will be constantly reinvented and not limited to these forty; the rivers, though listed in a geographically random order, will persist more predictably through later poets. Besides the Trojan rivers mentioned in *Iliad* 12, Hesiod lists, in order, the Nile and Alpheus (to whom we will return) and deep-eddying Eridanus,[8] the Strymon and Maeander and fair-flowing Ister, the Phasis and silver-eddying Acheloüs (which or who will be our prime example), the Haliacmon and Peneus and broad-flowing Hermus and Caïcus, and then the Sangarius and Ladon and Parthenius and Evenus and Aldeskon (Hesiod *Theogony* 337–45). As West (1966) shows, this is a strange selection, one omitting many important rivers but mixing with Greek mainland rivers like the Evenus rivers of the Black Sea, such as the Sangarius and Parthenius, which can have become known only shortly before Hesiod wrote.

It is natural, then, that rivers feature in Roman imperial or triumphalist poetry not only as markers of whole regions, but as boundaries to be leapt by Roman armies: in actual triumphs and in poetic panegyric their names and representations – no doubt painted or impersonated as powerful reclining males with symbolic urns or streams – symbolized conquered peoples.[9] The influence of Hellenistic poetry brought new interest in both the remote Phasis, the river of Colchis and destination of Apollonius' Argonauts, and the great fertilizing Nile, whose delta was dominated by Alexandria. Richard Thomas and Ruth Scodel (1984) were first to notice the role assigned to the Euphrates, initially in Callimachus' *Hymn to Apollo*, where the god rejects the verbose epic style of poetry symbolized by the vast current of the Assyrian river, and then in Virgil, who three times echoes Callimachus' placement of the name Euphrates six lines from the end of his work, but with a change of emphasis and significance. Six lines from the end of the first *Georgic* (1.509), the poet symbolizes external attacks on the empire with *hinc movet Euphrates, illinc Germania bellum* ('in this region Euphrates stirs up war, in that Germany'), but he reassuringly rounds off the fourth *Georgic* (six lines from the end) with *Caesar dum magnus ad altum / fulminat Euphraten bello* (4.560–1, 'while mighty Caesar thunders in war by the deep Euphrates'). The Parthian threat persisted until the year of Virgil's death, but in the description of Vulcan's prophetic shield of Aeneas in *Aeneid* 8, Augustus' triple triumph again features the Euphrates, this time as the first of three supposedly subjugated rivers from East and North and far East: 'The Euphrates now flowed more gently with its waters, and the Morini, remotest of men, and the twin-horned Rhine, the unconquered Dahae and the Araxes, protesting at its bridge.'

Euphrates ibat iam mollior undis,
extremique hominum Morini, Rhenusque bicornis
indomitique Dahae, et pontem indignatus Araxes.
(Virgil *Aen.* 8.726–8)

Why is there no image of the defeated Nile? Because Virgil has
ended his complex image of the battle of Actium with the figure
of father Nile compassionately reaching out to envelop and shelter the queen's fugitive fleet: 'But opposite he showed the Nile
grieving with his vast body, opening his embrace and inviting the
defeated with his entire cloak into his sea-grey arms and concealing streams.'

contra autem, magno maerentem corpore Nilum
pandentemque sinus et tota veste vocantem
caeruleum in gremium latebrosaque flumina victos.
(8.711–13)

It was not that Virgil was indifferent to the power of rivers in
full spate. Already in the *Georgics* he evokes the flooding Eridanus
(here his own Cisalpine river Po), the king of rivers, which in rage
at Caesar's death washed away the forests, wrenching them up
with its eddies, carrying the herds and their byres over all the
plains (1.481–3). The poet's catalogue of great rivers whose sources
lie beneath the sea (*omnia sub magna labentia flumina terra*,
4.366) moves rapidly through the Colchian Phasis and Anatolian
Lycus to Thessalian Enipeus, Tiber, and Anio, the rocky Scythian
Hypanis and Anatolian Caicus, to 'the Eridanus, its countenance
gilded with twin bullhorns: no other river flows more violently
through fertile farmlands into the dark red sea.'

gemina auratus taurino cornua vultu
Eridanus, quo non alius per pinguia culta
in mare purpureum violentior effluit amnis.
(*Georg.* 4.371–3)

It is Horace rather than Virgil who first uses the river in spate as
a symbol of inescapable fate: 'All else is swept away like a river

which now glides peacefully within its banks to the Etruscan sea, now rolls hollowed rocks and uprooted trees and flocks and houses together, with the roar of mountains and nearby forest when a savage flood provokes calm streams.'

> cetera fluminis
> ritu feruntur, nunc medio alveo
>   cum pace delabentis Etruscum
>   in mare, nunc lapides adesos
> stirpesque raptas et pecus et domos
> volventis una non sine montium
>   clamore vicinaeque silvae
>   cum fera diluvies quietos
> irritat amnis.
>   (Horace *Odes* 3.29.33–41)

But for Horace the river is also the positive image of Pindaric lyric; compare 4.2.5–8, 'like a river pouring down from the mountain which rains have swollen beyond its familiar banks, Pindar seethes and rushes beyond measure with his great deep voice.'

> monte decurrens velut amnis, imbres
> quem super notas aluere ripas,
> fervet immensusque ruit profundo
>   Pindarus ore.

Rivers have always appealed to the imagination, and that must be the reason why Virgil's poem of the Italian·land is rich with allusions to exotic rivers. There is virtually no Greek or eastern river in Ovid's great catalogue of *Met.* 2.241–59 which does not put in a cameo appearance in the *Georgics*, whether for its associations with Thessalian myth or the tale of Orpheus, or with the conquests of Alexander, who marched far beyond the Euphrates to the Araxes and Ganges and Hydaspes.[10]

But it is Ovid above all who delights in river catalogues, and the reason is probably his admiration for Callimachus, who wrote a work on the Loves of Rivers (now lost) and another, which may not be irrelevant, on Nymphs. Ovid made early use of the lost work in his invective (*Amores* 3.6) against the muddy stream whose spring spate supposedly obstructed his journey to his girl-friend; there, twenty lines evoke the love affairs of eight rivers celebrated in Greek myth before he settles down to the sympathetic version of Anio's love for Ilia, which we considered in the last chapter. Each of the Greek rivers is characterized either physically as a stream or anthropomorphically with some moral feature. His Inachus (whom we know better as the sedate father of Io) is said to have grown pale for love of Melie of Bithynia and heated his cool waters (25–6). Neaera ravished 'your gaze, O Xanthus' (27–8). Resolute love of the Arcadian maiden drove Alpheus (whom we will meet again) to flow to distant lands, and Peneus (sedate father of Daphne in the *Metamorphoses*) is supposed to have hidden Creusa, destined bride of Xuthus, beneath the earth of Phthia (29–32). Thebe, daughter of Mars and future mother of five, bewitched Asopus,[11] and – as Ovid approaches the end of his list – Acheloüs' loss of his horns, broken off by the angry hand of Hercules, bears witness that Deianeira was worth so great a loss; even the Nile with his seven mouths, so skilled in concealing the source of his waters, could not overcome with his eddies the accumulated flame of his love for Asopus' daughter Evanthe (33–42). Finally the Enipeus, who ordered his own water to retreat so that he could embrace the daughter of Salmoneus, and the water obeyed his orders (43–8).

Enipeus has been placed last in the Greek catalogue and given this act of self-denial (ordering his own waters to retreat) because Ovid wants the anonymous stream to emulate his behaviour and withdraw its muddy waters. Thessalian rivers had a long life in Hesiod's works, and twice in the *Metamorphoses* Ovid lists the usual suspects: at 1.577 the newly bereaved Peneus invites his local rivers (*popularia flumina*) Spercheus and Enipeus, old Apidanus, Amphrysus, and Aeas, and other unnamed rivers; only Inachus absents himself in grief over Io. Again, in 7.228–30, Medea flies over Thessaly to gather herbs and visits Apidanus, Amphrysus, Enipeus, Peneus, and Spercheus – Aeas is omitted. It is Ovid's pleasure to allude to offbeat myths, and searchers for their origins may find allusions in the fragments and testimonia of Hesiod's *Catalogue of Women*, or they may discover more scattered evidence in Gantz's

(1993) great collection *Early Greek Myth*, or, more likely, they may fail.[12] But Enipeus – or rather Tyro, daughter of Salmoneus and mother of the twins Pelias and Neleus – is a special case. Already in the *Nekuia*, Tyro was the first heroine to be introduced, and her curious love triangle was described most explicitly:

There I saw first Tyro of noble father, who claimed to be the child of excellent Salmoneus, and the wife of Cretheus the child of Aeolus. She was infatuated with the river, the divine Enipeus, which flows most beautifully of all rivers on earth, and she used to visit the Enipeus' glorious streams. So the earth-shaking Poseidon took on the river's likeness and lay with her in the estuary of the eddying river. A deep red wave-crest rose up like a mountain and concealed the god and the mortal woman [he untied her maiden girdle and poured sleep over her]. But when the god had completed his acts of love, he took her by the hand and addressed her. (Homer *Odyssey* 11.235–47, Rieu 1946/1961)

Poseidon told her that she would bear fine children to him, since unions with gods were never childless; for now she should go home and refrain from naming him; and at this point he names himself. In the Homeric narrative, then, the river-god shows no sexual initiative; although the woman desires him, it is not clear that *pôlesketo* implies any sexual union; this privilege is usurped by the god Poseidon in disguise. Later versions (a lost play of Sophocles; Diodorus 4.68; and Apollodorus *Bibl.* 1.9.8) preserve the river's innocence. Propertius twice alludes to the love-story in different versions, stressing Poseidon's deception in 1.13.21–2, *non sic Haemonio Salmonida mixtus Enipeo / Taenarius facili pressit amore deus*, 'not so did the god of Taenarus mingling with Haemonian Enipeus embrace Salmoneus' daughter,' but placing emphasis on Tyro's own desire in 3.19.13–14, *testis Thessalico flagrans Salmonis Enipeo, / quae voluit liquido tota subire deo*, 'Salmonis is witness: blazing with desire for Thessalian Enipeus, she was eager to yield utterly to the watery god.' Surely Propertius has chosen to be ambiguous here, so that the union can be read as that of girl and river? In fact both references allow for some physical confusion or blending between the beloved river and the lecherous god. Ovid himself makes Tyro's story one of Arachne's indictments of divine deceit in *Met.* 6.116–17, where Neptune, seeming to be Enipeus, begets the hubristic Aloiadae.

Nymphs could be as aggressive as rivers, as shall be illustrated in the last section of this chapter. In Prop. 1.20 the 'cruel' river Ascanius in Bithynia does not molest Hylas but is witness when the Dryads pull him under their pool. Another friend of Propertius (addressed by the pseudonym of Lynceus) seems to have included erotic tales of Acheloüs and Maeander in his narrative verse: 'Though you are telling of the course of Aetolian Acheloüs, how its waters flowed shattered by a great love, and how the stream of the Maeander wanders deceptively on the Phrygian plain, concealing the direction of its flow.'

> nam cursus licet Aetoli referas Acheloi
> fluxerit ut magno fractus amore liquor,
> atque etiam ut Phrygio fallax Maeandria campo
> errat et ipsa suas decipit unda vias.
> (Prop. 2.34.33–6)

THE MOODS OF ACHELOÜS: JEALOUSY, LOVE, AND COMPETITION

Along with the Acheloüs, the Alpheus, flowing past Pisa and Olympia in Elis, is given full masculinity and develops a quasi-human personality in erotic episodes of the *Metamorphoses*. There is no question of worship, only of (intermittent) superhuman powers; but the characterization of these rivers sets a model for the way rivers and their gods will be represented in later poetry. As Achilles pointed out, not least among rivers is the Acheloüs, which, after passing through Acarnania, empties itself into the sea opposite the islands called Echinades, and, according to Herodotus (2.10) and Thucydides, had already joined one-half of them to the continent by the late fifth century (2.102):

Opposite to Oeniadae lie most of the islands called Echinades, so close to the mouths of the Acheloüs that that powerful stream is constantly forming deposits against them and has already joined some of the islands to the continent and seems likely in no long while to do the same with the rest. For the current is strong, deep and turbid, and the islands are so thick together they serve to imprison the alluvial deposit and prevent its dispersing ... The islands in question are uninhabited and of no great size.

Thucydides mentions the alluvial delta of the Acheloüs in connection with the Delphic command to Alcmaeon permitting him to settle on land which had not existed when he murdered his adulterous mother, for he made his settlement at the mouth of the Acheloüs. Indeed, we know that Ovid himself was familiar with this and other natural phenomena, from Pythagoras' comments: 'Just so the condition of places has often been changed. I have seen what was quite solid earth become sea, and lands made out of the water's surface.'

> sic totiens versa est fortuna locorum
> vidi ego, quod fuerat quondam solidissima tellus
> esse fretum, vidi factas ex aequore terras.
> (Ovid *Met.* 15.262–4)

However, when Ovid introduces Acheloüs' reminiscences in *Met.* 8.549, he has created a peculiar context. It looks as though Ovid's larger purpose is to get from the saga of Theseus and the war between Athens and Crete to the saga of Hercules, while avoiding the better-known feats of either hero. So Ovid has Theseus, returning from Calydon, waylaid by Acheloüs, who insists on imposing overnight hospitality. Acheloüs is swollen with rain but seems unable to control his own waters, for he invites Theseus to enter his residence rather than trust himself to the violent waters, which often carry away solid tree-trunks and roll over dislodged rocks with a great rumble. In fact the river speaks at length of his stream's destruction of stables, and herds of oxen and horses, and even sturdy young men's bodies, when swollen by melting winter snows (550–7). It is safer, he announces, for Theseus to wait until the stream has returned within its banks.

It was surely the physical force of rivers in flood that first earned them worship, but Acheloüs seems to be boasting of his strength without any sense of a social duty to control it. Let us give the voluble hero of this extended narrative an in-depth moral or psychological analysis. Acheloüs has an elegant grotto and will prove a chatty host to Theseus and his friends; but even before they have tasted the feast and sipped the wine served by his barefoot nymphs, a question from Theseus, who is admiring the view, diverts the god into offering two preliminary tales of his troubled relationships with nymphs, first as neighbours and later with a single nymph whom he had wooed or probably seduced.

As Theseus looks from Acheloüs' dining alcove out to sea, he asks, 'what place is that? ... and tell me the name of that island, though it seems to be more than just one,' *quis ... / ille locus? ... et insula nomen / quod gerat illa doce, quamquam non una videtur* (8.574–6). The river replies without embarrassment that what Theseus is looking at is not one entity. There are five pieces of land, and the distance is deceiving him, concealing their separation: *non est ... unum, / spatium discrimina fallit.* Swiftly, in eleven lines (579–89), he explains that these Naiads had sacrificed ten oxen and invited the country gods to the feast, but held their party without him – or without gratitude to him (*immemores nostri* might suggest the latter). He proudly reports that his stream swelled to its maximum size, monstrous in fury and in waves (*pariterque animis immanis et undis*, 584). This time the river presents the destructive power of the current as his own deliberate purpose. He had retaliated by ripping away their woods and fields from their land mass and rolled the nymphs with their site into the sea (*cumque loco nymphas memores tum denique nostri / in freta provolvi*, 586–7). Together the force of the breakers and his own current had fragmented the continuous land into 'as many islands as the Echinades' – he names them for the first time – 'which you now perceive in mid-tide.'

So far, so good. Acheloüs has answered Theseus' questions with both the history and the name of the islands – though Bömer (1977, 178–82) is able to cite specific and individual names for several of them. But now comes what seems a conflicting story, that of the otherwise unrecorded nymph Perimele (8.590–610). It begins as if this nymph were one of the original islands: 'But as you see, one of them has withdrawn far, far away: an island dear to me,' *procul, en procul una recessit / insula, grata mihi* (590–1). He adds that sailors now call it (her?) Perimele. Was this, then, her name when she was still alive? Does this story begin after the flood which expelled the nymphs? So I originally thought, but this possibility is excluded, even contradicted by the following narrative.

Again without embarrassment Acheloüs reports that he loved Perimele and took her virginity, but her father was angry and hurled his daughter bodily into the deep from a cliff so that she would perish (594, *propulit ... periturae corpora natae*). Acheloüs caught her and, even as he supported her, appealed to Neptune to save her. Depending on how much of the following text we accept as Ovidian, Acheloüs may offer a swift appeal to Poseidon prefaced by ingratiating honorifics: 'O trident-bearer, thou who hast been allotted kingship over the second realm of the world, the wandering wave ... bring aid and grant a place to this girl drowned by her father's savagery, or may she herself become a place.'

> O proxima mundi
> regna vagae ... sortite, tridentifer, undae,
> adfer opem, mersaeque, precor, feritate paterna
> da, Neptune, locum – vel sit locus ipsa licebit.
> (8.595–6, 601–2)

Or he may instead amplify his appeal with a further six lines of justification.[13] I would encourage readers who think the deferral frustrating to skip the next two pages.

Ignoring the violation of urgency before reaching the specific appeal to Neptune, let us briefly review these intervening lines. Picking up the vocative *tridentifer*, they continue: 'You in whom all of us sacred rivers[14] who run our course come to our end, be present and hear me kindly, Neptune, as I pray. I have brought harm to this girl whom I am carrying. If Hippodamas had been mild and fair, if he had been a [real] father, or less disloyal, he should have taken pity on her, and pardoned us. To her for whom the earth has been closed off by her father's savagery ...'

in quo desinimus, quot sacri currimus amnes,	597
huc ades atque audi placidus, Neptune, precantem.	598
huic ego quam porto nocui; si mitis et aequus,	599

si pater Hippodamas, aut si minus impius esset,   600
debuit illius misereri, ignoscere nobis.   600a
cui quondam tellus clausa est feritate paterna ...   600b

Here we must resume with line 601 as above, but with an unwanted repetition, 'bring help and give a place to her, drowned by
her father's savagery, or she herself will be allowed to become a
place.' Tarrant has excised all these lines, and despite my innate
conservatism I cannot but sympathize. First, Neptune's already
lengthy honorific title is extended unnecessarily (598), and then
comes the justification, which postpones for four lines the actual
request. Certainly it would be possible to pass comfortably from
line 598, *audi ... precantem*, or even the first part of line 599, *huic
ego, quam porto, nocui*, to line 601, *adfer opem*, and the digres-
sion with its triple reproach of Hippodamas seems incongruous:
'if he was gentle and fair, if he behaved like a father, or even if he
were less disloyal, he should have pitied her and pardoned me.' I
sympathize with Anderson's complaint[15] that gods, even river-
gods, do not think they need or even ask for pardon; we might add
that such pardon is irrelevant to rescuing the drowning nymph.

How are we to explain the precise and pointless repetition (or
anticipation) of *feritate paterna* in line 600b, unless these lines
have been generated from the slimmer, two-line version which
editors generally take as authentic? Surely line 600b has arisen
from an attempt by Ovid to rewrite line 601 or provide an alternative sequence in lines 600b–602? I would not want to impugn
602, since the play on *locus* serves to bind the story of Perimele
to that of the other islands.

But there is more to come – in Tarrant's text, only two lines:
'And as I spoke new earth embraced her swimming limbs, and an
island grew over her; weighty with her transformed body.'

dum loquor, amplexa est artus nova terra natantes   609
et gravis increvit mutatis insula membris.   610

This time, however, it seems more likely that the additional lines
preserved in many manuscripts (603–8) are authentically Ovidian.
Acheloüs has already displayed a certain playboy-like attitude to

women. The suspect lines follow on 602, *sit locus ipsa licebit,* with Acheloüs' desire to continue his love-making: either *hunc (sc. locum)* or *hanc quoque complectar* – even if she become a place, I shall embrace it (or her) too. Lines 603–8 develop the action: 'The king of the sea gave the nod, shaking all the waters with his agreement. The nymph was terrified but kept on swimming, and I touched the breast of her, heaving with her panicked emotion as she swam. And while fondling her breast, I felt her body harden all over and her ribcage become buried in land that covers her over.'

> hunc quoque complectar. movit caput aequoreus rex
> concussitque suis omnes adsensibus undas.
> extimuit nymphe, nabat tamen: ipsa natantis
> pectora tangebam trepido salientia motu,
> dumque ea contrecto, totum durescere sensi
> corpus et inductis condi praecordia terris.

Here we begin to duplicate, for the next lines are unchallenged: 'While I speak, new land embraced her swimming limbs, and a heavy island grew around her transformed body.'

> dum loquor, amplexa est artus nova terra natantes
> et gravis increvit mutatis insula membris.
> (8.609–10)

Even by Ovidian standards this is quite lubricious, but does that argue for or against accepting the lines as an alternative version written by Ovid himself? Review of the language used here shows that both *salire* and *durescere* are used in a truly Ovidian fashion, of the throbbing of life and the hardening that marks its removal,[16] but there is less precedent for the plurals *adsensibus* in line 604 and *terris* in line 608.[17] Nonetheless, the conceptualization is Ovidian, as we can see from comparing the transformation of Dryope[18] in book 9 and the humanization of Pygmalion's statue in book 10. We may treat the lines intervening between 602 and 609 with suspicion, as does Murgia (1984),[19] because they seem to echo the formulation of the Daphne episode; but Ovid was a notorious self-imitator, and even if the first phase of transformation contains interpolated material, its presence should not predetermine our evaluation of the later phase. Without lines 603–8, both 602, with its strange construction *sit locus ipsa licebit*, turning the river-god's request into the statement 'she will be allowed to become a place,' and 609, *amplexa est artus nova terra natantes*, are awkward and incomplete. And there is no doubt that Ovid's Perimele did become earth, a piece of earth that can be called an island.

So what is the temporal relationship between Acheloüs' two tales of transformation? And how has Ovid conceptualized the river-god? Again, why does Ovid include both Acheloüs' angry spate that transformed the Naiads into islands and his helpless but loving appeal to Neptune to save the woman he apparently cannot save himself, introducing the otherwise unknown metamorphosis of Perimele by Neptune? In the first episode the river-god shows the jealousy for honours of a Greek hero like Achilles, but acts entirely as a river. In the second, he has already enjoyed Perimele, presumably in human form since she does not seem able to survive in his waters or the ocean – the unexplored assumption is that she is to be saved from drowning. We will see that nothing in Acheloüs' third narrative associates him with the river's waters, and his behaviour throughout assumes human form.

Ovid must have juxtaposed the first two stories in order to play them off against each other. Thus, for example, the first transformation is punishment and the second serves as rescue, but why did Acheloüs need to rescue Perimele from his own watery embrace? Daphne expressed some doubt as to whether her river-god father, Peneus, had divine powers to rescue her from Apollo ('bring aid, father, if rivers have divine power,' *fer, pater ... opem, si flumina numen habetis, Met.* 1.545). Thus river-gods may not be able to cause the transformation of other beings (Barchiesi 1989/2001, 276–84); certainly shape-shifters (like Acheloüs) can usually shift only their own shape. So they may need the help of Neptune – or, in the other story, the intervention of Nature or Earth herself. Acheloüs is equally capable of seeing the nymphs as religious offenders (since when did nymphs conduct sacrifices?) and of lusting after and seducing one of them, who has a mortal father who apparently discovers her offence. Or was Perimele only a vulnerable human girl?

While the tale of the Echinades depends on natural geography, that of Perimele combines a bourgeois morality tale with a story of supernatural intervention that can bring little satisfaction to the passionate god. But then Ovid's love of paradox may have prompted him to offer a supernatural and even titillating explanation of what he knows was a natural (alluvial) transfer of earth to earth.

But these are just preliminary diversions. Ovid separates Acheloüs' tales from the best-known myth of his unsuccessful erotic adventures by two memorable and antithetical tales: of the reward of the pious Baucis and Philemon by the gods to whom they gave hospitality, and of the punishment of the impious Erysicthon, with its coda of his daughter Mestra's successful shape-shifting to elude her captors. This double tale of father and daughter is told by Acheloüs, again in answer to Theseus, who is asking for examples of divine miracles (*facta ... mira deum*, 8.726–7), but it also reflects some of Acheloüs' previous themes. As an answer to Pirithoüs' doubts that gods can change their own shape, he cites Proteus, 'dweller in the sea which embraces the earth,' *complexi terram maris incola* (8.731), and approaches the story of Mestra through that of her impious father, 'who despised the divinity of the gods and kindled no incense on any altars,' *qui numina divum / sperneret et nullos aris adoleret odores* (8.739–40). Again, Mestra's special talent for shape-shifting is her reward from Neptune for her violation (8.850–1). Only after this coda does the river-god turn from Mestra to his own limited capacity (*finita potestas*) to appear as man (*qui nunc sum*, 881), snake, or bull. But the thought of his bull-like strength brings him to the sad loss of one of his horns – so it seems that even in human form his appearance is mutilated, showing only one of the expected horns. There was no mention of his horn(s) when Acheloüs first entered the narrative (8.549), nor was there any hint of his shape-shifting capacities in the earlier tales. With a groan, the river now turns to his famous defeat and humiliation.

Why does Ovid introduce the river in book 9 'with his hair unadorned and bound with reeds,' *inornatos redimitus harundine crines* (9.3)? We were not told that Acheloüs was garlanded for the feast, but that would be assumed by Ovid's readers. Perhaps his broken horn becomes visible now that he wears only a wreath of reeds. That would provide a fit setting for his narrative, which opens by compensating for his defeat by describing the greatness of his victorious rival; but later we are told that the reeds can conceal the damage to the river's noble brow.[20] The river-god's story starts from the beautiful Deianeira and the competition among her many suitors, including Acheloüs himself; indeed, all the other suitors withdrew from the contest, leaving only Acheloüs and Hercules. Hercules claims that Jupiter and the glory of his labours make him a fit son-in-law (9.14–15). The river-god stands on his divine dignity. It would be shameful for a god to yield to a mortal, and Acheloüs offers a very proper speech for a suitor. He is local where Hercules is foreign, Juno does not hate him, and he has no lists of chores to perform; indeed, either Hercules is lying in calling himself son of Jupiter, or his birth is adulterous. Enraged Hercules counters the river-god's eloquence with his own physical force, and confronts him for combat. Nothing so far has distinguished our speaker from any good Greek fighter, except perhaps the colour of his green robes (9.32), and what follows is strictly a wrestling bout to divert sporting readers. For all his imagery comparing himself with a rock assailed by sea waves, and their combat with that of bulls over a gleaming heifer, Acheloüs shows himself a static and defensive fighter: he can repel Hercules three times, but at the fourth attempt Hercules has him in his grip and forces him to the ground (51–61). Finding himself worsted in *virtus*, the river resorts to his specialty, shapeshifting. He is first a serpent, but Hercules is experienced in throttling snakes; he then falls back on his third shape, that of a grim bull (80–1), but Hercules simply presses him down by the horns, thus forcing him down into the sand, and snaps off the horn he has in his right hand.

If Ovid's readers wanted to hear the end of the tale of courtship, or of the river's frustrated violence, they are disappointed. This combat tells us nothing more about the river-god's personality. Throughout he is in human form, acting like any Greek princeling in, say, the courtship competition for Cleisthenes of Sicyon's daughter. River-god he may be, but he makes no use of the waters; he may own them, but he is not identified with them. Instead Ovid follows the destiny of the broken horn, which is taken by the Naiads, and filled with fruit and perfume to become the wealthy Horn of Plenty. After all, we have been listening only to an *aition*, and one that is implemented when a serving maid with streaming hair comes round offering in his *cornucopia* a whole autumn harvest and a dessert of prime-quality apples. The heroes leave his residence at dawn without waiting for the waters to subside, and Acheloüs hides his rustic features and crumpled horn beneath the waves.

ALPHEUS AND ARETHUSA: 'HANG YOUR CLOTHES ON YONDER TREE,
BUT DON'T GO NEAR THE WATER ...'

It turns out, then, that Acheloüs behaves in a fashion far more typical of river-gods when he first enters the narrative and gives full vent to his anger and lust, than in his final rivalry and encounter with Hercules. Let us contrast him with the Alpheus, who is seen in Ovid's narrative only through the words of Arethusa, his female victim, addressed to the goddess Ceres and reported by and to other females – the muse who repeats Calliope's verse epic to the goddess Athene. This time, surely the lechery of river-gods will go undisguised?

Arethusa enters the epic as *Alpheias* ('the beloved of Alpheus,' 5.487) speaking in her new home of Sicily, but rising from *Eleis undis*, again the Elean waters of Alpheus; it seems she has become the river-god's possession. But she postpones her story until Ceres has made sure of recovering her daughter. She resumes at line 577, introducing herself as an Achaean nymph, indifferent to her own charms, and returning weary from what one must assume is a hunting expedition. In the heat she finds a calm, clear stream, shaded by hoary willows and poplars, with sloping banks. Foolishly she hangs her clothes on a willow and swims this way and that in the waters. But now she hears a mysterious murmuring in the waters, panics, and tries to reach the water's edge. A hoarse voice accosts her and she identifies it as Alpheus: 'where are you hurrying to, Arethusa?' *quo properas, Arethusa?* (5.599). She is cut off from her clothes and escapes onto the land naked, feeling all the more exposed to his onslaught (*sum visa paratior illi*, 5.603). She starts to run, and the savage male (*ferus ille*), clearly quite distinct from the stream of the river itself, pursues her relentlessly, all over the Peloponnese. Proudly, Arethusa reports that he was no faster than she, but her endurance was running out, whereas he was practised in prolonged effort. With the sun behind her, she sees his long shadow – unless her own fear imagines it – and hears the thud of his feet and feels his mighty panting on her headdress (cf. 617, *ingens / ... anhelitus oris*). This last touch, along with the poet's reminder of the protective *vittae* which apparently she is still wearing, adds pathos and terror to the contrast of pursuer and victim. When her appeal to Diana provides her with a concealing mist, the river does not give up but circles twice round where she is hidden, each time calling, 'Hey Arethusa!' Arethusa's pursuit narrative is enriched by comparison of her with the lamb hearing the wolf or the hare the hounds, but this is not the usual comparison of predator and prey, since the essence of her situation is the need to be both still and silent. Dread and perspiration combine to turn Arethusa herself from human form into water, *in latices mutor* (636), but now that transformation empowers the river-god. He too 'casts aside his human form and reverts to his real nature as water in order to unite with her,' *positoque viri, quod sumpserat, ore, / vertitur in proprias, ut se mihi misceat, undas* (637–8).

After so many false climaxes, Arethusa cuts her story short. Diana splits the earth open, and Arethusa flows through underground caves to Ortygia (the island of Syracuse), which bears her patron goddess's name[21] and is beloved by her as the place which first restores her to the upper air.

Ceres (and Ovid's narrator) move away, leaving an open question. Why does Ovid (or his muse reporting Calliope's epic) say nothing of what became of Alpheus? Does Arethusa, or the narrating Calliope, want to leave this as a story with the happy feminist ending of virginity preserved? What did Ovid's readers expect as the outcome of the story? There was a later Hellenistic tradition that the human hero Alpheus drowned in the river for love of Arethusa, but it might not have been familiar to Ovid or his readers; what was familiar was the magical tradition that perpetuated the river's love of Arethusa even across the Ionian sea.[22] They would know from Aeneas' visit to Sicily that Alpheus too travelled under the sea to Sicily, and the two seem to have become lovers: 'Tradition is that Alpheus, the river of Elis, pursued a hidden path beneath the sea and now emerges through your mouth, Arethusa, blended with the Sicilian waves.'

> Alpheum fama est huc Elidis amnem
> occultas egisse vias subter mare, qui nunc
> ore, Arethusa, tuo Siculis confunditur undis.
>   (Virgil *Aen.* 3.694–6)

Is this not what Ovid implies by his opening identification of the nymph? He returns to the story in his exile poetry, when he recalls his own youthful visit to Sicily with Macer. There he saw Etna, and Palice and Enna, and the river Anapis (or Anapus), which mingles his waters with the spring Cyane (*ex Ponto* 2.10.26); last of all Ovid alludes to Arethusa and leaves her escape implied: 'and nearby the nymph who runs even now hidden (protected?) beneath the waters of the sea as she flees from the river of Elis,'

> nec procul hinc nympha, quae dum fugit Elidis amnem
> tecta sub aequorea nunc quoque currit aqua.
>   (Ovid *ex Ponto* 2.10.27–8)

Here, perhaps the poet prefers to contrast Arethusa's escape with the fate of the nymph Cyane, symbolically violated by Dis in *Met.* 5.419–24, but on her own account previously and happily mated with Anapis (5.415–19). The version he offers provides an upbeat ending. Does the idea lurk behind Arethusa's (doubly reported) narrative in *Metamorphoses* that she didn't know what was good for her, and the river was only 'doing what came naturally?' What was the gain if a nymph maintained her virginity? (But what was the gain anyway, if no precious heroic son was born of the union?) Even the vivid terror of the victim as (inner) narrator does not make Acheloüs or Alpheus or Anapis or other lusty river-gods into evil monsters. For monsters of lust we have to look elsewhere, to humans like Tereus and Cyclopes like Polyphemus.

Hylas and Hermaphrodite:
Gender Reversal and Sexual Aggression

Earlier in this multiple chapter we found abundant evidence that nymphs, whose very name denoted nubility (cf. Greek *nymphe* = bride), were often the sexual victims of supernatural aggressors, whether rivers or wilderness spirits like Faunus, *nympharum fugientum amator* ('lover of fleeing nymphs,' Hor. *Odes* 3.18.1). Only Pomona seems able to ward off the lecherous advances of 'country creatures,' by enclosing her orchards (*pomaria claudit, Met.* 14.635) to exclude the Satyrs, the Pans, and Silvanus, and even Priapus, 'who intimidates thieves whether with his sickle or his member,' *quique deus fures vel falce vel inguine terret* (14.640). When other nymphs were off-duty from their service to Diana as hunters or dancers, much of their activity was aimed at escaping coarse or inferior lovers, though they sometimes favour chosen lovers, as, for example, Galatea favours Acis in *Metamorphoses* 13. But gods superior in power they could not escape, except by sacrificing their identity, as Daphne and Syrinx escaped by exchanging their rational, quasi-human existence for that of trees.

In Ovid's *Metamorphoses* and *Fasti*, nymphs, whether Greek or Roman, were also great gossips, and behaved remarkably like modern teenagers. When they were not rejecting or deceiving lovers, their chief conversation seems to have been about their successful deceptions, or about the sexual pursuits of gods and demigods. A prime example is Scylla: 'many suitors sought after her, but she drove them away and went to the nymphs of the sea, being most welcome to the sea-nymphs, and would tell how she cheated the loves of young men.'

> hanc multi petiere proci, quibus illa repulsis
> ad pelagi nymphas, pelagi gratissima nymphis,
> ibat et elusos iuvenum narrabat amores.
> (Ovid *Met.* 13.735–7)

Where Jupiter was concerned, it was dangerous either to frustrate or to protect his adulteries. Thus in *Fasti* Jupiter summons all the local nymphs of Tiber and Anio and lectures them on why they should keep quiet his pursuit of Juturna, who had been evading him by hiding in woods or leaping into streams. His claim is that she is cheating herself of the pleasure and privilege of intercourse with him: 'Your sister is begrudging her own luck and avoiding what is in her interest, to sleep with the most almighty god. Take thought for both of us, for what is my great pleasure will be of great advantage to your sister. So block her path on the edge of the stream as she flees, so she cannot plunge her body into the river water' (*Fasti* 2.591–6).

As we saw in the previous chapter (p. 77), one nymph, Lara, despite her father's warnings to hold her tongue, immediately warned Juturna, and even told Juno what was going on. In fury Jupiter tore out her tongue and told Mercury to escort her down to Hades to live in the infernal marsh. Unable to cry out, she could not prevent Mercury from raping her, and became mother of the Lares. (Carna or Crane, honoured with offerings on the Kalends of June, suffered a similar fate at the hands of Janus.)[23] Normally it is as informers that nymphs and other creatures are punished by the gods. But in one case, that of Echo, a nymph was punished by Juno with loss of all independent speech for trying to help Jupiter conceal his affairs by detaining Juno in conversation. Echo, however, was unusual in another respect: she actually desired and wanted to woo a human, and failed bitterly, both because of her hampered speech and because she had been smitten with love for the wrong human. So nymphs too could fall in love and suffer for it.

But even before Ovid put his creative imagination to work improving on pre-existing myths, Hellenistic poets, with the fascination they felt for women's wrongful passions, had told of aggressive women, and specifically of aggressive nymphs. Hellenistic tradition, so fascinated by 'unnatural' passion, transmitted two notorious instances to our Latin poets. In Silenus' song recapitulating Hellenistic themes, including the love of Pasiphaë, a brief allusion to shores that echoed 'Hylas, Hylas' needs no further comment. As Virgil himself protested in his proem to the third *Georgic*, the ravishing of the boy Hylas by the nymphs of the spring Pegae, close to the estuary of the river Ascanius in Asia Minor, was one of the most commonplace tales of the poets: *cui non dictus Hylas?* 'Who has not told of Hylas?' (*Georg.* 3.6).

As scholars have pointed out, the boy Hylas was assimilated to raped virgins, and especially Persephone, in his role as an innocent victim of the desire he provoked in others. But unlike Persephone, he had a double appeal, as a blushing boy to his lover Herakles, and as an emerging youth to the passionate nymph or nymphs. Perhaps, like Horace's Ligurinus (*Odes* 4.1 and 4.10), he should be thought of as in transition between boy and man. The two Alexandrian narratives diverge in two respects. While the epic of Apollonius does not stress the sexual relationship between Herakles and Hylas, but, as we shall see, constructs a single enduring heterosexual relationship between nymph and boy[24] (comparable in reverse to that between Ovid's Anio and Ilia in *Amores* 3.6), Theocritus wrote *Idyll* 13 for his gay friend Nicias and assimilates the boy Hylas to Nicias' beloved; Hylas is the acknowledged beloved of Herakles and is seized not by one nymph but a whole crowd, who treat him almost as a plaything. Yet the two versions converge in the way they describe the emotional condition of the nymph(s).

First, here is Apollonius' narrative at this crucial moment:

Quickly he went to the spring which the local people call The Sources. And the dances of the nymphs had just occurred. For all the nymphs who dwelled in the lovely meadow constantly devoted themselves to singing nocturnal hymns for Artemis. And those who lived in the watchtowers or the mountains or the streams, and the guardians of the woodlands, were arrayed far away, but the water-nymph had just emerged from her fair-flowing spring. And she saw him nearby, blushing with beauty and sweet charms, for the full moon shining from the heavens struck his features. And Aphrodite sent the nymph's wits in a flutter and from sheer helplessness she could barely collect her spirit. But as soon as he dipped his jug into the stream, bending sideways, and the rushing water gurgled as it was taken into the sounding vessel, she placed her left arm on the thick of his neck, longing to kiss his rounded mouth, and with her right hand grasped his elbow. And she pulled him down into the midst of the eddy. (Apoll. *Arg.* 1.1221–39)

It is another water deity, the sea-god Glaucus, 'the knowing prophet of godly Nereus,' who completes the narrative by telling the mourning Argonauts that a divine nymph acting from love has taken Hylas to be her spouse (1.1324–5).

Theocritus may have known Apollonius' epic before he composed his thirteenth *Idyll* for Nicias, since he seems to have drawn on Apollonius again for *Idyll* 22. He too is clear about the female initiative, but since he is writing for a boy-lover he gives much more attention to the boy Hylas.

When Hylas went to fetch water for the feast of Herakles and Telamon, he came to the spring surrounded with grasses and sedge and wild parsley. In the midst of the water the nymphs were arraying their dance, those sleepless nymphs, dangerous goddesses for hunters, Eunika and Malis and Nycheia, whose glance was like spring. Then the boy held out his capacious jug for a drink, hastening to dip it in. But they all took him in their hands, for desire had panicked the tender wits of them all for the Argive boy. And he fell into the dark water headlong, just as when a brilliant star shoots headlong from the heaven into the sea, and a sailor says to his comrades, 'Lighten the sails, boys. The wind is good for sailing.' But the nymphs held the boy in their laps and comforted him with kindly words as he wept. (Theoc. 13.36, 39–54)

Where Apollonius offers a single nymph, apparently intent on a lasting marriage, Theocritus calls the nymphs dangerous *(deinai)*, as if this behaviour was to be expected from them, and depicts a collective kidnapping of the boy. Nothing is said of the future of Hylas, who does indeed hear Herakles call for him, but only faintly. But both poets lay stress on the desire felt by the nymph(s), which overcomes their or her wits (*phrenas ... eptoiesen / exephobesen*), and describe the moment when Hylas is drawn down under the water.

Many cultures have myths of water-spirits such as Ondine or the collective Nixies, who become enamoured of young men and pull them down under water – no doubt to explain mysterious instances of drowning, when bodies could not be recovered. I do not know of Italian versions of such a myth, and we shall see that Roman poets kept both Hylas and the more extreme case of Hermaphroditus in their exotic Asian setting. We do not know whether Varro of Atax in any way modified his version of Hylas' fate when he came to this part of Apollonius' narrative; and despite Virgil's scorn we have only one independent version, and one which is most probably later than the publication of the *Georgics* in 29 BCE: This is Propertius' extraordinary *Elegy* 1.20, for a Gallus who is almost certainly not Cornelius Gallus,[25] and may or may not be the same Gallus who is addressed in Prop. 1. 5, 10, and 13. I have called it extraordinary because of its almost parodic Hellenistic diction and narrative technique. Is it in fact possible that Propertius composed this poem very early in his career, in the thirties, and that Virgil knew and disliked it, but Propertius wanted to preserve it with the other more mature elegies of the *Monobiblos*?

Camps (1966, 93) sees the poem as modelled on Theocritus 13, because it too is addressed to a friend with a beloved boy and uses the sad tale of Hylas as a caution. Despite its stress on the Minyae and exotic Greek geography (the otherwise unknown river Ascanius), even exotic forms (*Theiodamanteo*, 6, and the datives *Adryasin*, 12, and *Hamadryasin*, 32), Propertius' message is a warning to protect his beloved Hylas ('not different in name,' 5) from Italian girls:

You must always, whether you follow by boat the rivers of the Umbrian forest, or dip your feet in the water of Anio, or you stroll on the shore of the Giants' coast, or anywhere in the domain of a wandering river, ward off from him the ravishing of passionate Nymphs (for Ausonian dryads feel no less a love), in case it fall to you endlessly to visit harsh mountains and chill rocks and new lakes untried.

> huic tu, sive leges Umbrae rate flumina silvae, [<rate> Richmond]
>   sive Aniena tuos tinxerit unda pedes,
> sive Gigantei spatiabere litoris ora,
>   sive ubicumque vago fluminis hospitio,
> Nympharum semper cupidas defende rapinas
>   (non minor Ausoniis est amor Adryasin),
> ne tibi sit duros montes et frigida saxa,
>   Galle, neque expertes semper adire lacus.
>   (Prop. 1.20.7–14)

Gallus is imagined holidaying in Umbria, or near Tibur, or near Baiae and the Phlegraean fields, where Jupiter quelled the rebel giants. No doubt it is living Italian girls, rather than the local Nymphs, who are compared for their passion with the nymphs of the river Ascanius who stole the original Hylas; but the warning presupposes – and then denies – the same expectation of innocence in the Italian landscape which Virgil contrasts so powerfully with Greece and Asia Minor in his Georgic *Laudes Italiae*. Safe in the foreign Greek context, Hylas is depicted as irresistible, even to his fellow sailors, the winged sons of Boreas, who dive-bomb him for kisses, which he desperately fends off with a tree branch. But he escapes one threat to his virginity only to fall victim to another yet unknown: 'Alas! woe is me, Hylas kept going, going to the Hamadryads,' *ah! dolor, ibat Hylas, ibat Hamadryasin* (32).

His quest for water is an excuse for a lush description of Pegae, with its fresh untended apples, lilies, and poppies, which beguile the boy into the fatal act of picking flowers. If this Hylas was commissioned to fetch water in a pitcher for Hercules and his comrades, he forgets, lingering to lean over the water gazing at pleasing reflections (both *formosis … undis* and *blandis … imaginibus* must refer to his own beauty reflected in the water). The nymphs seem to become aware of him only at the moment when he leans on the brink to scoop up water in his bare hands. Then indeed 'they are set aflame by his brilliant beauty and abandon their customary dances in wonder, easily drawing him down through the water as he slips forward.'

> cuius ut accensae Dryades candore puellae
>   miratae solitos destituere choros
> prolapsum et leviter facili traxere liquore.
>   (1.20.45–7)

(But where are they dancing? On the bank? Surely they must be under water, to drag him gently down?) The splash (*sonitus*) of Hylas' fall alerts Hercules, who calls on him three times, but the breeze from the distant mountains only echoes the name.

As with Theocritus, we are not told what becomes of Hylas. Both Greek and Roman readers knew that Hercules never recovered his beloved, but continued the vain search and let the expedition go on without him. Propertius adds only an injunction to Gallus to watch over his boy 'if he does not want to lose him again' (*formosum ni vis perdere rursus Hylan*). Why 'again,' unless he is implying that this boy has strayed before, when other nymphs laid their claim?

The myth of Hylas was not treated again in its own right until Valerius Flaccus composed his highly individual version of the whole *Argonautica*,[26] but it remained paradigmatic of the risk which boyish beauty suffered in the face of both female and, indeed, male lusts. Nymphs and Pans alike are incriminated in the melancholy comment of Seneca's chorus when Hippolytus has fled in revulsion at Phaedra's attempt to seduce him.

Why do you make for the wilderness? Beauty is not safer in out-of-the-way places. In a hidden wood when the Sun has paused at high noon, the wanton crowd of importunate Naiads will surround you, whose habit it is to trap the handsome in their springs, and the mischievous wood nymphs will lay ambush for your sleep, as will the Pans that range over the mountains.

> quid deserta petis? tutior aviis
> non est forma locis: te nemore abdito,
> cum Titan medium constituit diem,
> cingent, turba licens, Naides improbae.
> formosum solitae claudere fontibus,
> et somnis facient insidias tuis
>   lascivae nemorum deae
>   montivagique Panes.[27]
>   (Seneca *Phaedra* 777–84)

Propertius 1.20 is the poet's only elegy focused on the love of a boy, a topic which Tibullus explores on three occasions (1.4, 8, and 9) but which Ovid passes over in his love-elegy. And it would not be unfair to say that unlike Propertius, who devotes an entire elegy (3.19) to alleged female libido, from Semiramis to Cleopatra, Ovid excludes unprovoked female desire from the foreground of his contemporary elegies, in which girls are normally more desired than desiring.

He is less restrained in the *Metamorphoses*, where he introduces not only amorous or lustful women, but even nymphs in love. Echo is a special case, punished, as was mentioned, by Juno for distracting her with conversation to prevent her from catching Jupiter philandering with unnamed nymphs. Juno deprives Echo of independent speech and limits her to brief repetition of another person's words (*Met.* 3.356–69). And it seems that while Narcissus' death from self-love has several Hellenistic precedents, neither Echo's punishment by Juno nor her infatuation with Narcissus is the subject of any pre-Ovidian narrative.[28] The Echo who appears in Hellenistic Bucolic, in the *Syrinx* attributed to Theocritus and Moschus 6, is a conventional chaste nymph, pursued not pursuing, who is raped by Pan and gives birth to twins. It is Ovid who has turned her story into one of frustrated desire, when she falls in love at first sight with the frigid Narcissus. And Ovid leaves the reader to assume that, like Narcissus himself, Echo is a virgin, set aflame (*incaluit*, 371) because of her inexperience, so that her passion increases, flaring up like a sulphur torch as she comes near him. She longs to speak to him but stays hidden and can only repeat his words, until, misled by his 'let us come together,' she emerges to embrace him, and he flees. Ovid postpones Echo's fate until he has outlined a brief career for Narcissus of turning down water- and mountain-nymphs, and even male associates (402–3), which rejection brings down upon him the curse that leads to his self-infatuation and death.[29] Echo remains true to her love of the youth and fades away only after echoing his last farewell. But although Echo's fate is only marginal to this saga of self-love, it is also a preliminary to the much more lurid tale of the nymphomaniac nymph Salmacis, told not by Ovid in propria persona but by the Minyeid Alcithoe. Alcithoe passes over as too familiar (*vulgatos ... amores*, 4.276, as Virgil passed over Hylas!) the loves of the Idaean shepherd who was turned into a rock by an angry nymph for taking a mistress.[30] She passes more briefly still over the tale of Sithon, who changed sex, and three other transformations, to her theme: 'Learn how Salmacis became ill famed, and why she emasculates with waves evilly powerful, and softens the limbs she touches. The reason is hidden but the power of the spring is notorious.'

> unde sit infamis, quare male fortibus undis
> Salmacis enervet tactosque remolliat artus,
> discite. causa latet, vis est notissima fontis.
>   (Ovid *Met.* 4.285–7)

As with Narcissus, so the beautiful son of Hermes and Aphrodite, when he reaches fifteen, wanders from his home on Mount Ida to explore unknown places and streams, going to Lycia and the region of the Carians. There he sees a pond of deep, clear water, free of reeds and sedge, with an inviting lawn of fresh turf and grasses at its farthest point. But a Naiad lives there who is indifferent to the healthy exercise of hunting with Diana, and who indulges in perpetual ease, bathing, combing her hair and observing her beauty in the waters, reclining in her translucent robe, or picking flowers. As if she were some susceptible male god, she no sooner sees him than she wants to possess him. Her first approach is highly diplomatic, echoing Odysseus' speech conciliating Nausicaa (*Odyssey* 6.149–61). She calls him worthy to be a god, for he could be Cupid himself; but if he is mortal she blesses (or envies) all his family, and (going beyond Odysseus) even more happy would be his wife, if he has one: 'If you have such a bride, then let me enjoy adulterous pleasure; if you have none, let it be me, and us enter the same bedchamber.'

> haec tibi sive aliqua est, mea sit furtiva voluptas
> seu nulla est, ego sim, thalamumque ineamus eundem.
>   (4.327–8)

Ovid delights in visualizing the embarrassed horror of the boy with a triple simile, as he blushes like apples, or stained ivory, or the moon in eclipse; the nymph insists, asking now for sisterly kisses, but when he tells her to stop or he will leave, she pretends to go away and leave the pool for his enjoyment. As the poor fool first samples the water and then undresses, she bursts into flame with desire for his naked body (*nudaeque cupidine formae / Salmacis exarsit*) and her eyes glitter like the sun's reflection in a mirror. In words which would seem only too predictable if the subject were male, she can scarcely bear the delay, or postpone her joys; now she lusts to embrace him and, madly, can scarce control herself.

The prurient narrator allows herself another simile, in comparing the gleam of his naked body in the water with an ivory statue or lilies placed behind glass (354–5), but it is not the last. Now Salmacis leaps into the water, there seizing upon him and caressing his breast, wrapping herself round other unnamed parts (*invitaque pectora tangit / et nunc hac iuveni nunc circumfunditur illac*, 359–60), and entangling him as he tries to escape, like a serpent trying to free itself from an eagle, or ivy twining around tree-trunks, or an octopus clutching his prey under water by sending out its tentacles on all sides (361–7). The comparison of Salmacis with the serpent is particularly strange, since it is trying to escape from the eagle who is carrying it off, while she is trying to entrap the boy. But the scene is certainly a true nightmare to any male reader. What makes the tale more tragic and universalizes the evil are a pair of curses. First the nymph invokes the gods to make them inseparable, and her prayer meets with divine sanction. Their two bodies are fused and assume one appearance, like grafted branches, no longer two persons, nor anything that can be called boy or woman. This prayer is answered, when Hermaphroditus sees and feels himself turned into a half-man, by his entirely misdirected curse on any man who enters this spring; he wishes that his parents (Hermes and Aphrodite) may make this man (too) emerge a half-man as soon as he is softened as he touches the waters.

This unpleasant tale is perhaps designed to reflect the unpleasant nature of its teller. But the extreme instance of a lustful nymph was also a folk-*aition*. At 15.319, Ovid's Pythagoras includes Salmacis among his list of rivers and springs with alarming effects: 'who has not heard of Salmacis' obscene waters?' *cui non auditus est obscenae Salmacis undae*? In fact, outside the *Metamorphoses* there is little trace of this tale, and far more evidence of an interpretation that made both Hermaphroditus and his fountain of Salmacis beneficent. Clearly there was diversity of opinion in Hellenistic times, evidenced by ambiguous fragments of Callimachus (fr. 407 Pf.) and Ennian tragedy reporting that 'Salmacis won spoils without sweat or blood,' *Salmacida spolia sine sudore et sanguine* (fr. 181 V). Ennius in turn is quoted by Cicero *Off.* 1.61 and the Augustan Verrius Flaccus (ap. Festus, ed. Lindsay, p. 439.10 s.v. *Salmacis*):

Salmacis by name, a nymph, daughter of Heaven and Earth, is said to have been the origin of the name of the Halicarnassian spring Salmacis. Whoever drank this was made effeminate with the fault of unchastity. <?And the cause of this is that?> its approach, through the closeness of its walls, lavished the opportunity to wanton young men of violating boys and girls who went down in front of them because there was no escape.

Salmacis nomine nympha, Caeli et Terrae filia, fertur causa fontis Halicarnasi aquae appellandae fuisse Salmacidis quam qui bibisset vitio impudicitiae mollesceret. ob eam rem+que id+ eius aditus, angustate parietibus, occasionem largitur iuvenibus petulantioribus antecedentium puerorum puellarumque violandarum quia non patet effugium.[31]

   There is naturally much support for a more positive interpretation of this famous tourist site. The fountain house of Salmacis was not just a well-known Hellenistic monument, it was adjacent to one of the seven wonders of the ancient world, the tomb of Mausolus of Halicarnassus. In the generation before Ovid, it was described and discussed both by the Greek geographer Strabo and by Vitruvius (2.8.10–11), who praises the fountain, situated next to the temple of Venus and Mercury (i.e., Hermes and Aphrodite), and protests against allegations that its waters emasculated those who drank them.

I shall not shirk explaining why this opinion has been spread worldwide by false gossip. For it is not true, as is said, that men become soft and immoral from its water; the quality of the water is very clear and its taste is excellent.

Is autem false opinione putatur venerio morbo inplicare eos qui ex eo biberint. sed haec opinio quare per orbem terrae falso rumore sit pervagata non pigebit exponere. non enim quod dicitur molles et impudicos ex ea aqua fieri ... sed est eius fontis potestas perlucida saporque egregius. (Vitruvius 2.8.12)

Instead, Vitruvius claims, the local barbarians, driven out by the Greek colonists, had returned to the spring to drink at an inn nearby and had become civilized from their wild behaviour (*e duro +ferreoque+ more commutati in Graecorum consuetudinem et suvaitatem sua voluntate reducebantur*). The water won this reputation not from an immoral infection, but when the spirits of the barbarians were softened by the sweetness of civilization (*humanitatis dulcedine*, 2.8.12).

This obviously local Halicarnassan interpretation is confirmed by the splendid verse inscription discovered on the site of the spring a decade ago. An elegy of sixty-odd lines, datable to the second century BCE, adopts the mannerism of Callimachus' *Aitia* to invite Aphrodite to explain the reasons why the city of Halicarnassus should be proud of herself. Salmacis is praised in lines 15–22:

> Having settled the lovely promontory sung of as dear to the
>   immortals
> by the sweet stream of Salmacis, she [Halicarnassus] controls
> the beautiful dwelling of the nymph who once received
> our boy Hermaphroditus in her kindly arms,
> and bred him to become an extraordinary man, who invented
>   matrimony
> for mankind and was the first to fasten the matrimonial bed by law.
> She in turn, under the sacred streams dripping in the cave,
> tempers the savage minds of men.[32]

In the fascinating volume recently devoted to this discovery of patriotic local epic (Isager and Pedersen 2004), Christina Sourvinou-Inwood (2004) disentangles the layers of myth by arguing that in local myth Hermaphroditus, born the bisexual child of Aphrodite and Hermes, was not seduced or unmanned by the nymph(s), but reared and protected to become the founder of the Greek colony and its civilized institutions; indeed, she suggests that Halicarnassus was the origin of the cult of Hermaphroditus. This would be just one more example of the traditions of Greek civic *Ktistai* (founding heroes) bred by nymphs. And Ovid probably knew this positive version, for in both *Ars Amatoria* 2.477–8 and *Fasti* 4.97–8 and 107 Ovid credits Aphrodite with teaching men to discard savage ways (*feros habitus*) and softening their brutish spirits through marriage. If he knew this more flattering version, it did not prevent him from exploiting to the full, by means of his 'unreliable narrator,' last to speak among the daughters of Minyas, the lurid and almost blasphemous tale that distorts the benevolence of Aphrodite transmitted through her son, and turns the kindly nymph into a vicious trollop, a story parallel in spirit to that of the sisters' hostility to Bacchus, which brings on their well-earned transformation into fluttering bats.

But this is not the first or the last time Ovid will choose a sinister version of tales about the loves of foreign (if mortal) women: Salmacis of Caria will be followed by Medea of Colchis, Scylla of Megara, the Propoetides of Cyprus, Myrrha of Cyprus, and Byblis of Tyre. The drowning of handsome young men would naturally provide occasion for imaginative tales in which they were drawn down to a watery grave by enamoured or lustful nymphs. Perhaps the story of Salmacis differs only in its extension to provide a universal threat, albeit one that presumably went untested! In any case Ovid will provide a comic counter-myth of a fastidious sea-nymph, in the story of the human fisherman Glaucus, who deliberately eats grass (*Met.* 13.936, *gramine*; 943, *pabula*), which turns him into a blue-bearded sea-god with a fishy tail, and who is shockingly rejected by that other Scylla – whom Circe cruelly turns into the monster that will infest the straits of Messina throughout the *Odyssey* and the *Aeneid*.

CHAPTER FIVE

Gods in a Man-made Landscape: Priapus

No garden is complete without him ...

Here we leave behind strictly Italian gods, but follow our Latin poets into the (mostly Italian) landscape, as they offer Priapus a sacred grove or invoke his active protection for an existing garden or orchard. This is a man-made god in a man-made environment, with an absurd conventional form that fosters comic bravado and invites mockery. My introduction to his personality will concentrate on the collection called *Priapea*, the size of which permits a wide range of jokes and poetic styles, mostly in the form of addresses by the god to thieves or passers-by. I shall set examples of these versifying-statue poems against two foils: the incidental use of Priapus in different genres (satire, didactic poetry, aitiological elegy) and the selective use by Martial of epigrams based on the statue of the god.

The earliest surviving Latin reference to Priapus is fragmentary: 'Priapus, I dedicate and sanctify this grove to you, where your home is at Lampsacus, and where <..?..> Priapus. For the Hellespontine shore worships you especially in its cities, a shore more rich in oysters than all others.'

> hunc lucum tibi dedico consecroque, Priape,
> qua domus tua Lampsaci est, quaque <– u > Priape.
> nam te praecipue in suis urbibus colit ora
> Hellespontia, ceteris ostriosior oris.
>   (Catullus fr.1)

These lines, excerpted in a lost poem on metre by Caesius Bassus and preserved by later grammarians,[1] are unlikely to have been the first mention of Priapus in Latin poetry, but they would introduce a flood of highly varied addresses and allusions to the ithyphallic god. Catullus may have composed this poem during his trip to Bithynia, when he would have passed Priapus' city of Lampsacus on the southern shore of the Hellespont, or he may have wished to create that impression. In any case the poem resembles a real-life dedicatory inscription, except for the curiosity of its metre, the 'Priapean,' which combines the glyconic (– u – u u – u x) and its shortened end-form pherecratean (– u – u u – x).[2] There may be a special point in the reference to oysters, which were (and still are) thought to be aphrodisiac, for Priapus was the personification of aggressive virility, represented in the statues and paintings known to us with an outsize and erect penis.[3] In fact Catullus takes the god's name in vain when he denounces the governor, Piso, for his exploitation of Catullus' friends Veranius and Fabullus (47.4), just as he boasts of his own virility in a literal narrative (56) in which he claims to have sodomized a boy he had seen making love to a girl. Virility is a favourite metaphor for Catullus, which may explain his dedication poem to the virile god.

But Catullus need not have been prompted by his travels to attempt a poem to Priapus. The god was honoured in Ptolemaic Alexandria, where Philadelphus included in his famous procession two images of Priapus, child of Dionysus, each crowned with a golden garland. One stood beside Dionysus and wore an ivy crown of gold on a float depicting how Dionysus took refuge at the altar of Rhea; the other, apparently in the same float, stood wearing an olive crown of gold beside statues of Ptolemy and Virtue (Athenaeus 5.201d).[4] Hans Herter, whose monograph and article in Pauly's *Real Encyclopedia* (repr. as Herter 1932) remain the classic sources for the serious cult of the god, ascribes his popularity to 'the longing for country life which obsessed that epoch to an amazing degree; he began to be as beloved as Pan, whom he resembled in several respects.'[5] Two of Alexandria's most famous poets can be said to have contributed to the divergent tradition of representing Priapus that was available to learned Romans.

First Theocritus, who offers somewhat conflicting images of the god in three contexts connected with the herdsman poet Daphnis. In *Idyll* 1, where Daphnis seems to be dying of love, various gods come to comfort him, including Hermes and Priapus, who asks (1.82–3), 'unhappy Daphnis, why are you wasting away? Your beloved girl is searching for you borne on foot through all the glades and fountains.' His role seems in part to reproach Daphnis with languishing like a goatherd who neglects his (love-sick) flock because of his own condition (1.85–91). When Aphrodite comes, Daphnis dismisses her contemptuously but appeals to Pan. In one epigram, Theocritus (*Epigr.* 3, ed. Gow = Gow and Page 1965, 19; *AP* 9.338) associates Priapus and Pan in erotic pursuit of Daphnis – seen now as an object of homosexual desire; but in a longer epigram (Theoc. *Epigr.* 4, ed. Gow = Gow and Page 1965, 20; *AP* 9.437) the speaker asks a goatherd to beg Priapus either to cure him of desire for Daphnis or make Daphnis return his love. Two-thirds of this miniature elegy offers a vivid description of the god's physical form and his setting.

Turning along this path here, goatherd, you will find a newly carved fig-wood statue, three-limbed, bark-bearing, and earless, but able with its child-begetting phallus to achieve the works of Cypris. A sacred enclosure runs round it, and an ever-flowing stream splashes from the rocks on all sides onto the laurels and myrtles and fragrant cypress; there the grape, child of the cluster, spills down from the tendril, and the spring jackdaws echo in high-pitched songs the variety of their warbling melodies, to which fair nightingales reply with trills, uttering the sweet sound from their beaks. (Theoc. *Epigr.* 4.9; *AP* 437.1–12)

This poem is perhaps unique among the Hellenistic allusions, in its precise representation of the wooden ithyphallic statue (the third limb being its penis) set in a formal shrine. However, it shares with all the Greek references a seriousness which need not be reverent, but never allows any element of ridicule. Starting with Leonidas of Tarentum, the anthology contains many epigrams addressed to Priapus or reporting the dedication of his likeness by a named Greek, but none are mocking, and many resemble epigrams by the same poets honouring Pan.[6]

Is this why Virgil's two *Eclogues* (5 and 10) based on Theocritus' figure of Daphnis omit Priapus? As Micon's supposed dedication of a marble statue in *Eclogue* 7 (discussed below) makes clear, the god (and his power to fertilize their flocks) is part of the world of goatherds; but in both *Eclogue* 5, on the death and deification of Daphnis, and *Eclogue* 10, in which Gallus takes on Daphnis' role of dying languor, it is Pan who rejoices at Daphnis' elevation (5.59) and comes (after Apollo) to argue against the destructive power of love. Pan is even ruddy, like Priapus, with the juice of elderberries and cinnabar.[7] Was Priapus already seen in Italy as lacking proper dignity?

The other, even more influential, Alexandrian was of course Callimachus, although no allusion to Priapus survives in the fragments of his *Aitia*, or other poetic genres. What does survive is an iambic poem addressed to Hermes, but on a priapic theme. Only one line is preserved of Callimachus' ninth *Iambus*, 'long-bearded Hermes, why is your penis (pointing?) to your beard and not to your feet?' (Trypanis 1958, fr. 199). But it is given a full context by the scholiasts' *diegesis*: 'the lover of a handsome youth called Philetadas saw the ithyphallic statue of Hermes in a small palaestra, and asked if his arousal was due to Philetadas. The Hermes answered that he was of Tyrrhenian[8] descent, and was ithyphallic because of a mystic story. As for his questioner, Hermes accused him of loving Philetadas with dishonest intent' (Trypanis 1958, fr. 199 and pp. 136–7).' So this interview with a talking statue combines an *aition* with the kind of abuse appropriate to iambi. (Since Archilochus, iambi had been the poetry of insult and of frank sexual and scatological language.) This is not the only speaking statue found in Callimachus. In the *Aitia*, too, a statue of Apollo is questioned by the poet about his cult and gives authoritative replies (Trypanis 1958, fr. 114). But it is the lost poem of the *Iambi* whose bawdy and abusive tone provides a precedent for much that will be found in the Latin tradition. Yet of the Roman poets it seems that Tibullus (1.4) was the only one to take seriously Priapus' role as an expert and adviser in boy-love – an aspect quite distinct from his regular role in Tibullus and others as protector of gardens, which will be the concern of this chapter.

As scholars have seen, when Roman poets take over the figure of Priapus from the Hellenistic epigrammatists there is a different pattern in both theme and tone. The Greek poets of the *Palatine Anthology*, starting with Leonidas of Tarentum in the third century BCE and including poets associated with Rome such as Licinius Archias, the client of Cicero, and Crinagoras, the client of Octavia, produce serious if fanciful dedications rich in newly coined vocabulary, and their content is different.[9] They more often associate Priapus with figures set up in public, on harbour or seashore, by sailors and fishermen than with private images set up by individuals in their gardens. After Catullus' dedication poem, Priapus is featured by almost every Roman poet. Perhaps the best-known aspect of the god is his aggressive sexuality (usually directed against boys or young males). His penis is not only erect, but often visibly swollen (the Romans called this *tentigo*).[10] It is this memorable figure which Amy Richlin has taken as the patron of a wider range of sexual invective and scoptic poetry in her classic *Garden of Priapus*.

One minatory figure stands at the centre of the whole complex of Roman sexual humour; he will here be represented by the god Priapus ... The central persona ... is a strong male of extreme virility, occasionally even ithyphallic (as in the Priapic poems) ... This figure is active rather than passive and does not always restrict himself to foul descriptions of his victims, but sometimes threatens them with punishment, usually by exposure or rape, whether vaginal, anal, or oral. (Richlin 1992, 58)

Richlin's book is a powerful study of priapic invective in iamb, satire, and epigram and has become the definitive introduction to this kind of sexual invective. But there is some divergence between this figure and the common or garden Priapus who will be my theme – and I use both epithets, 'common' and 'garden,' deliberately.

For it is time to focus on the garden which is the Italian Priapus' milieu. Pierre Grimal in his ground-breaking study of Roman gardens traced a history in which gardens were originally protected by the Lar, but as Roman culture became more city-bound and restricted in space, the Lar was attracted towards more specific protection of the house and its interior (Grimal 1943, 42–6). But when Priapus came from the east to replace the Lar, despite the new god's oriental glamour and Dionysiac associations, he too was affected by the social decline of the *hortus* as kitchen garden. The master no longer thought of his villa but of his town house as his real home, and the kitchen garden lost status, becoming the territory of the *vilicus*, who was the continuing occupant of the villa. Thus the cult of Priapus became that of the slaves and freedmen who tended the gardens and orchards. And it is true that most Roman or Italian allusions introduce the god as a private servant, a personal tough guy or bouncer, the 'ruddy watchman over gardens'[11] set up as a scarecrow, and associated with humble genre settings, often with the actual humour of either parody or self-mockery. Despite constant allusions there is little hint of worship. The elder Pliny, in discussing gardens, claims that statues of satyrs were dedicated in the forum and in gardens only to ward off or cure the evil eye of jealousy (Pliny *NH* 19–50).[12] But while we know from Pliny and others of the popular statue of the satyr Marsyas in the Forum, I have not seen any evidence of satyrs in gardens (except as part of a decorative sculptural complex such as the luxurious gardens of Maecenas)[13] or of Priapus in the Forum.

But Grimal's explanation is not entirely compatible with the presence, even prominence, of this half-disreputable god in the Roman poets for more than a century after Catullus. He may have no place in epic, but he seems to have been necessary to the portrayal of gardens in didactic poetry and elegy, satire and lyric poetry, an object if not of reverence or respect, at least of familiar affection. So I shall cover in this chapter the role of Priapus in the neoteric and 'Augustan' poets, but treat only selectively the themes found in poems about or to the god in Martial and the body of eighty short poems in epigram, hendecasyllable, and choliamb preserved as the *Corpus Priapeorum*.

For our Latin poets, Priapus was above all guardian of edible plants, the vegetable garden or orchard – a function he had taken over from Venus, who originated as the protector of *olus* ('greens').[14] Typically he is a favourite with the neoteric poets associated with Catullus, whose personal poems set him in a garden. Furius

Bibaculus writes affectionately of the humble vegetable patch and plot of wheat belonging to the learned critic Valerius Cato, and the grapes, probably from a simple vine arbour rather than a more spacious vineyard,

If anyone sees the home of my dear Cato, its splintered stones painted with vermilion, and those little gardens of the protector Priapus, he must wonder by what expertise Cato achieved such wisdom – a man whom three cabbages and half a pound of emmer-wheat and two bunches of grapes nourish under one roof-tile into extreme old age.

> si quis forte mei domum Catonis
> depictas minio assulas et illos
> custodis videt hortulos Priapi,
> miratur quibus ille disciplinis
> tantam sit sapientiam assecutus.
> quem tres cauliculi, selibra farris,
> racemi duo tegula sub una
> ad summam prope nutriant senectam.
> (fr. 1, quoted by Suetonius *Gramm.* 11)

For lovers of Latin poetry any mention of gardens will spontaneously evoke the passage in the fourth *Georgic* where Virgil claims he must pass over gardens because his larger poetic task is urging him on. Yet he has already introduced Priapus to watch over the garden setting needed for the happiness of his bees. 'Let gardens breathing with crocus flowers invite the bees, and may the guardianship of Hellespontine Priapus, protector against thieves and birds with his sickle of willow, protect it, while the master brings thyme and pine saplings from the high mountains and sows them widely around the bees' dwelling.'

> Invitent croceis halantes floribus horti
> et custos furum atque avium cum falce saligna
> Hellespontiaci servet tutela Priapi.
> Ipse thymum pinosque ferens de montibus altis
> tecta serat late circum.
> (*Georg.* 4.109–12)

The poet's enthusiasm for Hellenistic culture delights in stressing the exotic nature of this otherwise simple country scarecrow. Given this transitional passage, it is unnecessary for Virgil to include Priapus a second time, as guardian of the apples and sloes and pears of the old Corycian's little plot, itself set near southern Italian Tarentum (*sub Oebaliae … turribus arcis*, 4.125). This does not deter Columella, writing on Roman agriculture two generations after Virgil. Columella has written the first nine books of his manual in businesslike prose, but in his tenth book, 'On the Garden,' he seizes the opportunity to versify offered to him by Virgil's professions of haste[15] and brings Priapus on twice. After specifying the streams and enclosing walls needed for his garden plot, Columella asks not for a work of art – a statue by Daedalus or Polycletus – but for a wooden Priapus to worship: 'Give worship to a rough-shaped trunk of some ancient tree, the godhead of Priapus, fearsome with his member, to stand at the garden's centre, threatening boys with his groin and robbers with his sickle.'

> truncum forte dolatum
> arboris antiquae numen venerare Priapi
> terribilis membri, medio qui semper in horto
> inguinibus puero, praedoni falce minetur.
>   (Col. 10.31–4)

Columella still preserves some sense of the god's divine power and special interest in boy-love. The planting of medicinal herbs like panacea leads him to enumerate aphrodisiac hyacinths, unnamed North African herbs, and the rocket (*brassica eruca*),[16] 'which is sown next to fruitful Priapus to arouse sluggish husbands to love-making,' *quae frugifero seritur vicina Priapo / excitet ut Veneri tardos eruca maritos* (10.108–9).

It is probably in general reminiscence of the *Georgics* that Horace's banker Alfius, in his dream of idyllic country life, includes pears and grapes as offerings to Priapus and Silvanus (*Epode* 2.19–22). But Virgil included a more fanciful version of such offerings in the singing contest of *Eclogue* 7. The first singer, Corydon, imagines his friend Micon offering to Diana the head of a boar he has hunted down and the antlers of a stag. If he is successful, then there will be a statue of Diana made of smooth marble, wearing purple hunting boots. To cap his offering, Thyrsus turns to Priapus: it is enough for him to expect a bowl of milk and the cakes he apparently is holding once a year. Just now he has erected Priapus in marble as a provisional tribute, but if his flock succeeds in lambing, *aureus esto!*, 'may you be made of gold!' (7.36). The absurdity of this lies less in the impossibility of Thyrsus paying for a statue of marble, still less of gold, than in the more obvious incongruity of Priapus, traditionally a simple god carved in wood, being represented in such sophisticated materials.

The generations after Virgil actually credited to him several poems of which the theme and focus was Priapus, a class of poem known as *Priapea*. These were almost certainly not by Virgil himself but composed by admirers who felt that he must have – or should have – written short personal poems before he moved on to compose the *Eclogues*, and later the *Georgics* and *Aeneid*. The academic name of *Pseudepigrapha* (falsely ascribed writings) offers a discreet way of avoiding calling these poems outright forgeries.[17] Whoever wrote them, these attractive poems probably come from the time of Augustus or Tiberius, and they are neatly combined to represent the god from different aspects. The first poem, in elegiacs, gives a sample of seasonal offerings from the farmsteader, contrasting the risk that in winter the peasants may need the wood from which he is carved to keep warm.

Since Callimachus had created a dialogue in which the statue of Apollo addressed the poet or his readers, it had been quite common for Roman poets to represent statues as speaking; compare Tibullus' poem, in which Priapus answers the poet's request for advice on winning over a boy beloved: 'then the countrified child of Bacchus who is always armed with a curved sickle, replied to me as follows; "beware of trusting yourself to the tender young crowd of boys, for they provide a stimulus for full-scale loving".'

... tum Bacchi respondit rustica proles
armatus curva sic mihi falce deus.
'O fuge te tenerae puerorum credere turmae
nam causam iusti semper amoris habent.'
    (Tib. 1.4)

Another instance of a talking statue is the statue of Vertumnus in Rome's *Vicus Tuscus*, who in a poem by Propertius describes his own superhuman versatility in disguise: 'give me a sickle and bind my brow with hay: you'll swear the grain has been cut by my hand.'

> da falcem et torto frontem mihi comprime faeno:
> iurabis nostra gramina secta manu.
>   (Prop. 4.2.25–6)

It was this elegiac self-presentation of Vertumnus which prompted Ovid to invent the god's own attempted courtship of Pomona through impersonation in *Met.* 14.643–6. But while there is nothing new in letting a statue or image speak for the god himself, for Priapus to stress the statue's humble material (in contrast with the fantasies of *Ecl.* 7.35–6) is to bring out how far this god is from divinity: 'In spring I am honoured with roses, in autumn with apples, in summer with ears of corn; only winter is a plague that makes me shiver: I am afraid of the cold, for fear this wooden god should provide a fire for the unwary farmers.'

> vere rosa, autumno pomis, aestate frequentor
>   spicis; una mihi est horrida pestis hiems.
> nam frigus metuo et vereor ne ligneus ignem
>   hic deus ignaris praebeat agricolis.
>   (Pseudo-Virgil *Priapea* 1)

The second poem, in iambics, falls into three sections. It actually starts from the god's physical material: 'Here I am, traveller, made with rustic craft, look! from dry poplar wood, I guard this little field on the left, and the little villa which you see and the garden of a poor master, and I keep away the wicked hands of thieves.'

> ego haec, ego arte fabricata rustica
> ego arida, O viator, ecce populus
> agellulum hunc sinistra stantem quam vides
> erique villulam hortulumque pauperis
> tueor, malasque furis arceo manus.
>   (*Priapea* 2.1–5)

In the next section (6–15) the god lists the gifts by each of the four seasons, first vegetable offerings from the smallholding, a multi-coloured garland in spring, a red-gold corn-ear under the hot sun, a sweet grape with green tendrils, and a grey olive picked in harsh cold, and then offerings of animal sacrifice; he claims entitlement to a kid and lamb and sacrificial calf. Renewing his appeal to the traveller, Priapus requests him to respect this god and keep his hands off; it is in his own interest, for the god's member is ready to punish him. This traveller seems quite happy with sexual punishment ('*velim, pol,*' *inquis,* ' "gladly," you say,' 19), but the poem imagines it is too late: here comes the bailiff, who will break off the prick with his sturdy arm to make a club that neatly fits his hand. The third poem, in Catullus' priapic metre, has the same tripartite construction; four lines identify the speaker: 'Young men, I sustain this place and the marshland cottage covered with woven rushes and bundles of figwood, I, a dried-up oak shaped by a country axe: the place is better off every year.'

> hunc ego iuvenes locum villulamque palustrem
> tectam vimine iunceo caricisque maniplis
> quercus arida rustica fomitata securi
> nutrior: magis et magis est beata quotannis.
>   (*Priapea* 3.1–4)

The middle section describes how 'the masters of the plot worship me and greet me as a god,' *huius nam domini colunt me deumque salutant* (3.5–16). The father removes weeds and brambles from his little shrine, the other brings little gifts in a generous hand, a garland, the first corn-ear, golden violets and milky poppy, gourds and fragrant apples and grapes grown red in the shade of the vine-leaves; these are conventional offerings, but they even sacrifice a bearded billygoat or hooved kid, whose blood is smeared on the god's weapon:

> sanguine haec etiam mihi – sed tacebitis – arma
> barbatus linit hirculus cornipesque capella.
>   (3.15–16)

Priapus asks his audience to keep this sacrifice of a he-goat secret (*sed tacebitis*), either because the *domini* are not the legal owners but subordinates whose absentee master would resent an expensive (and very tasty) sacrifice of a kid, or because blood sacrifices were not normal for this country god. The last five lines (3.17–21) explain Priapus' return for these honours: to provide all the produce and protect the master's little garden and vineyard. But he has a further point to make in keeping with the rough justice he advocates: 'So keep wicked thefts away from here, boys; the next-door neighbour is rich and his Priapus is careless: go steal from him, this path itself will lead you on to the place.'

> quare hinc, o pueri, malas abstinete rapinas.
> vicinus prope dives est neglegensque Priapus:
> inde sumite, semita haec deinde vos feret ipsa.
>   (3.19–21)

The comedy of a god made from a tree-trunk must derive at least in part from the old Roman habit of calling a fool a blockhead (*stipes*), and the god's sheer helplessness and lack of dignity appealed especially to Horace, who made Priapus the narrator of a satire set on the Esquiline near Maecenas' palace gardens. In it Horace continues his fantasies about the witch Canidia from *Epodes* 5 and 17, but despite his boasts Priapus will prove to be a helpless witness:

I was once a figwood stump, a useless piece of timber. The carpenter could not decide whether to make me a bench or a Priapus, but preferred me to become a god. Hence I am a god, a great bogey to thieves and birds: my right hand seizes thieves, and the red pole extending from my lusty groin, but a reed stuck in my head terrifies the pesky birds and forbids them settling in the newly made gardens.

> olim truncus eram ficulnus, inutile lignum,
> cum faber incertus scamnum faceretne Priapum
> maluit esse deum. deus inde ego, furum aviumque
> maxima formido; nam fures dextra coercet
> obscenoque ruber porrectus ab inguine palus,

ast importunas volucres in vertice harundo
terret fixa vetatque novis considere terris.
  (Horace *Sat.* 1.8.1–7)

True to the tradition, Priapus opens by introducing himself and
explaining his origin. At least part of the poem's purpose is to compliment Maecenas on his restoration of the old paupers' cemetery
(8–16), but the place is still not safe at night. Priapus cannot deal
with the witchcraft that Canidia and Sagana practise by moonlight,
and describes their rituals, which even the moon refuses to witness. In his identity as a statue, Priapus swears that he is telling the
truth: if he is lying may his head be whitened by crowshit, and may
Julius and Pediatia and the thieving Voranus come to him to pee
and defecate on him (1.8.37–9). But as a witness he too is unexpect-
edly able to avenge the spells and actions of the two furies, for 'the
figwood cleft in my buttocks split, farting as loudly as a burst blad-
der, and drives the women running back into town.'

nam displosa sonat quantum vesica pepedi
diffissa nate ficus; at illae currere in urbem.
  (1.8.46–7)

Bringing his audience into the story at the end, Priapus adds, 'you
would have found it a great laugh and joke to see them as Canidia
lost her teeth and Sagana her bowl and herbs and the magic bonds
on her arms.'

Canidiae dentes, altum Saganae caliendrum
excidere atque herbas atque incantata lacertis
vincula cum magno risuque iocoque videres.
  (1.8.48–50)

Tibullus is witness to two different strands in the portrayal of
Priapus. In his first elegy the wooden form of Priapus is mentioned along with the other country gods made from rough stumps
and stone that are worshipped on his estate: 'Let the ruddy watchman Priapus be set up in the apple-laden gardens, to terrify the
birds with his fierce sickle.'

pomosisque ruber custos ponatur in hortis,
terreat ut saeva falce Priapus aves.
(Tib. 1.1.17–18)

But in the fourth elegy Tibullus addresses himself to the god in a different capacity – as an expert in winning the love of boys. Certainly his description of the god evokes the usual garden statue, as he addresses the god (1.4.3–6) scruffy with ill-trimmed beard (*non tibi barba nitet*), and naked, reflecting his poverty. Naked, he endures the weather all year round, exposed to the snow and frost of midwinter (*hibernae producis frigora brumae*) and the heat of the summer dog-star (*aestivi tempora sicca canis*). How can this god be an expert in an art that calls for sophisticated refinement? Priapus provides an extended set of instructions in pederasty, and the elegy clearly draws on the Greek tradition, making little use of his garden setting.

Ovid too holds aloof in some ways from the Italian tradition. In *Amores* 2.4, we are told that an attractive woman can turn Hippolytus into a Priapus, treating the god as the epitome of lust. This notion also animates the story Ovid will tell twice in his *Fasti* with only minor variations, of Priapus gate-crashing a party of gods and nymphs and attempting to rape either a nymph (Lotis) or the chaste goddess Vesta:[18] the god is forestalled by the braying of a donkey, which the poet cites (1.439–40 and 6.341–6) as the origin of the unusual donkey sacrifice to the Hellespontine god of Lampsacus. But Ovid tells a similar story of Faunus' foiled attempt on Omphale in *Fasti* 2 (305–56), and shows a happy indifference to naming his rustic fertility god Pan or Faunus or Priapus.

Ovid does, however, as mentioned, offer one tale of love in an Italian garden. In the preliminaries to Vertumnus' courtship of Pomona, Priapus plays a most uncharacteristic role. He too is relegated from his usual position as a guardian or scarecrow inside the orchards, and shut out along with the satyrs and country spirits who try in vain to get near the nymph but cannot enter her orchards. Pomona was the most expert among the Latin hamadryads at cultivating gardens: the orchards were her love, her devotion; she even had no desire for sexual love (14.634).

But from fear of country violence she closed off her orchards and barred and shunned the approaches of males: what did the Satyrs, the young things keen on dancing, not try, and the Pans whose horns are garlanded with pine branches, and Silenus, always more youthful than his actual age, *and the god who terrifies thieves with his sickle or his member*, to gain possession of her?

> vim tamen agrestum metuens pomaria claudit
> intus et accessus prohibet refugitque viriles.
> .quid non et Satyri, saltatibus apta iuventus,
> fecere et pinu praecincti cornua Panes
> Silenusque suis semper iuvenalior annis
> *quique deus fures vel falce vel inguine terret,*
> ut poterentur ea?
>   (Ovid *Met.* 14.635–41)

The whole story depends on Pomona excluding *all* males from her orchard, so that it must survive without the regular guardian. In any self-respecting Italian orchard, Priapus would be there standing guard, but Pomona's orchard is unguarded, and his exclusion is the extreme proof of her resolve to stay enclosed. Yet apparently she admits members of her own sex, and Vertumnus gains admission as an old woman and teller of tales.

By now the parameters for Roman treatment of Priapus are established. He belongs in a private garden (or orchard, or occasionally vineyard or woodland grove).[19] He identifies himself as man-made, by the farm-bailiff or gardener, and his function is to scare away birds or thieves. He expects and receives small tributes of fruit or vegetable grown under his protection according to the season. But there is a discrepancy between the function men ask from him and his own purpose, conveyed by his obvious virility, displayed by his nakedness. Thus, while his presence may be a protection or even a source of fertility to the vegetable world, it is more often seen as a threat to invaders. Originally a lover of boys, the god boasts of inflicting violent sex in a choice of forms appropriate to any desirable person: anal rape (*pedicatio*) or sodomy for the boys, conventional rape for the girls, and oral rape (*irrumatio*) for the bearded – men grown past their boyish charms. Hence a range of short epigrams playing on the god's threefold punishment of thieves according to their sexual status: 'I warn you, boy, you'll be pierced from behind, you'll be knocked up, girl: the third penalty waits for the thief with a beard.'

> percidere puer, moneo, futuere puella:
> barbatum furem tertia poena manet.
> (*Priapea* 13)

The poet's unscrupulous imagination goes beyond this threat to include allegations that some visitors to the garden like what the god has to thrust upon them and have come to be raped; a similar assumption of interest in sex leads the poet to address the respectable married women who persist in reading his verse when warned that these are 'dirty poems,' *impudica verba* (*Priapea* 8.2); obviously they enjoy looking at his mighty member.

The Romans were extremely prudish, at least in formal company, and leery of nakedness and of naked language.[20] In fact, they were more like the generation of the 1950s than are modern scholars, who have been encouraged by contemporary frankness about all forms of sexuality to write about and freely translate collections like the *Priapea*. In the last fifty years, besides the lively discussions in Richlin's (1992) broader study of Latin sexual and scatological poetry and Parker's (1988) attractive and accessible bilingual edition of the *Priapea*, this collection of poems has been investigated in detailed scholarly studies, starting with Vincenz Buchheit's *Studien zum Corpus Priapeorum* (1962), and equipped with commentaries, of which the fullest is Christiane Goldberg's *Carmina Priapea* (1992).[21]

Others with more interest and expertise are welcome to analyse the psychology of Priapus as a surrogate for those whose private lives do not provide sufficient sexual gratification. Since my own interest in Priapus is in his relationship to the garden, I have been searching for more explicit evidence of belief in his power not only to protect plant life from thieves but to enhance its fertility. The *Priapea* inherited the raw material for a kind of verbal game in which poets could play with, rearrange, combine, and extend the kind of propositions I have just listed. Now that the collection, once falsely ascribed to Virgil, has been accepted as the work of a single poet, and we can see the kinship between these poems and the scattered epigrams of Martial focused on Priapus, it makes sense to consider the motifs of this corpus along with parallel motifs in Martial's work.

Priapus actually puts in more appearances in Martial's epigrams than in the few poems analysed in detail by Willenberg (1973). That scholar's concern is in determining whether the four epigrams focused on the god in book 6 (16, 49, 72, and 73) should be seen as a cycle. The first epigram is a four-line parody of the prayer form, relying on the common notion that the god is entitled to punish thieves by appropriate forms of rape. Instead of promising to pay the god a reward from the produce he has kept safe, the speaker wishes him a different reward – the sexual enjoyment of attractive young boy or girl thieves. The other three poems of book 6 do seem to be cumulatively if not mutually dependent: they have in common play on the material from which the image is made, durable cypress in 6.49:

I am not made of brittle elm, nor is my column, standing erect with stiff limb, made of some random wood, but created from living cypress that does not fear hundreds of passing generations, nor the rot of long old age. Fear it, bad boy, whoever you are, for if you damage even the smallest clusters with thieving hand, however much you deny it, a painful ulcer will afflict your arse from the thrusting cypress.

> non sum de fragili dolatus ulmo,
> nec quae stat rigida supina vena
> de ligno mihi quolibet columna est,
> sed viva generata de cupressu:
> quae nec saecula centiens peracta
> nec longae cariem timet senectae.
> Hanc tu quisquis es O malus, timeto.
> nam si vel minimos manu rapaci
> hoc de palmite laeseris racemos,
> nascetur, licet hoc velis negare,
> inserta tibi ficus a cupressu.
> (Martial 6.49.1–11)

Priapus is made of cypress again in 6.73:

See how I don't appear wooden, with my well-defined features, or bear a
weapon destined for firewood. Instead my prick of everlasting cypress is
stiff enough for Phidias' handiwork. I warn you, neighbours, celebrate
holy Priapus and spare my fourteen acres.

> aspice quam certo videar non ligneus ore,
>   nec devota focis inguinis arma geram,
> sed mihi perpetua numquam moritura cupresso
>   Phidiaca rigeat mentula digna manu.
> Vicini, moneo, sanctum celebrate Priapum
>   et bis septenis parcite iugeribus.
>   (6.73.5–10)

This makes a neat contrast with the more fantastic hendecasyllables of 6.72:

A Cilician thief of notorious thievishness wanted to strip a garden, but
there was nothing in the immense garden, Fabullus, except a marble
Priapus. Not wanting to return empty-handed, the Cilician stole Priapus
himself.

> Fur notae nimium rapacitatis
> compilare Cilix volebat hortum,
> ingenti sed erat, Fabulle, in horto
> praeter marmoreum nihil Priapum.
> Dum non vult vacua manu redire,
> ipsum subripuit Cilix Priapum.
>   (6.72.1–6)

Perhaps this was a strictly ornamental garden, with nothing edible (rather than no ornamental planting) and an unemployed or
useless Priapus made (as in *Ecl.* 7.35) of expensive marble.

This kind of contrast is also played up between two epigrams
featuring Priapus in the first and second part of book 3. Priapus is
innocent enough, even frustrated, in the exceptionally long epigram 3.58, which contrasts the productive villa-estate at Baiae of

his friend Faustinus with Bassus' pretentious urban villa (which has already been Martial's butt in 3.47, a trial run for the fully developed 3.58): 'But you (Bassus) own pure starvation on the edge of town, and from your lofty tower look on unmixed laurels, care-free since Priapus need fear no thief.'

> at tu sub urbe possides famem mundam
> et turre ab alta prospicis meras laurus,
> furem Priapo non timente securus.
>   (3.58.45–7)

As for Faustinus, one of Martial's lasting friends and addressees, the mere location of his villa at Baiae increases the surprise value of Martial's account for readers expecting a more luxurious and unproductive establishment. The whole long poem is a model for the extreme cases of old-fashioned fertility versus trendy dis-play.[22] Faustinus' villa (3.58.5–44) is brimming over *rure vero bar-baroque,* real uncivilized countryside: bursting wheat-ears in every corner, wine jars with the bouquet of six-year-old vintages, and late-ripening grapes in November, truculent steers and still harmless calves, a messy farmyard full not of regular chickens, but of geese and exotic fowl such as peacocks, flamingos, par-tridges, and pheasants as well as doves and pigeons (12–19), greedy pigs and soft suckling lambs, healthy home-bred slaves frolicking round a warm hearth, opportunities for game with fowlers catch-ing thrushes, fishing, and deer hunting, and country tenants bear-ing honey, milk, dormice, kids, and capons, while their sturdy grown daughters (*grandes ... virgines*) bring baskets of gifts from their mothers (39–40), most likely of eggs despite the reference to eggs in line 50 below, since poultry were the regular care of the farm wives. We scarcely notice that this picture of abundance omits the *hortus* and its rampant guardian god; are they just taken for granted? Instead Martial rounds off his picture with feasting with the neighbours after work.

Bassus' villa near town, 'all elegance and starvation' in Shackleton Bailey's pungent phrase, no doubt has the *ingrata lati spatia ... campi,* the unrewarding areas laid out with leisurely myrtle groves and barren plane and trimmed boxwood hedges which

Martial repudiates in lines 1–4, but Bassus feeds his vine-dresser in the country on town-bought flour, carting food from the market (vegetables, eggs, chickens, fruit, cheese, and unfermented wine[23]) to a villa covered with paintings, *pictam … ad villam* (45–51). This is not *rus*, simply a distant town-house.

Ten epigrams later (3.68) Martial warns chaste matrons against reading further, to avoid the risk of reading obscene language: 'my verse does not hint in ambiguous figures but openly names the private part which proud Venus welcomes in the sixth month,[24] which the bailiff set as guard in the midst of the garden, but the chaste maiden gazes on with her hand in front of her face.'

> schemate nec dubio, sed aperte nominat illam
> > quam recipit sexto mense superba Venus,
> custodem medio statuit quam vilicus horto,
> > opposita spectat quam proba virgo manu.
> (3.68.7–10)

The coy feminine pronoun conceals the outspoken *mentula*, or 'prick,' which features immediately in the next poem and four others before Martial again scolds the matron for peeping in 3.86. But this is simply a matter of verbal as opposed to conceptual obscenity, open naming instead of innuendo: 'I told you, chaste lady, not to read this part of my book, I warned you, but look, you keep on reading. But if you watch Panniculus and Latinus, chaste lady, these poems are no worse than the mimes – read on.'

> ne legeres partem, lascivi, casta, libelli
> > praedixi et monui; tu tamen, ecce, legis.
> sed si Panniculum spectas et, casta, Latinum,
> > non sunt haec mimis improbiora – lege.
> (3.86.1–4)

In this book Priapus is merely a useful symbol of fertile gardening, or of obscenity; as we saw, Martial gives the wooden god more attention in his own right in and after his sixth book.

Much of the *Priapea* poet's artistry lies in his command of these two traditional metres for short personal poems, and the less common 'limping iamb,' with its three dragging final syllables.[25]

Again Latin readers can appreciate the ingenuity of the poet's diction and pointed arrangement of words and ideas in a small compass. Typically, even minimal epigrams consisting of single distichs will consist of a build-up of expectation followed by a quick deflation or witty turn of thought.

To his (apparently male) reader, the poet speaks in *Priapea* 1 with a warning epigram. But it does not warn against reading; rather, it prepares the reader to adopt an open attitude appropriate to this god's uninhibited cult:

You who are about to read the wanton diversions of rude poetry, drop your frown, proper to Latin people. It is no virgin-sister of Phoebus or Vesta, nor the warrior goddess born from her father's head, who lives in this little shrine. It is the ruddy watchman of gardens, with outsize member, who does not keep his loins under any wraps. So either cast a tunic over his private part, or read these words with the same eyes you use on looking at it.

> Carminis incompti lusus lecture procaces,
>   conveniens Latio pone supercilium.
> non soror hoc habitat Phoebi, non Vesta sacello,
>   nec quae de patrio vertice nata dea est.
> sed ruber hortorum custos, membrosior aequo,
>   qui tectum nullis vestibus inguen habet.
> aut igitur tunicam parti praetende tegendae,
>   aut quibus haec oculis adspicis, ista lege.

Then, in *Priapea* 2, the poet turns to the god as his witness to a similar justification, this time in Catullan hendecasyllables:

I wrote these verses, with you as my witness, Priapus, more fit for a garden than a booklet, and not with too much toil. Nor did I invite the muses, as poets do, to such an unvirginal place. I would have been senseless and heartless if I had dared to escort the Pierian band of chaste sisters up to Priapus' prick. So take in good part whatever I have idly scribbled on the walls of your shrine, I beg you.

> ludens haec ego teste te, Priape
> horto carmina digna, non libello,

scripsi non nimium laboriose.
nec musas, tamen, ut solent poetae,
ad non virgineum locum vocavi.
nam sensus mihi corque defuisset
castas, Pierium chorum, sorores
auso ducere mentulam ad Priapi.
ergo quicquid id est, quod otiosus
templi parietibus tui notavi,
in partem accipias bonam, rogamus.

We should not be deceived by the reference to a shrine in these two poems and in *Priapea* 14 below. Buchheit (1962) plausibly suggests that the text itself contained a small illustration of a shrine as frontispiece; certainly the Priapi we will meet in these pages live out in the open, unprotected and exposed in every sense. Since the god is traditionally made of wood, poems may play on the vulnerability of wood to be converted into winter fuel, as in Martial 6.16. One particularly apt poem (25) exploits, as many epigrams do, the contrast between the dignified world of epic and the more playful one of epigram. Priapus begins by admitting that his rod (*sceptron*) will never sprout into leaves (the *adynaton* by which Achilles had sworn his oath in *Iliad* 1.234–6 and Latinus had sanctioned his oath in *Aen.* 12.206), but kings long to hold it and noble perverts lavish kisses upon it.

Columella had insisted that his Priapus should not be the costly work of a renowned sculptor (10.29–31);[26] as we saw, Martial implies the same judgment, and the author of the *Priapea* makes the same point: 'Praxiteles and Scopas did not make me, nor was I polished by Phidias' hand, but the bailiff hacked out the raw wood and told me, "you be Priapus!".'

non me Praxiteles Scopasve fecit,
nec sum Phidiaca manu politus,
sed lignum rude vilicus dolavit
et dixit mihi 'tu Priapus esto!'
  (*Priapea* 10.2–5)

Most of the poems speak from the god's point of view, and many complain of the discomfort and exposure of outdoor life. Why does Priapus expose his private parts? (*Priapea* 9). Well, don't other gods display their weapons? This is his only weapon, like Jupiter's thunderbolt or Hercules' club. A good-humoured argument based on this exposure (*Priapea* 14) is also unusual in crediting the god with a shrine (*sacellum*) in which a passer-by may need to take refuge. The shrine fits the religious play that will follow – on the prohibition, by many cults, of worshippers entering a sacred space after intercourse.

Come hither, whoever you are, don't think it troublesome to turn aside into the lusty god's shrine. Even if a girl was with you last night, there's no need to fear approaching for that. That concession is made to severe heaven-dwellers: we are just worthless little godheads of the tilled land; we stand quite shameless under Jove's eye with balls exposed. So anyone will be allowed to enter, even smeared with the black soot from underneath the arches.

> Huc, huc, quisquis es, dei salacis
> deverti grave ne puta sacellum,
> etsi nocte fuit puella tecum,
> hac re quod metuas adire non est.
> istud caelitibus datur severis:
> nos vappae sumus et pusilla culti
> ruris numina, nos pudore pulso
> stamus sub Iove coleis apertis.
> ergo quilibet huc licebit intret
> nigra fornicis oblita favilla.
>   (*Priapea* 14.1–10)

Priapus imagines worshippers too poor to have girlfriends or use a pricey brothel; their only sex is to be had with streetwalkers traditionally lurking under arches (*fornix* thus became the root of 'fornication'). So this shrine, although not roofed (*sub Iove*), seems to be an enclosed space (*intret*). Almost all other references imply that Priapus stands on open (if private) ground. The tenant who embarrasses the god in poem 70 has offered two kinds of sacred cake, *libum* and *quādra*, baked in hot ash, which have unfortunately drawn the neighbour's bitch to the scene. Parker's version assumes that the tenant has spilled food on Priapus' member and the dog is directing her attentions to it, causing the god unwanted arousal. The poem ends with instructions to avoid putting down any food offering, in case it attracts a crowd of starving dogs, 'for fear that, while worshipping me and my godhead, you end up with your guardians suffering oral rape,' *dum me colitis meumque numen, / custodes habeatis irrumatos* (12–13). The only other reference to a sacrifice, as opposed to a garden offering, comes in a poem (65) addressed to Priapus by the person making the sacrifice of a pig straight from the sty. It is being punished for uprooting Priapus' seedling lilies, but the sacrificer begs the god to keep his garden gate closed in future, so as not to scare the whole herd to death (*ne tamen exanimum facias pecus omne* probably puns on both senses of *exanimus* – terrifying the whole flock and causing its death). As we saw, other types of poetry have mentioned offerings of young animals – kids, lambs, calves – but these are too lavish for the world of the *Priapea*. When a speaker compares the offerings to Priapus with those to other deities (53), all are modest: despite a lavish vintage, Bacchus gets only a bunch of grapes; despite a generous harvest, Ceres is given only a garland of corn. Priapus then, as a lesser god (*dive minor*), should take in good part the few apples he receives.

And apples are what he seems to get. They may be glorified by comparison with mythological apples, like those which made Atalanta lose her race with Hippomenes, the apples from Alcinoos' orchard,[27] or the apple in which Acontius wrote the vow of fidelity for Cydippe (16): such is the superlative fruit which the devout owner of this flourishing plot has set on Priapus' altar table. Others seem to have had trouble finding even apples: in poem 21, the speaker has had to substitute for homegrown apples ones bought on the Sacred Way; in poem 42, Aristagoras has had a good vintage and offers Priapus apples made of wax. In return Priapus is begged to be content with the likeness, and ensure that the man harvests real fruit. It is not clear why the apple tree which laments its sterility in poem 61 has been laden by a poet with his bad verse, unless this too is a form of appeal to Priapus, who goes unmentioned in the poem. Most often it was apple orchards he was supposed to guard (*pomaria*, 71, 72; cf. *tua pomaria*, Martial 6.16), and he punningly excuses his ignorance of literature in the long and elaborate spoof of Homer (68) because he is a rustic god: 'I collect apples, instead of reading books,' *libros non lego; poma lego* (68.2).

What was in these gardens? Various poems mention stealing greens (*olus*) and grapes, but in one poem Priapus obligingly gives a list of fruit and vegetables and herbs, which maps onto the herbs and vegetables listed in Columella's garden poem (he deals with fruit trees in another book). Poem 51 is a complaint with a very brief final turnaround. Why do thieves rob me, when my fruit is no better than next door's produce? It opens with figs, and grapes, then apples and pears, glossy yellow plums and sorbs (a kind of crab apple), then mentions mulberries and filberts from Abella and almonds, before listing the garden's vegetables: 'I do not boast of growing cabbages' (*brassicarum caules*; cf. Col.10.129), or beet (Col.10.253–4), or leeks (Col.10.167), or cucumbers and gourds (Col.10.234), or basil (*ocimum*). Nor does he believe that anyone comes to take lettuce (Col.10.179)[28] or onions and garlic, or steal rocket, mint, and rue by night (Col.10.119–20). Although Priapus (or the smallholder) has all these things, the neighbour's gardens have just as many, which the thieves are neglecting in order to invade the speaker's laboriously tilled plot. They know what is coming to them – so there has to be another reason. Can it be that they are attracted by the prospect of being raped?

Before moving on from the Augustans to the volume of *Priapea*, we found Priapus enjoying cheerful semi-divine company. One sad poem in this collection, *Priapea* 33, contrasts his lot with that of Priapuses in the good old days.

The Priapuses of old used to have Naiads and Dryads, and there was something for the god's turgid member to enter, but now there is nothing, now my lust is so overflowing that I believe all the nymphs must have perished. Shameful as it is, to escape from bursting with tumescence I must put down my sickle and use a little help from my hand.

Naidas antiqui Dryadas habuere Priapi,
  et quo tenta dei vena subiret, erat.
nunc adeo nihil est, adeo mea plena libido est,
  ut Nymphas omnis interiisse putem.

turpe quidem factu, sed ne tentigine rumpar.
falce mihi posita fiet amica manus.

Martial offers a happier if more fanciful account of a garden well
supplied with divine denizens in a late epigram from Spain.
Addressing himself to Marrius, living in retirement at Atina,
Martial asks him to take care of the poet's own estate near
Nomentum:

I commend to you the twin pines, glory of the unplanted[29] grove, and the
holm-oaks of the Fauni and the altars of the Thunderer and rough Silvanus
built by a semi-skilled hand, altars which the blood of a lamb or kid has
often painted; and I commend the virgin mistress of the holy temple and
Mars, guest of his chaste sister, the originator of my birthday Kalends,
and the laurel grove of fastidious Flora, where she takes refuge when
Priapus chases her. You will placate every mild deity of the little plot
with either blood or incense.

has tibi gemellas barbari decus luci
commendo pinus ilicesque Faunorum
et semidoctas vilici manu structas
Tonantis aras horridique Silvani,
quas pinxit agni saepe sanguis aut haedi,
dominamque sancti virginem deam templi
et quem sororis hospitem vides castae
Martem, mearum principem kalendarum,
et delicatae laureum nemus Florae
in quod Priapo persequente confugit.
hoc omne agelli mite parvuli numen
seu tu cruore sive ture placabis.
　　(Martial 10.92.3–14)

The envoi (15–18) explains that in Martial's absence Marrius as
priest will placate these gods; they in turn are to believe that
Martial is present and give to both men whatever one alone will
ask for. We readers are to imagine that Martial has made himself a
sacred grove; the invisible and aniconic Fauni do not need altars,
but there are altars for Jupiter and Silvanus, Minerva and Mars,

with a laurel grove dedicated to Flora. Priapus is surely without an image or altar, but there will be company for him if he appears.

The cult of Priapus seems to have been maintained in a humorous or whimsical spirit by the sophisticated, to whom he appealed with his uninhibited licence, and as one of the cheerful lesser gods of mythological fantasy. It is most unlikely that he had any formal public shrine or cult, but at a simpler level the smallholders and labourers of the countryside could have made themselves dummies with fluttering ribbons to scare the crows. Instead they carved and erected the virile god, both to give his fertility to their crops and to drive off thieves – or perhaps to take responsibility for any violence the peasant himself inflicted.

CHAPTER SIX

Gods in Statian Settings

The Villa Gardens of the *Silvae*

Recent years have seen a multiplication of studies on the Roman pleasure garden.[1] Increased Roman wealth and acquaintance with Hellenistic luxury in the second century BCE brought the development of both private estates and public parks that provided shady, well-watered spaces for walking and resting. Cultured and well-travelled Romans like Cicero aimed to create gardens in the grounds of their villas that would reflect their Hellenic and philosophical tastes, with generic or specific Greek names like *xystus* (a covered walkway), *gymnasium* or *palaestra*, and *Amaltheum*, a grove honouring Amaltheia, the nymph who nurtured the baby Zeus and was associated with the legendary Horn of Plenty. Indeed, when Cicero commissioned an agent to obtain statuary for his villa, he was offended when the man offered him Bacchants instead of Muses; they did not fit his self-image, and both the layout of the garden and its program of statuary were intended to represent Cicero's own values.[2] But Muses were a highly esteemed component in many ornamental gardens; many statues and statue groups survive, and were recently displayed in a *mostra* on Muses and the intellectual life in the Colosseum.

This kind of conspicuous consumption was not yet universal among the wealthy. Nepos, for example, speaks proudly of the simple town-home and rural estates of Atticus, the Philhellene citizen of Athens who also owned substantial estates in Epirus. Atticus' practical living arrangements earn Nepos' commendation just because they are already exceptional:

His house, once owned by Tamphilus, was on the Quirinal hill; it had been bequeathed him by his uncle, and its charm lay not in the building, but in its woodland, for the structure itself was built long ago and had more character than luxury. (*Life of Atticus* 13.2, Horsfall 1989, translation modified)

He had no park, no luxurious villa near Rome or by the sea, nor any country estate in Italy, but for those at Arezzo and Nomentum. All his financial income consisted of properties in Epirus and Rome. (14.3, Horsfall 1989, translation modified)

Even before Cicero's prime, men of the previous generation, like his teacher Lucius Crassus, had set great value on the luxury both of their domestic interiors and of their gardens. We have Cicero's evidence for features of the grounds at Crassus' Tusculan villa, but also a secondary, if more garbled, tradition reporting the luxury of his Palatine town-house. The villa is the setting of Cicero's first dialogue, *De Oratore*, which introduces the discussion of book 1 by settling Crassus' guests in a formal seating area (probably an exedra). In imitation of Socrates – or at least the literary Socrates of Plato's *Phaedrus* – this first discussion is opened under a plane tree; in contrast, book 2 is set in a so-called *palaestra*; and book 3 takes the conversation farther away from the villa into an actual woodland on Crassus' estate.[3] As for Crassus' place in town, we are given an idea of its luxury by an anecdote taken from the public quarrels and mutual accusations of Crassus and his fellow censor Domitius Ahenobarbus in 92 BCE.

Censors were traditionally supposed to monitor and repress public luxury, but Ahenobarbus began the dispute by offering an astronomical sum for the purchase of Crassus' home. Crassus retorted that he would accept the offer only if he were allowed to exclude a half-dozen shade trees, *lotae* (Pliny *NH* 17.4–5, trans. in Rackham's Loeb edition as 'nettle-trees'). When Domitius said he would not offer even a small percentage of his first price for the house without the trees, Crassus retaliated that the value his rival was prepared to place on a mere six trees proved Domitius was more luxurious. But, as Pliny reports, Crassus surpassed the luxury of his garden with the six columns of Hymettian marble he had imported some fifteen years earlier for public display during his aedileship and then transferred to the atrium of this mansion.[4]

While Crassus and the elder Catulus, and later Cicero, had their
luxurious mansions on the Palatine, the prominence of this fashionable area will have placed a limit on the size of their grounds.
But contemporaries of Cicero, like Lucullus and Caesar and the
slightly younger Sallust, enjoyed private *horti* around their houses
on the edge of town;[5] and Pompey, as the newly enriched con-
queror of the East, not only brought exotic balsam and ebony trees
back in his triumph, but gave away to the Roman people the large
part of his own estate on the Campus Martius which lay between
his town-house and his porticoed theatre temple. This area seems
to have been the first real public park for the Romans to promen-
ade in.[6] (Caesar too would give his gardens to the people in his
will, but they were less central.) For Ovid and other men about
town, Pompey's new park and sculpture garden were the choice
rendezvous. Propertius actually reproaches his Cynthia with her
constant trips out of town to Praeneste and Lanuvium. Isn't the
portico of Pompey good enough?

I suppose Pompey's portico with its shady columns, noble with Attalid
tapestries, is too shabby for you, and the dense series of plane trees soaring to equal height, and the streams which pour from the drowsy satyr
Maro, with the sound of waters lightly murmuring around the basin
when Triton suddenly swallows back the water in his mouth.

> scilicet umbrosis sordet Pompeia columnis
>   porticus, aulaeis nobilis Attalicis,
> et platanis creber pariter surgentibus ordo,
>   flumina sopito quaeque Marone cadunt,
> et sonitus lymphis toto crepitantibus orbe[7]
>   cum subito Triton ore refundit aquam.
>   (Prop. 2.32.11–16)

Later, when Cynthia catches Propertius cheating on her with two
street women, she orders him not to doll himself up and stroll in
Pompey's shade, *tu neque Pompeia spatiabere cultus in umbra*
(Prop. 4.8.75). In Martial's time the portico and the two planta-
tions (*Pompeia dona, nemusque duplex*, Martial 2.14.10) were
still good places for parasites like Selius to hang around in, in

hope of cadging a meal. But always this and other gardens are associated with the welcome coolness of water and shade, especially the shade offered by the large leaves of the non-indigenous plane trees. Horace may criticize the luxurious and productive gardens of wealthy men with their 'sterile' plane trees and violet beds;[8] but just as modern Greek villages cherish a plane tree (or more than one) to shade the *cafêneion* in the market square, so the oriental plane tree admired by the Persians had been imported first to Syracuse by Dionysius in the early fourth century, and then to Italy, whence it had even been carried to the northern coast of Gaul in Pliny the Elder's time. Romans had learned from their reading of Xenophon and from actual eastern travels to plant tall, straight-growing plane trees in courtyards and gardens.[9]

Although the gardens are lost, we know something of their chosen decor. The layout might be rigorously geometrical, or in other parts deliberately informal, with art cultivating the imitation of nature's irregularity by means of winding paths, unpruned trees, and grottoes of rough tufa studded with shells around bubbling springs.[10] Owners chose statuary to reflect their literary or ethical values. Ann Kuttner (1999b) has described the development of Roman aristocratic pleasure gardens in these terms:

By the first century BC such *horti* came up to the city's edge. In central courts and in those beyond the house core, trees and shrubs were cultivated for pleasure of appearance and shade, supplementing or replacing functional 'kitchen gardens' just as useful vine-arbors now doubled as pleasant pergolas. An ideal estate contained grottos, woods and meadows as well as formalized garden precincts with ordered plantings, walks, fountains, porticoes and pleasure suites.[11]

We can only guess at the arrangement of the bronzes recovered from the Villa of the Papyri, once owned by Cicero's contemporary, the Epicurean Calpurnius Piso, at Herculaneum, because the early excavators simply dug tunnels under the fossilized mud and brought out whatever they could lay hands on; but there are more than fifty busts and statues from both the house and its grounds in the Museo Nazionale at Naples. There will never be absolute certainty as to their original location, but the current guide to the four rooms containing the villa bronzes includes two satyrs, one dancing, one playing the tibia, from the *atrium*; a series of busts of Greek scholars from the *tablinum*; and an Athena Promachos (identified by the Romans with Minerva, goddess of poetry and scholarship?) and five bronze statues of maidens from one of the peristyles – these were once called nymphs or dancers, but have now been identified as Danaids, perhaps copied from the same Hellenistic model as the famous Danaids of Augustus' Palatine library portico. In the other peristyle there were busts of kings, generals, and philosophers. Parts of the garden celebrated Dionysus and his retinue (a drunken satyr has survived), and another part imitated a gymnasium with a 'resting Hermes' and statues of runners in action.[12] The documentary sources for Pompey's statuary report women poets, muses, famous mothers, and the drunken satyr Maro from the retinue of Dionysus, who is mentioned by Propertius.[13] Both Maro and (more predictably) Triton seem to have been fountains.

Prose writers like the younger Pliny, even when they are most enthusiastic about their villas, will not people their estates with supernatural beings, but rest content with human gardeners and the occasional altar to Silvanus.[14] But just as Bucolic poets speak freely of nymphs and fauns in the woodland and pasture, so, perhaps more surprisingly, Statius animates the villa estates of his friends and patrons with nymphs of the springs and seashore and river-gods. His *Silvae* are written to honour these friends, and praise them through the praise of the houses and gardens they have designed: praise of place is fused with praise of patron.[15] Romans of the governing class had always associated their villas with leisure – that is, leisure from political and social commitments to spend most often in composition of history or memoirs. Even in the time of Seneca and under the capricious autocracy of Nero, leisure had to be justified, and we can usefully quote from *Epistulae Morales* 55, a letter Seneca wrote to Lucilius, who had apparently been expressing sadness that he could not be in Campania, as Seneca was. Seneca has been going for rides and takes as an example the villa of Servilius Vatia, advantageously situated between the shore of the curved bay near Cumae and Lake Acheron (55.2). First Seneca deplores the idleness of Vatia's leisure spent without philosophy: 'The common crowd thinks a man at leisure is retired and carefree and self-sufficient, living for himself, but none of these conditions can arise except in a philosopher,' *Otiosum enim hominem seductum existimat vulgus et securum et se contentum, sibi viventem, quorum nihil ulli contingere nisi sapienti potest* (*Ep. Mor.* 55.4). But Seneca also stops to describe what he has seen of the grounds of the villa in passing.

There are two great grottoes, the size of any atrium however generous, and constructed by hand, one facing away from the sun, the other able to receive sunshine right into the sunset. A canal flows to divide his plantation [or avenue? Seneca uses the Greek *platanôna*] of plane trees, and draws water from both the sea and Lake Avernus, like a Euripus, full enough to nourish fish even though it is constantly being emptied ... The villa's greatest advantage is that it has Baiae beyond its enclosing walls: avoiding the nuisances of the place the villa benefits from its pleasures.

Speluncae sunt duo magni operis, cuivis laxo atrio pares, manu factae, quarum altera solem non recipit, altera usque in occidentem tenet. platanona medius rivus et a mari et ab Acherusio lacu receptus Euripi modo dividit, alendis piscibus, etiamsi adsidue exhauriatur, sufficiens ... hoc tamen est commodissimum in villa, quod Baias trans parietem habet; incommodis illarum caret, voluptatibus fruitur. (Seneca *Ep. Mor.* 55.6–7)

We should imagine the villa gardens of Statius' wealthy friends and patrons in similar terms. Almost all these friends either are retired or are men of leisure, and Statius himself honours both leisure and luxury in these poems. But while the 'villa' poems celebrate tranquillity, the poet imparts a sense of humming activity through his evocation of the non-human denizens of gardens and pools. The sense of luxury is fostered by his celebration of costly materials (typically, coloured marble) and of the play of light on water and the dappled shadows of leaves in shimmering settings.[16]

The poet's approach to his ekphrasis of each villa is as varied as are their settings, but all share the motivation of bestowing compliments on his patrons and friends, compliments based on the interpretation of Nature herself, or on appropriate, if lesser, gods, as paying homage to the villa and its owner. In *Silvae* 1.3, Manilius Vopiscus[17] has erected a villa near Tibur with separate and symmetrical wings facing each other astride a calm reach of the river Anio. In many ways the river is the hero of this poem and stands for Nature's glad obedience to Vopiscus' designs; accordingly, Statius will twice depict the river-god in action. The transition from river to villa is eased by the personalized verbs describing the intercourse between the partnered river banks and the competition of the twin villas to defend their master, as well as the good behaviour of the summer constellations, as the Dogstar refrains from barking and the Lion from glaring, while (Epicurean) pleasure and Venus anoint the rooftops (9–10; the text is damaged). As lofty woods brood over the waters and their elongated reflection plays upon the stream, the river pays its own homage:

> Ipse Anien (miranda fides!) infraque superque
> saxeus, hic tumidam rabiem spumosaque ponit
> murmura, ceu placidi veritus turbare Vopisci
> Pieriosque dies et habentes carmina somnos.
> (Statius *Silvae* 1.3.20–3)

Everything inanimate seems actively benevolent; the mansions keep safe their banks without complaint, so near that sights and sounds and almost touch can pass from bank to bank. Among the luxuries praised by the poet are piped and running water (37, *emissas per cubilia Nymphas,* 'nymphs unleashed through the bedchambers') and the outdoor pools that steam on the river's grassy verge, where the stream connected to the steaming furnaces laughs at the nymphs gasping for breath although the river is close at hand. The first nymphs, then, are personified plumbing, the second group the living spirits of the stream.

Statius himself had been permitted by Emperor Domitian to draw water from the public aqueduct for his Alban villa,[18] and perhaps for that reason he speaks of aqueducts with affection and enthusiasm. Thus, when he is called upon by Claudius Etruscus to praise his new baths at Rome, Statius diverts the address of his proemium from Helicon and the Muses, or Apollo and Dionysus, or even Mercury as inventor of the lyre, to invoke the Naiads as mistresses of the waves and Vulcan as god of fire: 'Come, green goddesses, and turn your clear faces to me, and bind your glass-green hair with young vine tendrils, all unclothed, as you surface from deep springs and torment lustful Satyrs with the sight.'

> Ite, deae virides, liquidosque advertite vultus
> et vitreum teneris crinem redimite corymbis,
> veste nihil tectae, quales emergitis altis
> fontibus et visu Satyros torquetis amantes.
> (1.5.15–18)

As he does elsewhere, Statius associates water-nymphs with watery colours, here *viridis* and *vitreus* (the green of bottle-glass), elsewhere *caeruleus* and *glaucus*. And as he will again, he provocatively visualizes their nudity. But he is not content to invoke the Naiads; he specifies the proper guests. Not the evil nymphs like Salmacis or the bereaved daughter of Cebron, dried up with mourning, or the (unnamed) nymph who stole away Hercules' protégé Hylas,[19] but the good nymphs of Latium, of Tiber and Anio (not the river in this case but the aqueduct, Aqua Anio, whether *vetus* or *nova*), and the Aqua Virgo, offering a welcome to swimmers, and Aqua Marcia, who together bring cool waters: 'you ... who raise the Tiber with fresh streams, you whom the rushing Anio and the Virgo, welcoming swimmers, delight, and Marcia, bringing Marsic snows and chill, whose wandering water swells on towering masses and is conveyed suspended through the air on countless arches. It is your achievement I undertake to sing, your home which I lay open in gentle verse.'

> vos mihi quae Latium septenaque culmina, Nymphae
> incolitis Thybrimque novis attollitis undis,
> quas praeceps Anien atque exceptura natatus
> Virgo iuvat, Marsasque nives et frigora ducens
> Marcia, praecelsis quarum vaga molibus unda
> crescit et innumero pendens transmittitur arcu.
> vestrum opus aggredimur, vestra est quam carmine molli
> pando domus.
> (1.5.23–9)

Both aqueducts are praised for gathering in the chill mountain waters on lofty piers, conveyed on high on countless arches; when Statius declares that his enterprise is their work, his theme their home, he surely is including the river-nymphs with those protecting (and inhabiting?) the aqueducts.

Nature, lavish in the physical beauty of the site (1.3.16–17), is glad to be tamed for Vopiscus' pair of villas; the ground delights (*gaudet humus*, 56) in its multi-coloured mosaic, and the tree in the courtyard surges upwards to the clear sky, immune to felling. Now perhaps some slippery Naiad or Hamadryad (*vel lubrica Nais / vel ... Hamadryas*) owes her length of years to Vopiscus (59–63)! Even the aqueduct (apostrophized simply as Marcia [67], so that the gentile name suggests a noble lady) is able to cross the river inside her pipe, competing with the river Alpheus, who flowed unsullied from Elis to Sicily. So inviting is the site that the river-god leaves the grotto at his source, at dead of night, casts off his grey-green robes, and sweeps the moss this way and that before him or dives into the pools and splashes the glassy waters as he swims (70–4). Other local streams are in attendance: Tiburnus reclines in the shade, and Albula longs to dip her tresses (74–5). Statius slips from personification to mythical comparison as he imagines the charms of this spot 'separating Diana of the Arician grove from her attendant Egeria or emptying cool Taygetus of its Dryad bands, or enticing Pan from the woods of Lycaeus.'

> haec domus Egeriae nemoralem abiungere Phoeben
> et Dryadum viduare choris algentia possit
> Taygeta et silvis accersere Pana Lycaeis.
> (1.3.76–8)

Did Statius know Peloponnesian Lycaeus, or again Taygetus? No, but he knew well their role in Virgil's *Georgics*, where Pan is invited to leave his ancestral woodland *saltusque Lycaei* (1.16; cf. 3.2 and 314; 4.539), and Virgil himself longs to visit Spartan Taygeta (2.488) shortly before he calls blessed the man who knows the country gods (*deos qui novit agrestes / Panaque Silvanumque senem Nymphasque sorores*, 2.493–4). For Statius neither the famous beauty spots of Greece nor the favourite resorts of Latium can compete with Vopiscus' *quies*. What crowns the charm of the place is its owner's personality: his calm virtue and 'sober elegance' (I owe this to Shackleton Bailey) and enjoyment free of luxury (*luxu ... carentes / deliciae*, 92–3) such as Epicurus himself would prefer. Not only Vopiscus' mansion but his art – in this case his lyre – delights the Fauns of Tibur and its local god Hercules, and founder Catillus, whom the great Virgil once sang.[20] Master and property are assimilated in the poet's final blessing *Macte bonis animi* (106), in his setting so glorious that the gold-bearing river Hermus or Tagus should flow through Vopiscus' estate, as he reaches a ripe (Nestorian) old age in *docta otia* – learned leisure.

There are many similarities between Statius' celebration of Vopiscus and *Silvae* 2.2, the first of his poems for Pollius Felix. Although the second book is dedicated to Atedius Melior (to whom we shall return), the poet implies in his preface that friendship will lead Melior to welcome both poem 2.2, 'the Surrentine villa of my dear Pollius, which deserved a thorough treatment as an honour to his eloquence,' and 2.7, honouring the anniversary of Lucan's birthday in response to the request of his widow, Polla Argentaria. (We owe to Robin Nisbet [1978] the firm identification of Pollius' wife Polla with Lucan's widow, the daughter, or granddaughter, of the declaimer and poet Marcus Argentarius.) Statius will also devote *Silvae* 3.1 to Pollius' new temple of Hercules at Surrentum, and 4.8 to the birth of his new granddaughter; but only 2.2 pays extensive attention to the country demigods.

A major reason for this is the extraordinary site of the villa. I was with a group from the American Academy in Rome who visited the site in 1994, and can more easily recall than describe its exceptional layout. The villa site offered a panoramic view of the Bay of Naples, including Misenum (77), Prochyta (Procida), and Inarime, and the ancient site of Naples itself (marked by the temple of Aphrodite Euploia, 'of fair sailing,' 79–80). As a further enhancement, because the sea had eaten into the coastline and wrapped itself around the promontory in which the villa stood, the establishment enjoyed a private inland harbour, with a private sea facing every chamber, and its own land across the water obedient to every window (*omni proprium thalamo mare, transque iacentem / Nerea diversis servit sua terra fenestris*, 74–5).

Statius opens his poem by locating the villa near the cliffs of the Sirens and temple of Minerva, the demigods and goddess associated with the charm of poetry, and looking across the Bay of Naples to Dicaearchia (the Greek name of contemporary Puteoli), in land favoured by Dionysus, where the grapes are a match for the famous wine presses of Falernum. It seems, too, that the villa's high-quality grapes grew close to the shore, which Statius will exploit as a fruitful source of unusual mixed mythology. Statius has been drawn to this serene place (cf. *placido ... recessu*, 13) by the poetic eloquence of its serene owner (*placidi facundia Polli*, 9) and the youthful[21] charm of his elegant wife Polla.

As in 1.3, Nature is prominent, paying tribute to art, and Nature frames the description in lines 15 and 52: she has cooperated, *dat Natura locum montique intervenit unum / litus et in terras scopulis pendentibus exit*, 'so that one shore interrupts the rising hillside and runs inland between overhanging cliffs'; there *gemina testudine fumant / balnea, et e terris occurrit dulcis amaro / Nympha mari*, 'twin baths steam with vaulted domes and a sweet Nymph (literally, fresh water) runs from land into the salty sea.' Here the parade of Hellenistic sea-gods[22] and nymphs are eager to bathe, Phorcus' frolicsome band and Cymodoce with moistened locks, and even Galatea in the green of youth (*viridisque cupit Galatea lavari*). There were temples of Neptune and Hercules near the house at the edge of the harbour (21–4), perhaps alongside each other, the temple of Hercules facing inland as Neptune resists the wild breakers (*gaudet gemino sub numine portus: / hic servat terras, hic saevis fluctibus obstat*); but in this sheltered pool the sea is wondrous calm, and its pools respect the calm of their master's manners (26, 29): *mira quies pelagi ... / stagna modesta iacent, domini servantia mores*. The poet resorts to supernatural aid (from Apollo and the muses, 36–42), relying on the topos of inexpressibility to evoke the immense length of Pollius' portico, which his eyes can scarcely take in or his steps follow. The house offers prospects of both sunrise and sunset, the noise of the surf and the calm to landwards, as Nature smiles on the place: she yields, defeated, to her cultivator and has grown tame and obedient to human requirements.

his favit Natura locis, hic victa colenti
cessit et ignotos docilis mansuescit in usus.
(2.2.52–3):

The very architectural and engineering feats that used to provoke
the anger of Sallust and Horace win praise from Statius.[23] As home-
owner, Pollius has triumphed over nature, and as poet he has surpassed the creative poets whom nature and her creatures obeyed
– Arion of Lesbos, who charmed the dolphin; Amphion, who
charmed the rocks into forming the city wall of Thebes; and
Orpheus, who drew rocks, trees, and animals to his music (60–2).

The second half of the poem celebrates the furnishings of
Pollius' mansion – his collection of bronzes, appropriately pro-
grammatic with statesmen and poets and sages, and the exotic
and many-coloured marbles – and calls a blessing upon Pollius, as
a townsman born in Greek Dicaearchia, for his love of Greek culture and objets d'art.

The country gods return, however, as the poet honours the produce of Pollius' estate (98–106). Because Pollius has created fields
where the sea once flowed (*pontoque novalia ... iniecta*, 98–9),
the cliffs are steeped in the juices of Bacchus, and the demigods of
sea and land compete to pluck the grapes and grow tipsy with the
vintage. In a unique paradox, the poet shows the rustic and mar-
ine deities prompted by wine and desire to intrude on each others'
territory. This at least is how I understand the daring Nereid who
climbs the cliffs as the grapes mature to wipe her eyes with the
ripe <fruit of the> tendril (*palmite maturo*, 102) and steal sweet
grapes from the slopes, and the reverse movement of the Satyrs,
who fall (or are swept?) from the land into the water when the
waves splash over the vintage, and the mountain-dwelling Pans,
who lust to seize the naked Doris in the waves.

Statius has been invited to celebrate the land itself, so he combines his parting blessing on Pollius and his wife with a wish that
this estate may surpass their other homes at Tibur and Puteoli
and Tarentum, whatever his patron's poetic endeavours. As with
Vopiscus, these (no doubt dilettante) compositions introduce the
last phase of the compliments from poet to poet(aster), whether

Pollius is meditating Epicurean protreptic and didactic poetry[24] or lyric or elegiac or even iambic verse. Returning to his opening motif, Statius evokes the Siren hastening from her cliff to hear compositions superior to her own,

> hinc levis e scopulis meliora ad carmina siren
> advolat, hinc motis audit Tritonia cristis,
>   (2.2.116–17)

and Minerva (*Tritonia*), listening as even the dolphins surface and approach the cliffs to hear Pollius' lyre. Given the ring-composition, I suspect that what follows, lines 121–42 addressed to Pollius and the lines addressed to his wife Polla (rearranged by Gronovius and subsequent editors, including both Courtney and Shackleton Bailey), may be an afterthought of the poet, who realized he had not done justice to Pollius' philosophical aspirations. This realization would explain the belated allusions to his patron's superior insights penetrating the obscurity of material things from his Epicurean citadel: 'you look down from the lofty citadel of your mind upon the wanderers … you see the truth with the darkness of matter dispelled,' *celsa tu mentis ab arce / despicis errantes* (132–3) … *discussa rerum caligine verum / aspicis* (138–9). Pollius has steered the ship of his life into the traditionally metaphorical safe harbour and calm tranquillity (*securos portus placidamque quietem*) that recalls the literal harbour and tranquillity with which the poem began. Despite the series of good wishes (*vive … felix*, 121–2, *sic perge nec umquam … demitte*, 141–2, and *discite securi … ite per annos … et priscae titulos praecedite famae*, 143–6),[25] Statius probably knew that he had not finished with Pollius, who is in fact the dedicatee of the next book, book 3, which begins with Pollius' new shrine to Hercules (3 *Praef.* 9–10): *Hercules Surrentinus … quem in litore tuo consecratum, statim ut videram, his versibus adoravi*, 'Your Hercules of Sorrento, consecrated on your shore, which I worshipped with these verses as soon as I had seen it.'

The first poem of book 3 (3.1) is addressed to Hercules, who will occupy the limelight in Statius' narrative, keeping other gods and demigods in the background. It opens apologetically, with Pollius returning to the cult of Hercules after a year of inaction while the new shrine was being constructed, a greater *Tholos* with a gleaming doorway and a roof resting on columns of Greek marble. Where did this new court come from? Only recently this site was barren sand and rocks shaggy with thickets, land unfit for any human traces. What good fortune enriched the cliffs with these walls? Were they raised by the lyre of Amphion or Orpheus? Statius suspends his account to address Hercules with a cletic hymn, asking him to come in peace (23–36 and 39, *pacatus mitisque veni*) to his sacred couch, where there is an innocent athletic contest and a still more innocent priest, Pollius' grandson, whose name his grandfather has entered on the temple's dedicatory inscription, since the child was still an infant like Hercules (*parvus adhuc similisque tui*) when he strangled his stepmother's snakes (43–8).

To tell the *aition* or origin of the new shrine, Statius calls on Calliope, who opens with an epic narrative motif; it was the time (52, *tempus erat*) of Arician Diana's festival on 13 August, and Statius himself was a now familiar guest (65, *non hospes*) at Pollius' home. They were enjoying a seaside picnic when a storm brewed equal to the storm cloud which Juno brought to Libya when wealthy Dido was given to her husband, and the Nymphs bore witness, howling in the wilderness.[26] So far, then, the Nymphs are absent from Statius' own narrative. The guests (even Polla's elegant female friends) took refuge in the old rustic shrine, fit only to shelter shipwrecked sailors and deep-sea divers, where the tables and couches were set up; but the building could not handle them, so the god, embarrassed, inspired Pollius with an idea. It is now the god who becomes Statius' spokesman (91–116), in reminding Pollius of his transformation of the terrain and lavish previous construction, of the portico and the shore where Pollius has enclosed the hot Nymphs under their double domes.[27] Hercules is still happy to enter even the primitive shrine on the shore, but Juno (his old enemy) can look down on him. He appeals to Pollius to give him a temple and altars that Jupiter and the gods, including Hercules' sister Minerva, would wish to visit. Pollius must not be discouraged by the solid hillside that blocks construction, since he, Hercules, will help, and the toil will be accomplished more swiftly than was the building of Amphion's Thebes or Apollo's Troy.

Statius resumes control of his narrative, describing the plans and excavations which Hercules himself promotes, eliminating cliffs overnight to the amazement of the workmen, until after a year he can look down on the waves from above and challenge the nearby building of his stepmother, inviting Pallas into a worthy temple (135–9). This is all exuberant invention, and now at last the green Nereids can leap up from their pumice grottoes and cling to the damp cliffs, unashamedly watching the naked wrestlers (this is the inversion of the nudity in 2.2). In fact all the beauty spots named in 2.2 (Nesis, Limon, Euploia, Misenum, and Parthenope) smile at the local rites and the naked contests. Statius reports this as his own verses uttered in Bacchic exhilaration before the altars, then returns to impersonate Hercules himself uttering the god's final blessing of Pollius for converting barren Nature's shame (167–8, *infecundaeque pudenda / Naturae deserta*) into this worthy shrine, which will be as dear to him as Nemea or Argos, western Gades or Tibur. This may seem a small harvest of allusions to the local nymphs, but the association of this poem with its predecessor, 2.2, serves to explain how Statius has used mythology to recall and to complement his first tribute to Pollius.

Were such fancies peculiar to Statius or his new genre of praise-poetry? We saw that Martial could populate his beloved Nomentine estate with demigods (10.92), perhaps with the nostalgia he felt from his distant retirement in Spain. But an epigram of Martial honouring a legendary plane tree that had been planted by Julius Caesar at Cordoba is just as fanciful; the note is struck early by the exaggeration that the gold-dust of the Baetis colours the flocks, adorning them with gold-leaf. The plane tree would be at least 140 years old, but it soars to the stars in pride at its divine originator (*auctorem dominumque*): 'Here the drunken fauns[28] often play, and late at night the sound of the pan pipes scares the silent house: the dryad often hides under its foliage when she is fleeing across the fields from Pan at night.'

> saepe sub hac madidi luserunt arbore Fauni,
>   terruit et tacitam fistula sera domum;
> dumque fugit solos nocturnum Pana per agros,
>   saepe sub hac latuit rustica fronde Dryas.
>   (Martial 9.61.11–14)

It seems that the house gives hospitality to Bacchus himself as a reveller (*comissator*) with his semi-divine escort: just as the pan pipe is heard at night from an unseen source, so the dawn finds the evidence of rose petals and last night's garlands strewn on the grass. These Bacchic associations of the plane tree *dilecta deis* suggest that this kind of fantasy may have been a common folk-belief, just as it was commonly represented in house decoration and popular art.[29] Such fantasies provide a basis for the more elaborate and circumstantial myth that will be developed by Statius.

I have reserved as the last 'villa poem' a myth of this kind, another *aition*, offered to Atedius Melior, the dedicatee of book 2. The book actually opens with Statius' lament for Melior's quasi-adopted child, the dead Glaucias, and then, after the praise of Pollius' Surrentine villa (2.2) which we have already considered, Statius returns to Melior. He offers two occasional poems (*in arborem certe tuam ... et psittacum*, on your tree and your parrot), described as light *libelli* written to serve as epigrams (2 *Praef.*). Melior's villa is not in Latium or Campania but in Rome itself. He may have done business at Rome, and seems to have been not only childless, but probably unmarried; there is no mention of a wife in any of the poems, and the only allusion to family or friends is to Melior as a loyal witness to the lost glory of Blaesus (2.76–7). Readers of *Silvae* 2 in book form would recall Statius' more emotional tribute to the long-dead Blaesus as a special friend in 2.1.191–207.[30]

Silvae 2.3, a relatively short birthday offering of seventy-seven lines, has been much admired as Statius' own mythological invention, and as narrative it certainly resembles Ovid's tales of the transformation of Daphne and Lotis and Byblis[31] into trees – but the form of the *aition* is not Ovidian. The Nymph pursued by the lustful Pan and subsequently paid his Platonic homage is not transformed into a tree, and it is difficult to see what Statius thought became of her. While the poem tends to identify her with Melior's pool, the pool itself belongs both to the prehistory of the mythical pursuit and to the time before Melior acquired his villa and grounds. Nor is Pan, her pursuer, turned into the tree, which itself exists before the mythical pursuit. In fact interpreters have differed quite considerably in how they have read the story in its physical details, which are less well handled than its emotional implications. There is clearly a sense in which the tree stands for Pan, just as the pool stands for the fleeing Nymph, but there are difficulties in this reading, and a number of other uncertainties in the narrative as a whole.

Statius begins with the tree[32] that shades the transparent waters as it bends over a pool. It has a most unusual shape, 'curved over the waters from the base of its trunk, [and] then changes direction, soaring with upright stem, as if it were born again from the midst of the waves and dwelt in the glass-green current with its unseen roots.'

> Stat quae perspicuas nitidi Melioris opacet
> arbor aquas complexa lacus; quae robore ab imo
> <in> curvata vadis redit inde cacumine recto
> ardua, ceu mediis iterum nascatur ab undis
> atque habitet vitreum tacitis radicibus amnem.
> (*Silvae* 2.3.1–5)

Who will help Statius tell this tale? He invokes the Naiads and Fauns, claiming that his theme is too modest for him to appeal to Apollo. To be sure of his setting, let me continue with a close translation. 'The Nymphs were once fleeing from Pan, who chased them as if he wanted them all, but really he was pursuing only Pholoë. She ran through the woods and streams to escape his hairy steps and wanton horns.' Now Statius surprises, by shifting the tale from the never-neverland of Arcadia or some wild Italian hillside to Rome itself. Pan traces a recognizable if erratic route as the tender crowds of nymphs flee from him. But although he acts as if he lusted after them all, Pan has eyes only for Pholoë.

> Nympharum tenerae fugiebant Pana catervae.
> ille quidem it cunctas tamquam velit, it tamen unam
> in Pholoën. silvis haec fluminibusque sequentis
> nunc hirtos gressus, nuc improba cornua vitat.
> iamque et belligerum Iani nemus atraque Caci
> rura Quirinalesque fuga suspensa per agros
> Caelica tesca subit ...
> (2.3.8–14)

Pholoë runs from him through woods and streams, 'shunning now his hairy steps and now his wanton horns, and now she draws near to the wood of warring Janus and the dark lands of Cacus, through the fields of Quirinus, to the thickets of the Caelian hill.' Terrified and exhausted (like Daphne *victa labore fugae, Met.* 1.544), Pholoë clutches her robes and sinks down by the water's edge, where Melior's welcoming and honourable home now stands.[33]

There, despite the urgency of pursuit, she apparently either sleeps or faints. Pan catches up and becomes confident of consummating his union (*sua credit / conubia,* 18–19); in fact he is already poised and hovering over his prey in passionate expectation, when Diana (who is wandering over the seven hills in pursuit of a hind on the Aventine) turns in that direction. Now Statius deliberately slows his narrative pace to prolong the suspense. Distressed at the sight, Diana voices her indignation that she must constantly try (and fail?) to stop this foul beast (*foedum pecus,* 25) from his greedy sexual assaults on her followers (24–6). Borrowing the motif of using diminished force from Jupiter in *Met.* 3.305, Statius has Diana take a light arrow from her quiver and invert it, tossing it lightly with one hand so that its blunt end grazes the left arm of the sleeping Naiad (*quod neque ... solito torquet stridore sed una / emisit contenta manu*). The position of the disclaimer in line 30 (*aversa fertur tetigisse sagitta*) suggests that at this point the poet was not entirely comfortable with his own invention. Restored to daylight (from sleep or unconsciousness?) the nymph sees her predator, leaps fully clad into the pool, and wraps herself in the weeds on its bottom (31–4). From this moment on, Statius says no more about the Naiad, but turns to Pan, the frustrated rapist (*subito deceptus praedo*), adopting his point of view: what can he do? Unable to swim, Pan laments the cruelty of Bromius (his patron, but how is he to blame for this situation?) and the malicious envy of the pool and the arrows.

Here begins the poet's account of the young plane tree, apparently already half grown, with a long stem and many branches, so that its tip is capable of reaching to the sky, *cui longa propago / innumeraeque manus et iturus in aethera vertex* (39–40). This Pan plants close by and piles up fresh sand, sprinkling it with the longed-for waters (*optatae* presumably by Pan, who cannot swim in them), before giving the tree his instructions (43–52). It is to live on as his surrogate, a pledge of Pan's desire, and bend over the hidden couch of the unyielding nymph to offer her love, covering her with the shade of its leafy branches. Pan's words *tu saltem declinis ama* (45) suggest that the tree, at least, is to express (or implement) the love which Pan could not satisfy; in fact it is to do the nymph loving service by sprinkling the waters and disturbing them with its leaves (48) so as to prevent her suffering from scorching heat or hail. In return Pan will long cherish and protect both the tree and the mistress of this kindly abode (*dominamque benignae / sedis*, 49–50) and earn for it the admiration of trees patronized by other gods.

The tree responds: inspired by the god's old passion, it leans tenderly over the fertile pool with sloping trunk and contemplates the waters with loving shadow. It (or he?) even hopes for an embrace, but the exhalations from the water ward it away, forbidding contact. We are actually watching the tree grow (as if in the accelerated motion used by nature films), and its growth will match the opening description of lines 1–5, but contains its own inconsistencies. When the poet speaks of it 'struggling through to the breezes and balancing *fundo* (58) before it cleverly rears up its smooth tip (*enode cacumen*), as if it was sinking to the depth of the lake from a different trunk,' is the tree, after all, rooting itself beneath the surface of the pool? Is *fundus* the bottom of the pool, or (less probably) a base formed by its own trunk? If the exhalations from the water deny it contact, what are we to understand by lines 60–1? *iam nec Phoebeia Nais / odit et exclusos invitat gurgite ramos*, 'now the Naiad protégée of Diana no longer shuns the tree but invites the branches shut out from the pool.'

There must be two stages, both in time and in space. As the tree grows stretching its trunk down towards the waters as if opening its arms in an embrace, it is first made to change direction and grow skywards, and then, as the trunk continues to form, slanting upwards but towards the centre of the pool, its upper branches curve down and are permitted to enter the water. The erotic language is quite delicate, limited to *vota* (classic of a lover's desire for sex), *amare, amplexus,* and the verb *excludere,* traditionally used of the locked-out lover.

Psychologically, then, Statius has made this a story in which the (untypical) fidelity of the lustful Pan earns him a delayed and vicarious satisfaction. The nymph's change of heart matches the yielding of chaste Pomona in *Met.* 14.766–71 to the urging of Vertumnus, but the mediation of the tree and disappearance of the nymph from the scene have shifted the courtship into the mode of allegory. And there have been scholars to argue that the whole tale is indeed an allegory of Melior's own career. Basing his argument on some pointed phrases like *sine fraude lares* (16) and the language of lines 66–9, but more particularly on the awkward and implausible invention of Diana's warning shot, Vessey[34] suggested that Melior had participated in public life until a friend's warning had led him to make a strategic retirement. Certainly if, as Peter White first suggested, Melior's long-dead friend Blaesus was the Junius Blaesus who first supported and then was forced to take poison by Vitellius,[35] Melior himself will have been associated with the wrong side in Flavian eyes; hence, perhaps, the poet's stress on his innocence of *iniqua potentia nec spes / improba* ('abuse of power and immoral ambition,' 66–7), his avoidance of civil strife (*tumultus*), and his private life open to public scrutiny (*secrete, palam quod digeris ordine vitam*, 69), to balance the final affirmation of Melior's loyal testimony to the glory of Blaesus, *te sub teste ... revirescet gloria Blaesi* (76–7). But it is easier to accept a political subtext to lines 64–71 and 76–7 than to apply it in the interpretation of the adventures of Pan and Pholoë. As Nauta (2002) points out, Melior's analogue would surely not have been the endangered nymph, but the protective plane tree, and there is no appropriate equivalent of the nymph or her reconciliation. We should also ask about the tact of Statius in choosing to remind his patron of past danger or misjudgments. It does far more credit to Statius' invention to read the tale as a deliberate fantasy designed to compliment his host's special plane tree with a flattering explanation of its abnormal growth.

Statius loves to animate the landscape, and to make gods and demigods the vehicle of his compliments. For his emperor, indeed, no human spokesperson would have been adequate. Hence the primary speaker of *Silvae* 4.1, inaugurating the civic year, is Janus, god of the year's beginning, whose shrine was once at the centre of the old republican forum and is now incorporated into Domitian's new Forum Transitorium.[36] When the poet turns in *Silvae* 4.3 to honouring Domitian's new coastal road, the Via Domitiana, by which the emperor 'had eliminated the burdensome delays of the sandy terrain,' to quote Statius' preface to book 4, he calls upon two more than human beings to do the honours for him: geography dictates that the second of these is the Sibyl of Cumae, who is the ideal vehicle for a prophecy of prolonged happiness for the emperor (4.3.124–63), but the first divine spokesperson is a river-god, Vulturnus (72–94), whose unruly natural course has been channelled and dignified by the emperor's engineering. He is introduced as Statius evokes the admiring response of Cumae and Liternum and the small stream Savo to the clang of the roadworks.

Not only does Vulturnus have the hoarse voice and shaggy dripping locks (here tawny, because impregnated with sand) of a river-god; as he surfaces, draped in reeds, he takes up position at the keystone of the arch of Domitian's new bridge, where in fact the emperor had set his inscription.[37] The river's speech is in keeping with the poet's own admiration for human control of nature; more significantly, it is in keeping with the emperor's pose as a disciplinarian and even a moral reformer. Domitian is the *camporum bone conditor meorum* (72), 'good establisher of my plainland,' who has forced the river's straggling course to obey the laws of a proper river bed (*qui me ... recti legibus alvei ligasti*, 73–5), and Vulturnus boasts of his new obedience (*vix passus ... / iam pontem fero*, 77–8) and pride in having the emperor as his lord (*servitusque tanti est / quod sub te duce, te iubente, cessi*, 81–2). Henceforward the emperor will be read (in Statius' poem, but also in the unmentioned inscription) as greatest of masters and eternal victor. And Statius deliberately gives to his deity the language of morality and purity. He expresses his gratitude to the emperor for cleaning up the shame (*malum ... pudorem*, 86–7) of his neglected and muddy flow. Thanks to Domitian, the river-god can now compete with the calm sea and nearby Liris in his shining flow and clean current (*nitente cursu*, 92; *puro gurgite*, 94). As Statius has previously offset Nature with the achievement of human design and construction,[38] so here he first evokes the whole business of engineering, and then its triumphant outcome in the lofty arch of the marble bridge, gleaming with the victory trophies of the warrior leader, which now crowns the stream.

Country Gods in the Pastoral World of Statius' *Thebaid*

As with Ovid, the contrasting genres of Statius' poetry invite us to consider whether he treats the country gods in a different way when they are Greek, not Roman, antique rather than modern, and living in natural landscapes, not manicured parks. The nymphs and satyrs of the *Silvae* are residents of Italy, of his own Campania, or Latium, or, in Pholoë's case, a *Romana di Roma*, so we can treat them as a part of Statius' Italian inheritance, however coloured by his own immersion in Hellenistic poetry and art. But even in the warlike world of the *Thebaid* the demigods are an active presence, particularly in pastoral Nemea, the neutral and peaceable land through which the Argive expedition must pass; indeed, these rustic nymphs and river-spirits provide a poignant physical and emotional contrast to the sheer brutality of the human conflict.

Three times Statius engages the country demigods in his Nemean sequence, from books 4 to 6. There is one clear difference: nymphs, fauns, and Pan appear as part of Bacchus' retinue, and their actions are obedient to his commands. Bacchus is returning to his birthplace, Thebes (*materna moenia*, 4.656), in his chariot drawn by tigers, with a triumphal procession of Maenads and personified passions (4.661–2; Anger, Frenzy, Fear, Courage, and intoxicated *Ardor*), when he sees the dust of the approaching Argive force and acts to delay it. It is high noon, and the fields beneath the sun pant and gape (*hiantibus ... arvis*) for lack of moisture when he summons the stream-goddesses (*agrestes fluviorum numina Nymphae*, 4.684) and asks the nymphs to endure and carry through (both are implied in *perferte*) the task he is imposing. They are to block the rivers of Argolid and bury them in dust. All waters must disappear from Nemea, from its underground sources (*ex alto*) just as Phoebus is already aiding this process from above (*summo limite*), and even the stars, especially the dog star Erigone, are collaborating. Now they must go underground, but soon he will compensate them:

'Afterwards I will entice you out in full spate, and your honour will have the most lavish gifts in my cult, and I shall ward off the stealthy assaults of wanton hoofed Pans and the lustful rapes of Fauns.'

> post vos ego gurgite pleno
> eliciam,[39] et quae dona meis amplissima sacris
> vester habebit honos, nocturnaque furta licentum
> cornipedum et cupidas Faunorum arcebo rapinas.
> (Statius *Thebaid* 4.692–6)

The nymphs are not just symbols; they share the affliction of their streams. A sickly neglect (*tenuior situs*) spreads over their faces, and the green moisture falls from their hair. Their suffering is transmitted to the land, drained by fiery thirst, as springs and pools become dusty and rivers harden with seething mud. Statius pictures the misery of the cattle as famous marshes and springs dry up, all except the little Langia, which still feeds its stream at Bacchus' command. The situation resembles and surely echoes the earth and river beds scorched by Phaethon's dangerous driving in *Met.* 2.237–71, especially lines 238–9, *tum nymphae passis fontesque lacusque / deflevere comis*, 'then the nymphs lamented with loosened hair their springs and lakes.' When the chieftains meet Hypsipyle, she guides them to the Langia, but the army rapidly drains and muddies the stream dry (800–5). We hear no more of the nymphs until Hypsipyle has completed her Lemnian narrative (5.498), and they return to find the sacred serpent has killed her nursling Opheltes. The serpent is ranging round desperate for moisture because the frightened nymphs are buried in dust (*trepidaeque*[40] *latent in pulvere nymphae*, 519), and accidentally it crushes the crawling toddler with its thrashing tail (5.538–40). When the hubristic Capaneus kills the serpent, and it flees into the temple of its protector to die, all Nature grieves: 'The indignant pools of his kinsman Lerna, the nymphs accustomed to sprinkle him with spring flowers, the land of Nemea where he crawled, and you woodland Fauns, lamented him in every grove on broken reeds.'[41]

illum et cognatae stagna indignantia Lernae,
floribus et vernis assuetae spargere Nymphae,
et Nemees reptatus ager, lucosque per omnes
silvicolae fracta gemuistis harundine Fauni.
   (5.579–82)

As for the nymphs, they reappear when the preparations for the child's funeral require the felling of the forest.

This scene of wood-felling had a long epic history, from the felling of forests on Mount Ida for Patroclus' funeral in *Iliad* 23.114–20 through a key scene in Ennius' *Annales* 6 (175–9 Skutsch), preserved by Macrobius (*Sat.* 6.2.27) for comparison with Virgil's scenes of felling timber for the pyre of Misenus in *Aen.* 6.179–82 and the Latin dead of 11.135–8. But Statius seems to be the first to involve the rural demigods in the devastation. Not surprisingly, the modernizing Lucan is explicit that no familiar gods or spirits dwell in the Massilian grove, which is felled on Caesar's orders to provide his siegeworks (3.399–425).

The *nemorum ruina* (6.85) is humanized from the beginning. Before rehearsing the range of trees felled, Statius inserts his own lament.

Immediately the wood is laid low, its ancient locks unfelled by steel: no wood more lavish in shade had reared its head above the stars between the Argive wilderness and those of Lycaeus. It stands sacred with the godhead of antiquity, and is said not only to have surpassed human ancestors, in its venerable age, but even to have outlived the bands of Nymphs and Fauns. Now a pitiable destruction threatened the grove. The wild beast fled and birds fled from nests still warm (driven by fear).

sternitur extemplo veteres incaedua ferro
silva comas, largae qua non opulentior umbrae
Argolicos inter saltusque educta Lycaeos
extulerat super astra caput: stat sacra senectae
numine, nec solos hominum transgressa veterno
fertur avos, Nymphas etiam mutasse superstes
Faunorumque greges. aderat miserabile luco

excidium: fugere ferae, nidosque tepentes
absiliunt (metus urget) aves.
   (6.90–8)

Now (6.110) the country gods leave their beloved haunts of leisure weeping, hoary Pales and Silvanus, protector of shade,[42] and
the half-divine creature (Faunus), as the wood groans with their
departure, and the Nymphs, embracing the trees, will not let go.

> linquunt flentes dilecta locorum
> otia cana Pales Silvanusque arbiter umbrae
> semideumque pecus: migrantibus adgemit illis
> silva, nec amplexae dimittunt robora Nymphae.
>   (6.110–13)

Statius even amplifies the tragic scene further by a preliminary
comparison with the natural disaster of a hurricane on Ismara or
a firestorm from the southern wind (107–10). Finally, the flight of
the country gods is compared with the ultimate human disaster,
the fall of a great city abandoned to plunder, suffering worse violence than during the preceding war.

While the collective life of the nymphs seems to be confined
to the Nemean interlude, where they serve almost as a tragic
chorus, book 9 involves the personal loss of an individual nymph,
Ismenis (or is this simply her filiation as daughter of river
Ismenus?), when her child by Faunus, Crenaeus (or fountain-
born), born and bred in his grandfather's trusted waters (9.319–22),
is killed by Hippomedon. Crenaeus has a local loyalty to Thebes
and to his family, and he challenges Hippomedon for having entered Ismenus' waters (342–3, *sacrum amnem, sacrum (et miser
experiere!) deumque / altrices inrumpis aquas*, 'you are intruding
on a sacred river, sacred, I say, and waters that have nourished the
gods'). When he is killed at the first blow, the waters themselves
shudder at the abomination (347, *horruit unda nefas*), and Statius
follows his last cry to his mother with the nymph's desperate
search for her son's body, until she reaches the rearing waves at
the river's mouth, and 'the Nereids take pity and waft the corpse
from the control of the high breakers into the mother's arms.'

possessum donec iam fluctibus altis
Nereidum miserata cohors ad pectora matris
impulit.
  (9.371–3)

Ismenis' lament differs from so many mothers' laments in two
ways: in her anger that an immortal grandfather and two half-
divine parents (*semidei parentes*) could not protect the boy, and
in her regretful pride that 'his safety had made her a greater goddess and queen among nymphs because the other nymphs clustered around her home begging to serve him.'

  quo sospite maior
diva et nympharum longe regina ferebar.
heu ubinam ille frequens modo circa limina matris
ambitus orantesque tibi servire Napaeae?
  (9.383–6)

Her angry demand that her father avenge his grandchild's death
provokes Ismenus to action, and provides opportunity for a vivid
description of the river-god, with no details omitted:

He raises his neck rough with moss and hair weighted with frost; he lets
go the full-grown pine which falls from his hand, and the dropped urn
rolls away. The woods and lesser streams feel wonder as he projects his
face over the banks, shaggy with age-old mud. So great he is when he
rises from his pool. He lifts his foaming head and his breast dripping with
streams from his blue beard in a resounding splash.

  levat aspera musco
colla, gravemque gelu crinem, ceciditque soluta
pinus adulta manu dimissaque volvitur urna.
illum per ripas annoso scrupea limo
ora exsertantem silvae fluviique minores
mirantur; tantus tumido de gurgite surgit
spumosum attollens apicem lapsuque sonoro
pectora caeruleae rivis manantia barbae.
  (9.408–15)

Only the garland of reeds is missing from the usual image, and it is compensated for by the slightly incongruous combination of pine staff and urn. But Statius is building up to a full-scale battle of man and river-god to match that of Achilles and Scamander. Like Scamander Ismenus is angry that his waters are choked by corpses and cannot reach the sea. But at his signal Cithaeron swells his waters with winter snows and Asopus pours in his currents, while like a diver (*scrutator*) Ismenus scoops up additional waters from the depths of earth and pools and marshes (447–53). Ismenus dominates for over a hundred lines (404–521), overcoming a series of diversions (the tree, Hippomedon's protest, and Juno's intervention), until Jupiter himself turns his attention to Thebes, and the rivers subside at the sight of his nod (521, *viso sederunt flumina nutu*). It seems as though Statius has constructed the whole tale both to provide a counterpart of Achilles' battle and to create a semi-divine equivalent of the (approaching) death of young Parthenopaeus.

Here, as in the Nemean episode of books 4 and 6, Statius' narrative combines pictorial vividness with sentiment. Within these episodes I see no difference of tone or technique between Statius' epic and the narrative moments of his descriptive landscape poetry. Both take the reality of our demigods to the edge of fantasy and beyond.

But in illustrating how Statius reanimated the *di agrestes* to populate and enliven his villa poems, I have inevitably played down other aspects of these descriptive encomia, by passing over many allusions to the Olympians, who symbolized power, and the gods and muses who patronized poetry. Now that so many scholars have discovered the complex charms of this poetry, I feel excused for limiting my account. Instead let me close with a great scholar and poet who so loved Statius' *Silvae* that he composed *Silvae* of his own. When Politian came to gather the four poems of his *Silvae*, he named the third poem, on the life and art of Homer, *Ambra*, after the villa of his Medici patron, and both began and ended the poem with a vivid image of the villa's presiding nymph, to whom he is offering his verse as a floral tribute.[43]

Notes

Chapter One

1 On Marsyas, and the role of his statue by the Comitium and in the fora of Roman colonies, see Wiseman 1988/1994. Servius on *Aen.* 3.359 maintains that augurs were sent from Phrygia by King Marsyas in the reign of Faunus to teach the Italians the science of augury.

2 As Borgeaud notes (1979/1988, 93), Lucretius is thinking of Pan, since 'Faunus is no musician.'

3 The J.L Myres lecture for 1964, delivered by B. Ward-Perkins as director of the British School at Rome.

4 The following books have proved useful: Potter 1979; Frayn 1979; Frayn 1984; Barker et al. 1978; Barker 1981.

5 This passage (D.H. 1.38) continues from the praises of Italy cited in my preface.

6 Tibullus reverses this; see 2.5, quoted below.

7 *Inter duos lucos*: cf. Cic. *Att.* 4.3.4, reporting of the election man-oeuvrings of 56, where, however, Shackleton Bailey ad loc. reads simply *inter lucos*.

8 See Cic. *Att.* 4.3.4 and *De Div.* 2.40.

9 On Faunus, see *Neue-Pauly* IV, s.v. 441–2 (Fritz Graf), and *Kleine-Pauly* II, s.v. 521–2 (Werner Eisenhut), as well as the older hand-books *RKR* and *RRG*. For the derivation of his name from *favere* and/or *for, fari*, and *fata*, see O'Hara 1993, 187 and 254; and chap. 2 below.

10 A reader for the press has suggested that this temple (outside the ritual Pomerium, reserved for Rome's original gods) may not have

been the first shrine erected to Faunus. I would note that the source of the fine money in illicit grazing may have dictated the aediles' choice to honour Faunus as god of the grasslands and of animal fertility.

11 Cf. Varro *LL* 7.26–7 for the form *Casmenae*; he quotes a line from Ennius, *musas quas memorant nosces nos esse Camenas* (*Ann.* fr. 2 V?), and from an unknown *carmen Priami*: *veteres Camenas cascam rem volo profarier*. But the derivation is complex; see the discussion in Habinek 2005.

12 Varro *LL* 5.71: *Ab aquae lapsu lubrica lympha. Lympha Iuturna quae iuvaret ... a fontibus et fluminibus ac ceteris aquis dei, ut Tiberinus a Tiberi et ab lacu Velini Velinia, et Lymphae Commotiles ad lacum cutiliensem a commotu, quod ibi insula in aqua commovetur.* On Juturna's name and associations, see p. 10; and on *lymphae,* n16 below.

13 Compare Cicero's discussion of Faunus in *De Natura Deorum,* cited p. 18 below.

14 On this, see Wiseman 1988/1994.

15 Larson 2001 does not, perhaps, contain radical new material, but it offers a substantial alternative in English to Hans Herter's authoritative article 'Nymphen' in *Kleine-Pauly* IV, 207–15.

16 Where the Greek word *nymphe* is affected by its use for brides and other young women seen as beddable, the Latin word overlapped with *lympha,* water, a name sometimes applied directly to them: in Varro *RR* 1.1.6, Lympha is the goddess identified with water (for irrigation), since all agriculture is dry and wretched without *Lympha*; again at 3.17.2 we are told freshwater fish pools are profitable when *lymphae,* the nymphs/waters, supply (*ministrant,* a word proper to human service) water for the fish. Another indication of the equation *nympha=lympha* is that in Italy a man believed to be possessed by nymphs (Greek *nympholeptos*) is called *lymphaticus.*

17 Cited from *AE* 1902, 185: EFFIGIEM CA[RAE MIHI CON]IUGIS ALBULA L[YMPHA]. / VOLTUS TU DEA [NUNC ACCIPE VIRGINEOS] / QUOS EGO DESCRIP[SI RA]RO FULGENTE M[ETALLO] / ET COMPOS VOTI N[UMI]NIS AUXILIO / [FONTI]BUS ECCE TUIS POSUI LAETUSQUE SALUTE / CO[NIUGIS] ... NYMPH[.] I owe this reference to Dr Tana Allen, who is writing a book-length treatment of Italian spas and baths.

18 DEFIXIONUM TABELLAE QUOTQUOT INNOTUERUNT (Au-
dollent 1904, #129). Essentially curses were simply the inversion of
vows; hence Tibullus (2.6.54) includes, among his vows for his girl
to relent towards him, curses (dirae) on the old bawd who has
alienated her from him.

19 Cf. Varro LL 6.22, Fontanalia a fonte quod is dies feriae eius; ab eo
tum et in fontes coronas iaciunt et puteos coronant.

20 See Cic. Leg. 2.56, 'The tradition is that our king Numa was buried
in a tomb not far from the altar of Fons' (haud procul a Fontis ara).
For other Fontes in Rome, see Richardson 1992, s.v. fons.

21 See Gerhard Radke, Kleine-Pauly V, s.v. Tiberis, 813–14, and add to
the Augustan references Servius on Aen. 3.500, Thybrim vicinaque
Thybridis arva, who lists Tiberis, Thybris, Tiberinus, the sacred
name, and the archaic name Albula.

22 = 26 Skutsch, who assigns the line to Ilia.

23 I owe this reference to Eden's commentary on Aeneid 8.

24 Compare Pythagoras' lecture in Ovid Met. 15.308–36, and Pliny NH.

25 Recent scholarship points in opposite directions. While Wiseman
(n28 below) plausibly suggests identifying certain wild and shaggy
figures in C4–C3 Etruscan bronze mirrors as Faunus, iconographers
such as Pierre Pouthier and Pierre Rouillard (1986) suggest that
Faunus was a very ancient god, eclipsed because he had been
absorbed into Rome's foundation legend. In contrast, Catherine
Johns (1986) discusses the late fourth century CE treasure recently
found at Thetford in Norfolk, which includes a bronze statuette
crowned with branches and carrying an uprooted tree, and associated
ritual spoons labelled DEI FAUNI or DEI FAU followed by an
abridged name of a Celtic god. Other iconographic elements seem to
associate this deity with Bacchic cult. It would appear, then, that
despite a lack of epigraphic record the god's cult survived informally
to resurface centuries later.

26 Cf. Dorcey 1992, and appendix to chap. 1 here.

27 Cf. Wiseman 1995b, 77–88.

28 See the plates illustrating the article cited in n25, one associating
this 'wild man' with the capture of the prophet Cacu, another
showing the discovery of the twins by Faustulus, and others showing
the wild man rousing a drunken bridegroom.

29 This version of Aeneas' vision is replaced by Tiberinus and a stationary sow in *Aeneid* 8. It seems that the Augustans preferred to leave
such warnings anonymous: the ominous prophetic voices heard at
Rome on the verge of civil war between Caesar and Pompey in *Georg.*
1.476–7 and Lucan *BC* 1.569–70 are not attributed to any god.

30 This is assuming the manuscripts of Pliny *NH* 15.77 correctly
reproduce the date, given as equivalent to 404 BCE.

31 Compare the grove of Silvanus beneath the Capitoline hill in Prop.
4.4.3–6: 'there was a fertile grove buried in an ivy-clad grotto, and
many trees whispered to the natural waters – this was the branchy
home of Silvanus, whither the sweet pan pipe invited the flocks to
drink after the heat,' *lucus erat felix hederoso conditus antro /
multaque nativis obstrepit arbor aquis. / Silvani ramosa domus,
quo dulcis ab aestu / fistula poturas ire iubebat oves.*

32 Note that when it comes to thinning a grove for the Lucaria, Cato
prescribes an alternative form of prayer for forgiveness to any
unknown god inhabiting the grove: *si deus, si dea es quoium illud
sacrum est* (*Agr.* 139).

33 For Horace's preference for the country, compare his fable of the
town and country mouse (*Sat.* 2.6), or the letters contrasting his
preference with Aristius Fuscus' love of the town (*Ep.* 1.10.1–2) or
his bailiff's hankering for city pleasures (*Ep.* 1.14.10–11).

34 Cf. [Tib.] 3.14: *invisus natalis adest, qui rure molesto et sine
Cerintho tristis agendus erit,* 'my hateful birthday is here, which I
much pass in the tiresome country and without Cerinthus.' Propertius too thinks of the country only because his Cynthia has withdrawn there (2.19). Because she is there he can contemplate hunting,
but even by the lovely Clitumnus he will be happy only because he
can hope she will be kept away from rival admirers.

35 We need not take too literally the elegist's boast of personal spade
work (1.1.8); he is more likely to spend his time, like Propertius in
2.19.17f., in hunting not farming.

36 Tibullus may well be thinking of the *cippi*, boundary markers identified
with the divinity Terminus; certainly his language is echoed by Ovid's
appeal to Terminus on the day of his festival (*Fasti* 2.641–2).

37 Priapus will have a chapter to himself (chap. 5 below).

38 For the Parilia, besides Tib. 2.5.87–90, see Prop. 4.1.19–20 and
4.4.73–8; Varro *LL* 6.15; and Ovid *Fasti* 4.721f., discussed below.

39 O'Hara 1993, 275, notes Tibullus' 'systematic etymologizing' of Pan, Pales, Palatia, and *pasco, pastor* in this dense passage. But the loving description of the pan pipe surely depends on Virgil's third *Eclogue*; see chap. 2 on *Eclogues* 2 and 3.

40 In fact Propertius, who pays little attention to other country gods, speaks in 4.4.3–6 of a grove of Silvanus beneath the Arx (citadel) of the Capitoline.

41 Tibullus is treating the gods as cultural heroes and bringers of civilization; he offers a similar cletic hymn in 1.7 to the river Nile (23–8), identified first with Osiris (29–38), then Bacchus (39–42), and then again Osiris (43–8).

42 Nisbet and Hubbard ad loc., who compare *Ep.* 1.19.3–4: *ut male sanos / adscripsit Liber Faunis Satyrisque poetas*, 'Bacchus enrolled poets as crazy fellows with Fauns and Satyrs.'

43 Horsfall 1997 argues that the poet Calpurnius Siculus is aiming at the effect of writing in the time of Nero; he provides a full bibliography of the controversy.

44 This is my version. *CIL* #12.103=*Carmina Latina Epigraphica* 19, Courtney 1995, #149.

45 *CIL* 9.3375=*Carmina Latina Epigraphica* 250, Courtney 1995, #150, from Aufinum (Capestrano), self-dated to 156 CE. The identification of the dedicator depends on a supplement, which Courtney rejects in favour of a less impressive person; in his reading, this is Athenio, freedman of Annius Lateranus, superintendent with the steward Eutyches.

46 Virgil *Ecl.* 3.25–6, *fistula cera / vincta* (or *iuncta*).

47 *Nitidis argenteus undis;* this is Narcissus' pool in Ovid *Met.* 3.407.

48 From Virgil *Georg.* 1.20.

49 Again, my translation.

50 Many Renaissance manuscripts of Virgil prefaced the first book of the *Aeneid* with four pseudo-autobiographical lines beginning *ille ego qui.*

51 *Laeti bene gestis corpora rebus / procurate viri ... et ... sperate parari.*

Chapter Two

1 Aristaeus is not just a woodsman; he also pastures three hundred snow-white oxen on Ceos, and will return in book 4 as a beekeeper.

2 See Clausen ad loc.

3 Clausen ad loc. cites Theocritus 4.58–61; and 5.41–3, 87 and 116–17.

4 Compare Servius Auctus on 5.56 and Clausen, p. 152n4; the idea may find support in the supposed quotation from Menalcas at *Ecl.* 9.47: 'Lo! the star of Venus-born Caesar has gone forth,' *ecce Dionaei processit Caesaris astrum.*

5 A strange choice, since these liquids were the *inferiae* normally offered to the dead.

6 We know from Wiseman 1988/1994 that Romans were accustomed to see Satyr dancers in processions. Notice that although Satyrs do not participate in the action of these poems, *Eclogues* 6 speaks vividly of the Fauni, dancing along with the wild creatures (6.27).

7 The epithet *miti* is odd. This is surely wine, but Macrobius (*Sat.* 3.11) claims Virgil was in error, since wine was never offered to Ceres; he suggests the phrase is a reference to *mulsum* (sweetened grape juice). Mynors ad. loc. refutes him, citing Cato *Agr.* 134 as evidence for wine offered to Ceres. I have kept the ambiguity in translation.

8 Cf. *cuncta ... pubes agrestis* (343) and *omnis chorus ... et socii ... ovantes* (346–7), nicely discreet on whether these participants are free labourers and neighbours or include farm slaves.

9 Note that here as at *Georg.* 1.17–18, Pan is glossed as Faunus by the epithet *favens* (cf. O'Hara 1993, 254–5). The god's name is variously derived from *favere* and *for, fari, fata;* hence *fatidici genitoris* in *Aen.* 7.82.

10 The Thessalian valley of Tempe had become so famed at Rome that its name was adopted to represent any idyllic landscape, natural or artificial.

11 Gransden 1976, intro., 20, notes, 'Virgil associates this instinct (*religio*) with the indigenous inhabitants and animistic local deities of Italy: it is a "religion of place," a sense of awe, associated with the landscape, as intense in his poetry as it is in Wordsworth's.' But Evander's people are not indigenous, nor is Aeneas. With *Aen.* 8.350–1, *hoc nemus, hunc ... collem ... habitat deus,* compare Ovid's description of the grove where Numa worships: *numen inest* (*Fasti* 3.296).

12 *In unoquoque virorum bonorum quis deus incertumst, habitat deus. Si tibi occurrerit vetustis arboribus et solitam altitudinem egressis*

frequens lucus et conspectum caeli ramorum aliorum alios prote-
gentium umbra submovens, illa proceritas silvae et secretum loci
et admiratio umbrae in aperto tam densae atque continuae fidem
tibi numinis facit. si quis specus saxis penitus exesis montem
suspenderit, non manu factus, sed naturalibus causis in tantam
laxitatem excavatus, animum tuum quadam religionis suspicione
percutiet. Magnorum fluminum capita veneramur; subita ex abdito
vasti amnis eruptio aras habet. coluntur aquarum calentium fontes,
et stagna quaedam vel opacitas vel immensa altitudo sacravit.
(*Ep. Mor.* 41.2–3).

13 Cato *Origines* fr. 58, *HRR*.
14 See Thomas 1988, 261–74; and on restrictions operating in sacred
 groves, Bodel 1986/1994. Cato *Agr.* 139 reports a prayer to be offered
 to the unidentified god when clearing a grove, that is, any grove not
 known to be sacred to a specific god.
15 *Aen.* 2.781–4, *et terram Hesperiam venies ubi Lydius arva / inter*
 opima virum leni fluit agmine Thybris. / illic res laetae regnumque
 et regia coniunx / parta tibi.
16 See Horsfall ad loc.
17 *Aeneid* 7.691, with Horsfall, pp. 691–705n; cf. Oebalus, 7.734,
 with Horsfall, pp. 733–43n; and Halaesus, 7.723, with Horsfall,
 pp. 723–32n.
18 On these details, see Gransden 1976 on *Aen.* 8.328–9.
19 Latinus can wear the sun crown at 12.164 because the Sun, grandfather of Circe, is his great-grandfather (*avus,* taken loosely). As wife
 of Picus, Circe is mother of Faunus. Moorton does not explain the
 presence of Italus and Sabinus, but they can either be seen as
 collateral ancestors or included on the same principle as the non-
 Julians in Augustus' forum.
20 Although Palmer 1970, 81, quotes evidence for an incubation shrine
 at Tor Tignosa, Albunea here is generally identified with Zolfatara
 near Ardea, not the better-known Albunea near Tibur. As we shall
 see, the abundance of sulphurous springs in the region of Rome leads
 to a number of names like Albula ('White river' – the Tiber) and
 Aquae Albulae ('Whitewater').
21 *est locus Italiae medio sub montibus altis / ... Amsancti valles;*
 densis hunc frondibus atrum / urget utrimque latus nemoris,
 medioque fragosus / dat sonitum saxis et torto vertice torrens. /

*Hic specus horrendum et saevi spiracula Ditis / monstrantur,
ruptoque ingens Acherunte vorago / pestiferas aperit fauces, quis
condita Erinys / ... terras caelumque levabat,* 'There is a place in
the heart of Italy beneath the lofty mountains, the valleys of
Amsanctus. On either side the dark flank of a forest presses upon
this spot with its thick foliage, and in the midst a crashing torrent
resounds with rocks and twisted eddies. Here a dread cavern and the
breathing holes of savage Dis are to be seen, and a vast chasm opens
its poisonous jaws where Acheron is split open, into which the
Erinys plunged, relieving earth and heaven.'

22 Horace's vow of his clothes to the deity of the sea in *Odes* 1.5.13,
whether read as *deo* (male Neptune) or *deae* (female Venus), is
metaphorical, an act of thanks for his rescue from the shipwreck of
love. See also n48 below.

23 On this episode, see Thomas 1988, 261–74.

24 In this he is following Livy 1.5.2. See Wiseman 1995a, appendix, for
other testimonia.

25 As mentioned in my preface, I owe much in this chapter to the early
chapters of Larson 2001.

26 These nymphs call themselves heroic protectors of Libya (*Heroissai
Libyes timeoroi*) and claim to have acted as nurses tending the
newborn Athena at Tritonis.

27 Cf. Aigle's speech, Apoll. 4.1432–49.

28 See McDonough 2002, 9–19, citing Servius on *Aen* 7.697: 'Hercules,
returning from Spain, is said to have planted the iron bar with which
he trained, and when it was planted in the earth and could not be
carried away by any man, he removed it on request, and a vast
quanity of water followed, which formed the Ciminian lake,'
*defixisse dicitur vectem ferreum quo exercebatur. qui cum terrae
esset adfixus et a nullo potuisset auferri, eum rogatus sustulit, unde
immensa vis aquae secuta est, quae Ciminum lacum fecit.*

29 Cf. Anchises' question at *Hom. Hymn Aph.*, 185–90, 'Are you
Artemis, or Leto, or Aphrodite, Themis, or Athene, or one of the
Graces or the nymphs?' Aphrodite tells him after their intercourse to
inform the Trojans that his son is the child of a nymph (284–5).

30 I make this suggestion because one reason why the marriage is
vitiated and doomed may be that Dido's foreignness (like that of her
model, Cleopatra) is understood to disqualify her for Roman marriage.

31 For the temple of Tellus, see Richardson 1992, s.v. Tellus: *aedes*,
378–9; for Spurius Cassius, see Val. Max. 6.3.1b; and Pliny *NH* 34.15
and 30. For Tellus as giver of life, cf. Lucr. 1.7–8 (*tibi suavis daedala
Tellus / summittit flores*), 193, 228, and 873; 2.1156; 5.234, 790, 837,
917, 926, and 942; and 6.790; Virgil *Ecl.* 4.18–20 and 39; *Georg.* 1.7–8
and 27; 2.173 (*magna parens frugum, Saturnia Tellus*), 423, and 460;
and cf. *volentia rura*, 2.500.

32 'those who plough your lands, Tiberinus, and the sacred shore of
Numicus, and work the Rutilian hills with the ploughshare,' *qui
saltus, Tiberine, tuos sacrumque Numici / litus arant, Rutulosque
exercent vomere colles.*

33 See Rehm 1932, 40–9, 50–5.

34 On these wordplays, see O' Hara 1993, 68, 108, 186, 226, and 240.

35 While Virgil has invented the metamorphosis, he has taken two
visual elements from Apollonius' account of the Nereids bringing
help to Thetis, as Nelis 2001, xx–xxx, shows: the simile comparing
the nymphs to dolphins, and the plunge of the ships before their
transformation.

36 *Aen.* 11.852–3, *hic dea se primum rapido pulcherrima nisu / sistit*;
and 867, *Opis ad aetherium pennis aufertur Olympum.*

37 Diana has already declared that she herself will protect Camilla's
body from violation.

38 *Aen.* 8.26, *nox erat et terras animalia fessa per omnis*, differing only
in the last two feet from *Aen.* 3.147, *animalia somnus habebat.*

39 On this, see Momigliano 1966, 609–39; Jenkyns 1998, 401f.; and
Cairns 2006a.

40 There is an Etruscan name Thebris; cf. Varro *LL* 5.30 (note also
Servius on *Aen.* 8.330): 'The account of the name of the Tiber is
ambiguous. For both Etruria and Latium believe the name is theirs,
since there were those who said it was named after Thebris, king of
the Veientines, and so was first Thebris. Others have reported in
writing that the Tiberis was called Albula, an ancient Latin name,
and later changed because of Tiberinus king of the Latins, because
he drowned there: for this, as they say, is his tomb,' *De Tiberis
nomine anceps historia. Nam et suum Etruria et Latium suum esse
credit, quod fuerunt qui ab Thebri vicino regulo Veientum dixerint
appellatum, primo Thebrim. Sunt qui Tiberim priscum nomen
Latinum Albulam vocitatum litteris tradiderint, posterius propter*

Tiberinum regem Latinorum mutatum, quod ibi interierit: nam hoc eius ut tradunt sepulchrum. But the Sibylline oracle preserved in Zosimus 2.6, *en pedio para Thubridos apleton hudor,* shows that Hellenistic learning had already adopted the 'Etruscan' explanation.

41 See Nelis 2001, 335–7.

42 Accius, *Medea sive Argonautae* (frr. 1, 2, and 3, ed. Dangel), cited by Cicero *ND* 2.89 as the speech of a shepherd marvelling at this first of all ships.

43 Cf. Ovid *Fasti* 1.499–508 for Carmenta on shipboard, and 233–4 for the coming of Saturn by ship, Janus' answer to Ovid's request for an explanation of the ship on early Roman coinage (229–30).

44 On the mysterious identity of Virbius (reborn Hippolytus, or his son?) and his protection by Egeria in Diana's grove at Aricia, see Green 2007, chap. 9.

45 9.583–5: 'whom his distinguished father Arcens had sent, reared in his mother's groves around the streams of Simaethus, where stands the rich and propitious altar of Palicus,' *insignis facie genitor quem miserat Arcens, / eductum matris lucis, Simaethia circum / flumina, pinguis ubi et placabilis ara Palici*; and 673–4: 'whom woodland Iaira had reared in the grove of Jupiter,' *quos Iovis eduxit luco silvestris Iaira.*

46 Turnus is reported as son of the nymph Venilia, and here of Pilumnus, but in 10.76 Pilumnus is his *avus* and at 10.619 his *quartus pater,* or great-grandfather.

47 For the ritual meaning of Greek *dechesthai*, Latin *accipere, excipere,* see Nock 1972. But our scene may be the odd man out, since most of Nock's examples are of nymphs or deities accepting people who meet their death by drowning, whereas Turnus, like Horatius Cocles, is saved by the river.

48 Compare n22 above, and Hor. *Odès* 1.5.13–16: 'the sacred wall shows with a votive tablet that I hung up my drenched clothing to the powerful deity of the sea,' *me tabula sacer / votiva paries indicat uvida / suspendisse potenti / vestimenta maris deo.*

Chapter Three

1 'It is Virgil's delight to be able to tell of the Actian shores of our guardian Phoebus and gallant Caesar's ships, Virgil who now is rousing the warfare of Trojan Aeneas, and walls raised on Lavinia's

shores. Give way, ye Roman writers, and give way Greeks: something greater than the Iliad is coming to birth,' *Actia Vergilium custodis litora Phoebi, / Caesaris et fortis dicere posse ratis, / qui nunc Aeneae Troiani suscitat arma, / iactaque Lavinis moenia litoribus. / Cedite Romani scriptores, cedite Grai! / nescioquid maius nascitur Iliade.* An alternative interpretation, however, reads his words as an indication that Propertius did not know the actual focus of the *Aeneid* and expected it to be a contemporary encomiastic epic honouring Actium.

2 Both legends had been told by Livy: Tarpeia at 1.11.6–9; the story of Hercules and Cacus by both Livy (in a flashback before his foundation narrative, 1.7.3–15) and Virgil (*Aen.* 8.184–279). The Capitoline hill had two summits. Before the construction of the temple of Jupiter Optimus Maximus, it was known for the citadel (*arx*) on the other summit (now S. Maria Aracoeli), and Tarpeia's name was given to the rock from which traitors were thrown; but later the adjective Tarpeius could refer to the entire Capitoline including the temple of Jupiter.

3 See Fantham 1997; also Hubbard 1974 and Hutchinson 2006.

4 On Verrius and the *Fasti Praenestini*, see Kaster 1992, chap.17, on Verrius; and Fantham 1998, intro., 29–30 and 40.

5 Writing from exile to Augustus in *Tristia* 2.560, he will refer to this end-date as 'up to your times,' *in … tua tempora.*

6 On the Ovidian *Fasti*, see Scheid 1992.

7 The story of Terminus' refusal to be moved, interpreted by Roman augury as a presage of the durability of Rome's future empire, was told by Livy at 1.55.3–6. On the shrine of Terminus, see Boyle 2003, 108–9.

8 Cf. *Fasti* 1.126: 'Jupiter himself comes and goes through my services,' *it redit officio Jupiter ipse meo*, 202, 236, 293. See also Labate 2005.

9 Ovid's Saturn is closely modelled on Virgil's presentation in *Aeneid* 8. Besides Steven Green's new commentary on *Fasti* 1 (Green 2004, 113–15), see, on Virgil and Callimachus, George 1974, 38,83, and 120; Eden's commentary on *Aeneid* 8, pp. 105–6; and, on the scanty pre-Virgilian tradition on Saturn, Schiebe 1986, 43–60. Parker 1997 nicely sums up the transformation of Greek Kronos into a kinder, gentler – indeed civilizing – Saturn.

10 *Maiestas convenit ipsa deo* (1.224) is deliberately ambiguous; the majesty of the golden temple on the Capitol fits both Jupiter, the god to whom it is dedicated, and its dedicator, who can be alluded to as divine.

11 Green 2004 on 1.241–2 notes the Virgilian *stringere* as precedent for *radit*, and the substitution of *harenosi* here for the frequent and evocative *flavus*.

12 Cf. *Aen.* 8.357–8, *hanc Ianus pater, hanc Saturnus condidit arcem: / Ianiculum huic, illi fuerat Saturnia nomen.* Evander's Saturnian *arx* has to be the other summit of the Capitoline hill, the one still called *arx* by Virgil's contemporaries. But the implication that the hills had been fortified (*disiectis oppida muris*) fits Evander's narrative, whereas Janus is reporting a more ancient phase of settlement. Although I have taken *colui* in line 241 literally, of arable tilling, the verb may mean little more than 'inhabit.'

13 Despite the difference in vowel quantity, Romans associated *Saturnus* (long –a) with *serere, sator* (short –a). On the role of Saturn before Virgil, see the references quoted in n9 above.

14 This is the form of her name at *Fasti* 1.499 and thereafter, as also in *Aen.* 8.336, 339, etc., but she is also called *Carmenta* elsewhere.

15 1.502, *sparsas per loca sola casas* = *Aen.* 8.98–9, *rare domorum / tecta.*

16 Here Alton, Wormell, and Courtney read *nemorum silvae,* citing *Cul.* 382; I have retained *nymphae.*

17 Compare the last stage of Aesculapius' voyage from Antium to Rome, in *Met.* 15.719–44.

18 Cf. Cicero *ND* 3.39; and on the whole episode, Littlewood 2006 ad loc.

19 It is unfortunate that Boyle 2003 does not have a separate section on the river.

20 See Littlewood 2006 ad loc.

21 Is there any parallel for 5.626, *fatidici ... Iovis*?

22 With Ovid's *harundifer,* cf. *Aen.* 8.34, *crines umbrosa tegebat harundo.* Virgil offers no model for *rauca ... ora.*

23 Cf. *Aen.* 1.167, *vivoque sedilia saxo,* with *Fasti* 5.661–2, *vivo rorantia saxo / antra.*

24 This reverses logic, since the king's name, Tiberinus, clearly derives from Tiberis.

25 On the Lupercal at the foot of the Palatine beneath Augustus' residence, see Boyle 2003, 126–7. A frescoed grotto apparently from the early imperial period has recently been excavated under the Palatine hill, and tentatively identified with an imperial reconstruction of the Lupercal.

26 On the location of the Numicus, see Horsfall's commentary on
Aeneid 7.797.

27 *Litus adit Laurens, ubi tectus harundine serpit / in freta flumineis
vicina Numicius undis.* Here Ovid has taken over Virgil's relocation
of the Numicius, from its position as a small stream near Lavinium,
to enter the mouth of the Tiber.

28 On the Lotis episode, see Fantham 1983, 185–216.

29 *Te quoque lux eadem, Turni soror, aede recepit, / hic ubi virginea Campus obitur aqua.* She is mentioned as pursued by Jupiter in 2.585–8.

30 For raped nymphs who do not bear children but are given privileges,
compare Juturna, *Aen.* 12.143–4, 878, and Caenis, *Met.* 12.195–207.

31 On Crane/Carna, see McDonough 1997.

32 See Boyle 2003, 84–7.

33 Livy makes it clear that the Sabines had already taken the citadel
and the battle was to protect access to the Palatine.

34 Cf. Coarelli 1987, 165f., and bibliography; cited by Horsfall in his
commentary on *Aen.* 7.761–82.

35 Cf. *Fasti* 5.147–58; Boyle 2003, 130–1.

36 On *Camenae*, cf. Varro *LL* 6.75 and 7.26–7: *Casmenarum priscum
vocabulum ita natum ac scriptum est alibi; Carmenae ab eadem
origine sunt declinatae ... quare e Casmena Carmena, e Carmena r
extrito Camena factum,* 'the old name of Casmenae originated and
was written like this elsewhere. Carmenae are derived from the
same origin ... so Carmena arose from Casmena and by pushing out
the r, Camena was formed.' See also *Enc. Virg.* s.v. *Camenae.*

37 Ovid's Egeria, like his Hippolytus, is strongly influenced by *Aen.*
7.761–82, in turn influenced by the lost version of the Hippolytus
resurrection myth in Callimachus' *Aitia.* On Egeria and Numa, see
Littlewood 2002, 179–94; and Fantham 2002, 222–7.

38 On this story, perhaps originating in a mime, see Fantham 1983,
185–216.

39 Compare Varro *LL* 5.50 for the *lucus ... Iunonis Lucinae* on the
Esquiline, and 5.69: *videtur ab Latinis Iuno Lucina dicta vel quod
est e<t> Terra, ut physici dicunt, et lucet; vel quod ab luce eius qua
quis conceptus est usque ad eam, qua partus quis in lucem, <l>una
iuvat, donec mensibus actis producit in lucem, ficta ab iuvando et
luce Iuno Lucina,* 'Juno Lucina seems to have been so-called by the
Latins either because she is also Earth, as the natural philosophers

say, and gives light, or because from the day-light on which someone is conceived to the day when he is brought into the light, she gives aid, until the months having passed she brings him into the daylight, so that Juno Lucina is formed from *Juvare* and *Lux*.'

40 The story of the Ancilia is also told briefly by Livy (1.20) and at greater length in Dionysius (2.70–1) and Plutarch (*Numa* 13). In some other versions of the myth, Numa is accompanied by twelve good men and true – the future Salii – but in Ovid he is alone.

41 See Enn., *Ann.* fr. xlv, 72–91, ed. Skutsch.

42 See Littlewood's (2006) helpful note ad loc. *Vesta eadem est et Terra: subest vigil ignis utrique: / significant sedem terra focusque suam. / Terra pilae similis nullo fulcimine nixa / aëre subiecto tam grave pendet onus,* 'Vesta is the same as Earth (Terra); an ever-watchful fire sustains each of them. The earth and the hearth stand for their dwelling place. The earth is like a ball, resting on no support, is suspended, a heavy burden on the air beneath'; and again 6.299: *stat vi terra sua,* 'the earth is kept stationary by its own force,' as neatly translated by Littlewood.

43 *Lanae* seem to stand in for *infulae,* which are metrically inadmissible except in the nominative singular. See my contribution to *Roman Dress and the Fabrics of Roman Culture*, ed. J. Edmondson and A. Keith, Phoenix Studies in Greek and Roman Social History 1 (Toronto, 2008), pp. 163–6.

44 Cf. *Fasti* 1.685–6 and 688–92, with *Georg.* 1.178–86.

45 We remember the obsessive hairdressing of Ovid's nymphs, whether Doris and her daughters (*Met.* 2.11–13), or Galatea (*Met.* 13.738), or even the dreadful Salmacis (see chap. 4 below); compare Diana's anger with Actaeon at her interrupted toilet (recorded in detail in *Met.* 3.155–93).

46 See the introductory note in Schoonhoven 1992, 221–52; my translation is based on Schoonhoven's text.

47 Statius alludes to the sad poems (*Tristia*) of Ovid's exile in his mini-history of Roman elegy, *Silvae* 1.2.254–5: *nec tristis in ipsis / Naso Tomis,* 'and Naso, not sad even in Tomi.'

Chapter Four

1 Livy 1.20.2 lists only the *Flamen Dialis*; cf. Plutarch *Roman Questions?*

2 We can compare Ovid's welcome to Venus 'in the city of her son Aeneas' at *Fasti* 4.119–24 (also *Amores* 1.8.42; *Ars Amatoria* 1.60), or his justification of Romulus' deification by Mars at *Fasti* 2.481–90.

3 There seem to be two variants of the incident. In Val. Max. 2.10.8 and Seneca *Ep. Mor.* 97.8, the common people did not dare to call for the actresses to strip because of Cato, although he had in fact walked out; instead they restored the games to their ancient dignity. Martial limits himself to mocking Cato's behaviour.

4 Also in Epigram 1.35.8–9. See Howell 1980 ad loc.

5 For her shrine outside the city, see Festus 296L s.v. *Pomonal*; Radke 1965, 257–8; and *RRG* 37, 73–4.

6 See Myers 1994.

7 On the Hesiodic list, see West 1966, 259, a rich source of further information.

8 On the Eridanus, a river in northwest Europe, equated by Apollonius with something like the Rhône but by Virgil with the Po, see West 1966, 261, and the quotations from Virgil discussed below.

9 See Jones 2005.

10 I list here in alphabetical order the exotic rivers of the *Georgics* (excluding Italy, Sicily, and the underworld): Alpheus (3.19; cf. 3.180), Amphrysus (3.2), Ascanius (3.270; not in Ovid *Met.*), Caicus (4.370), Caystros (1.384), Enipeus (4.368), Euphrates (1.509; 4.561), Ganges (2.137), Hebrus (4.463, 524), Hermus (2.137), Hister (2.497), Hydaspes (4.211), Hypanis (4.370), Lycus (4.367), Nilus (3.29; 4.288f.), Peneus (4.317), Phasis (4.367), Strymon (4.508), and Tanais (4.517); but not Simois and Xanthus, which stand for epic history rather than geography, and so appear approximately eight times each in the *Aeneid*.

11 This is problematic. According to West 1985, Thebe was not the beloved of Asopus but his daughter, although Asopus is credited with many daughters. The story of Arachne includes another such seduction, at *Met.* 6.113: (Jupiter) *Asopida luserit ignis.*

12 I have not been able to trace Evanthe in any mythological manual.

13 Hollis 1970 ad loc. offers a clear parallel table of the two texts, and seems sympathetic to the idea that the longer version might have been Ovid's first draft; but Tarrant (xxxiv–xxxv) finds this less acceptable.

14 Hesiod *Works and Days* 737–41 implies the sacrosanctity of rivers by its taboos on their violation. Coleridge seems to have distinguished 'Alph the sacred river' as exceptional in Xanadu!

15 In his commentary ad loc.

16 *Salire* of the flayed Marsyas' veins, *salientia viscera* (6.390); and of Galatea's statue coming to life, *saliunt temptatae pollice venae* (10.289). *Durescere* of the transformed Aglauros (2.831) and of coral hardening in the air (15.417); cf. *indurescere* of victims of Medusa (4.745 and 5.233), of the transformed Lichas (9.219), and of a newly formed hill in Pythagoras' list of marvels (15.306).

17 For plural *adsensibus*, cf. 1.245, but it is a true plural, as many gods assent; in 7.451 the collective people give a singular *adsensus*. *Terrae* may also be a true plural in 15.263.

18 Cf. 9.351–70 (especially 357–8, *materna rigescere sentit / ubera*) and 388–91.

19 Murgia treats this episode incidentally; his discussion is, however, primarily concerned with the secondary version of the text in the Daphne episode.

20 When Ovid picks up the theme at 9.99–100 in order to make the contrast with Nessus, he stresses that Acheloüs is unharmed apart from his broken horn, and can hide it well enough with willow branches or reeds.

21 Ortygia was also the name of Delos, Diana and Apollo's birthplace.

22 This tradition is later than Homer (*Iliad* 11.728) or Pindar (*Nemean Odes* 1.1) and is found in Pausanias 8.54.3 and 5.7.2–3. Such sentimental stories of heroes who drown or hang themselves for unrequited love are typically Hellenistic, as are aitiological stories of rivers named after heroes who drowned from other causes.

23 See chap. 3 for Carna and her protective powers.

24 Nelis 2001, 169, calls Hylas' fate 'a bizarre kind of wedding, one which means death for the boy at the very moment the nymph fulfils her passion'; cf. p. 170, 'the drowning is at once a death and a wedding.'

25 The most detailed examination of the identity or identities of the 'Gallus' addressed by Propertius in book 1 is Cairns 1983. Propertius mentions Gallus as newly dead in his list of elegiac poets at 2.34.91–2; but given Gallus' seniority as an officer on Octavian's Actium campaign whom Octavian then made prefect of Egypt (30 to approximately 27 BCE), it is most unlikely that Propertius was on intimate terms with him and is addressing him here. And the Gallus of 1.20 seems to have sexual preferences different from those of the Gallus who competes for Cynthia in 1.5, 10, and 13. The cognomen is very

common, and there need be no connection, either, with the kinsman Gallus who was killed trying to escape from the siege of Perugia (1.21).

26 Hylas appears in Valerius' narrative at intervals until the crisis of 3.535–44, when Juno (from hatred of Hercules) offers him as a spouse to Dryope, the nymph of Pegae, and sends a stag decoy, which he pursues to her spring. There Hylas falls victim (3.560–4) 'to the sound of the nymph surfacing for kisses. She casts her greedy hands upon him and pulls him down, calling, alas! too late for aid and reiterating the name of his mighty friend. Her strength is aided by his weight as it falls,' *Nil umbra comaeque / turbavit sonis surgentis ad oscula nymphae. / illa avidas iniecta manus heu sera cientem / auxilia et magni referentem numen amici / detrahit; adiutae prono nam pondere vires.*

27 Quite apart from Valerius Flaccus, Hylas is not forgotten two generations later. Statius compares the insistent repetition of Stella's appeals to Violentilla to the Hylas episode (*quantum non clamatus Hylas, Silvae* 1.2.199), whether his primary reference is to Hercules' despairing calls or to the poets who dwell on the theme.

28 On Narcissus, see Forbes Irving 1990, 282, and the commentary on the *Metamorphoses* by Barchiesi and Rosati, II, 205. The story bringing Echo and Narcissus into disastrous contact seems to be Ovid's own invention (Gantz 1993, I, 62); since she is not involved in a metamorphosis, she is absent from the literature of transformation. Ovid most probably omitted her role as one of Pan's sexual victims (I am indebted to the discussion of Pan and his loves in Gantz 1993, I, 110) as too close to that of Syrinx, which he had told in *Met.* 1.689–712. In *Daphnis and Chloe* 3.23, Echo succeeds in rejecting Pan, who has her torn apart by shepherds.

29 The tale of Narcissus forms one of the most powerful examples of the dangerous landscapes illustrated by Segal (1969) from Ovid's poem. See also the comments of Parry (1964) on the dangers of such apparently peaceful *loci amoeni*.

30 Ovid is surely making fun of his readers, and this transformation, far from *vulgatus*, is truly recondite. I have assumed that *nymphe paelicis ira / contulit in saxum* (4.277–8) means 'the nymph, in anger over a mistress, turned him into a rock.'

31 See the discussion by Gagné 2006.

32 This is Isager's translation in Isager and Pedersen 2004, 224, repr. from the *editio princeps* in *ZPE* 123 (1998).

Chapter Five

1 Caesius Bassus (*GL* 6.260) on metre; Victorinus *Ars Grammatica* (*GL* 6.151).

2 A similar combination of (3) glyconics and pherecratean in short stanzas is used by Catullus in his wedding poem 61, in imitation of Greek lyric. The Priapean, with choriambic base, should be not confused with the shorter ithyphallic, – u – x u u u, a Greek form not used in Latin poetry.

3 The most notorious image, sold on thousands of postcards, is the Priapus in the kitchen entrance of the house of the Vettii at Pompeii, depicted wearing a Phrygian cap and tunic, somewhat disarranged by the enormous erection he is apparently weighing in a pair of scales.

4 The source is Callixeinos of Rhodes in his fourth book, *On Alexandria*. On the whole procession, see Rice 1989.

5 See Herter 1932; repr. in *RE* xxii s.v. The quotation is translated from the Latin of *De Priapo*, p. 13: *desiderium vitae rusticae quod mirum quantum saeculum illud tenebat non minus in deliciis esse coepit quam Pan, cui nonnullis rebus non ita dissimilis fuit.*

6 Cf., e.g., *AP* 10.1–2 and 4–9 to or about Priapus, with 10.10–11 to Pan, and 10.12 to Hermes of the wayside; or *AP* 6.21–2 to Priapus, with 11–16 to Pan. The index of dedicatory epigrams in vol. 6 lists about 40 poems to Pan, 10 to Priapus, and about 30 to Hermes.

7 Compare the sleeping Silenus, painted with mulberries by Aegle in *Ecl.* 6.21–2.

8 This suggests either that the statue was Etruscan ('Tyrrhenian') or, perhaps, that Callimachus thought the cult itself Etruscan.

9 The choicest samples from the Greek anthology are discussed by W.H. Parker in his introduction to *Priapea* (Parker 1988). For Leonidas, see *AP* 10.1; 16.236, 261; for Archias, *AP* 10.7, 8; for the dedicatory epigram of Crinagoras, *AP* 6.232.

10 For *tentigo*, 'tumescence,' cf. *Priapea* 23.4–5, *hac tentigine quam videtis in me / rumpatur,* 'may he burst with the tumescence you see in me now.' Also, Hor. *Sat.* 2.118, Martial 7.67.2, Juvenal 6.129; and cf. *tensus, Priapea* 6.5; 27.6; 68.16. Like *prurigo* (sexual itch, Martial

11.73.3, *longa prurigine tentus*), it belongs to a word group denoting an inflamed or unhealthy condition (*impetigo, robigo, vitiligo*).

11 *Ruber hortorum custos*, Tib. 1.1.17; Ovid *Fasti* 6.333 (cf. *Fasti* 1.415, *ruber hortorum decus et tutela Priapus*); *Priapea* 1.5.

12 *hortoque et foro tantum contra invidentium effascinationes dicari videmus in remedia saturica signa*, 'and we see statues of satyrs dedicated in the garden and marketplace only as remedies against the evil spells of the envious.'

13 A recent and welcome rearrangement in the Palazzo dei Conservatori of the Capitoline Museums has devoted four rooms and part of a corridor to the refined statuary of Maecenas' gardens.

14 The same chapter, Pliny *NH* 19.50, quotes from Plautus a reference (not found in the surviving plays) to Venus as protectress of the vegetable garden. Cf. Schilling 1955.

15 Cf. Columella 10, preface 3, 'those parts of the Georgics omitted by Virgil, which, as he himself indicated, he left for later writers to handle.'

16 On rocket (*eruca salax*, Col. 10.372) as an aphrodisiac, see also *Priapea* 46, 47, and 51; Martial 3.75.5, *erucae bulbique salaces*; and Pliny *NH* 19.154–5, as *concitatrix Veneris* it is best mixed in salad with frigid lettuces. While this tangy herb certainly improves the tedium of lettuce, I know of no modern evidence that it has any erotic effect.

17 They may have been composed as exercises in the new poetic style, without intent of fathering them on Virgil.

18 On this story, see Fantham 1983, and most recently, Murgatroyd 2005, 81–8 (with updated bibliography). There is also a passing allusion in *Met.* 9.347–8 to Priapus' pursuit of Lotis, which led to her transformation.

19 The only example known to me of Priapus guarding a woodland is probably a witty fiction. In Martial 8.40, Priapus is *rari nemoris ... custos, ex quo natus es et potes renasci*: by making him the guardian of the copse from which he was originally made, Martial implies that he can easily be replaced, and – since we are told the copse is simply firewood for his master's hearth – explicitly threatens him with becoming firewood if he fails in his guardianship.

20 For anxiety about nakedness, cf. Cic. *Off.* 1.129, on men reluctant to bathe with their sons and sons-in-law; for avoidance in speech even of words whose sound recalled obscenities, see Cicero's discussion with Paetus, *Fam.* 9.22.

21 See the useful collection of O'Connor (1989).

22 See Purcell 1995.

23 In 3.47, Bassus' cart conveys garden produce, cabbages, leeks, lettuces, and beets, with thrushes, a hare, a suckling pig, and eggs, not from the country but to his country place from town.

24 Whether we understand the sixth month to be June or, according to the old Roman reckoning, *sextilis* (August), scholars cannot suggest a particular feast day of Venus appropriate to the display of a phallic procession.

25 The *Choliambus* or 'limping Iambus' of Archilochus and Hipponax, which substitutes a long syllable for the short of the final iamb: u – u – / u – u – / u – – x.

26 In a display of learning, he mentions not just Daedalus but Polycletes, Phradmon, and Ageladas.

27 More briefly evoked in poem 60: 'If you had as many apples as lines of verse, Priapus, you'd be as rich as Alcinoos.'

28 *Sessilesque lactucae:* this variety of lettuce, also called Laconicum (cf. Pliny *NH* 19.125), occupies the same sedes in Martial's list of *(h)olus*, 3.47.8 (see n23 above).

29 Here, Martial's grove is barbarian not so much because it has not been made into a formal garden (like Faustinus' productive Baian estate in 3.58), but because it has been left as natural woodland; given all the allusions to Fauns and Pans, it is also possible that Martial expects his readers to associate the pines with the Phrygian cult of Attis, which Romans tended to consider barbarian.

Chapter Six

1 See especially Purcell 1996, and (arguing for the continued high valuation put on the horticultural and other productivity of villas) Purcell 1995.

2 On Cicero's Amaltheum, see *Att.* 1.16, 15, and 18. It seems to have been modelled on a feature of Atticus' Greek estate; on Cicero's dissatisfaction with the agent, Q. Fabius Gallus, see *Fam* 7.23, and note especially 'but where is there a place for Bacchants in my estate? ... I usually buy statues to adorn a place in my *palaestra* in the fashion of *gymnasia*.'

3 Compare *De Or.* 1.28, where Crassus says pointedly that he believes the plane tree in *Phaedrus* grew as much from Plato's conception as

from the actual stream of the Ilissus. We know that Crassus put a high valuation on trees – as high, indeed, as his esteem for the Greek marble columns he erected in his atrium.

4 I have followed Pliny's version of the story, no doubt taken from his copious notes, rather than that of Val. Max. 9.4.1, in which the house prices are inflated from one to six million sesterces, and the (ten!) Hymettian columns belong to Crassus but the trees (ten again! and of unknown species) to Domitius. Pliny indicates that the trees had been consumed by Nero's great fire in 64, but that he himself had seen the nettle trees in his youth, when the owner of the house was Caecina Largus, and the trees still flourished.

5 Compare Tacitus' account in *Hist.* 3.82 of the advance guard of Vespasian's supporters approaching Rome from the northeast past the *horti* of Sallust.

6 On Pompey's portico and gardens, see Gleason 1994; Kuttner 1999a; and *LTUR* 4 s.v. *porticus Pompeii*.

7 This is the reading in Goold's edition; he adopts Heyworth's *sonitus* (for *sonitus* meaning splash; cf. Prop. 1.20.48, quoted in chap. 4), restoring Heinsius' *lymphis* for *nymphis* and preferring Heinsius' *toto ... orbe* to most editors' *tota ... urbe*. Even if *nymphis* is retained, it would be difficult to understand *crepitantibus* without interpreting *nymphae* as symbolic waters.

8 For plane trees as a symbol of non-productive planting, compare Hor. *Odes* 2.15.4–5, *platanusque caelebs / evincat ulmos*, and Virgil's allusion to *steriles platani*, at *Georg.* 2.70.

9 For the Persian cultivation of plane trees and their spread westwards, see Pliny *NH* 12.6–8. Cicero, who had translated Xenophon's *Economicus* in his youth, makes his Cato quote Xenophon's account of Cyrus' pleasure garden (*Paradeisos, Economicus* 4.20) in *De Senectute* 59. Cato does not name the *proceri arbores*, but they were probably interpreted as plane trees by Roman readers. The famous aria 'ombra mai fu' in Handel's opera *Xerxes* is sung to a plane tree.

10 Cf. Acheloüs' dining room at *Met.* 8.562–4: 'he entered the hall constructed of spongy pumice and heavy tufa; the ground was moist with soft moss, and shells alternating with murex were the ceiling of the lofty roof,' *pumice multicavo nec levibus atria tofis / structa subit; molli tellus erat umida musco, / summa lacunabant alterno murice conchae.*

11 Kuttner 1999a, 343–73 (note especially pp. 364–5, on plane trees).
The quotation is from Kuttner 1999b, 9.

12 I base this selective account on autopsy (in 2003) and Rosanna
Cappelli's report on rooms 114–17 (Cappelli 1999, 2001).

13 On Maro, see Kuttner 1999a, 347, 357.

14 Compare K.S. Myers' comments on Pliny's accounts of his villas,
Myers 2005, 111–29. Grimal (1943) cites an altar to Silvanus in the
garden of the Acilii from *CIL* VI.623, 583, 640, and Martial includes
one in his own estate at Nomentum (*Ep.* 10.92, cited in chap. 5,
p. 158).

15 On Statius' relationship with his patrons, see Hardie 1983, and
Nauta 2002, especially 193–248 and 290–323; Newlands 2002,
119–53, and 154–98; and Myers 2000, 103–38. Betty Rose Nagle
offers an informative introduction in her attractive new translation
of *Silvae* (Nagle 2004).

16 Hubert Cancik 1965, 66–90, was the first to distinguish this visual
aspect of Statian mannerism.

17 Vopiscus, unlike most of Statius' patrons, may have been a senator;
he was certainly of senatorial family. His father had been consul in
60, and the consul of 116 BCE is almost certainly his son (cf. Nauta
2002, 226).

18 Cf. *Silvae* 3.1.61–3: *quamvis ... rus proprium magnique ducis mihi
munere currens / unda domi ... sufficerent*, 'although my own
country estate ... and supply of running water, by the gift of the
great leader ... would be enough.'

19 On Salmacis, see chap. 4, pp. 128–31. Although the nymph(s) go
unnamed in most accounts of the ravishing of Hylas, Valerius
Flaccus names his captor as Dryope. Nothing is known of Cebron's
daughter beyond Statius' allusion.

20 Hardie 1983, 178, was perhaps the first to stress what he calls the
'curious treatment of local deities ... a roll-call of country gods
follows at 70ff.,' and suggest that Statius' allusions to Dryads, Pan
(78), and perhaps the *sorores* of line 80 are a deliberate recollection of
Georg. 2.493–4. But Hardie has not noticed that the allusion to
Vopiscus' poetry delighting the fauns (1.3.99) is surely intended to
echo *Ecl.* 6.27, where Virgil imagines the fauns and wild creatures
playing and dancing to Silenus' song. Thus Statius does not need to

name Virgil in the next line, but simply speaks of 'a greater lyre
[than mine].'

21 As Nisbet 1978, 3, notes, *'iuvenilis'* does not claim that Polla is
young; indeed, as widow of Lucan, who committed forced suicide at
twenty-six in 65 CE, she must have been over fifty in 89 CE. Rather
she is elegant (*nitida*) and well preserved.

22 Statius has combined Phorcus and Cymodoce from *Aen.* 5.823–6
(*et senior Glauci chorus … / Tritonesque citi Phorcique exercitus
omnis*, followed by a list of nymphs with Cymodoce bringing up the
rear) and Galatea, from *Eclogues* 7 and 9, but perhaps best known
from Ovid's episode of Galatea and the Cyclops (*Met.* 13.738–897).
Ovid often depicts sea-deities as sea-coloured, whether blue, grey,
or green. Galatea herself is not depicted as green by either Virgil
(*candidior Cycnis, Ecl.* 7.38) or Ovid (*candidior folio nivei … ligustri,
Met.* 13.789), but she is compared by both poets with young green
leaves.

23 Cf. Sallust *Cat.* 13 and Hor. *Odes* 2.18.17–22 and 3.1.33–7. But
Statius proudly reiterates his patron's domination of nature, *domuit
possessor* (56), and her willing submission, *gaudet humus* (58,
echoing 1.3.56).

24 Another echo of 1.3: cf. *Pierias artes*, 112, with *Pieriosque dies* of
Vopiscus' poetic leisure in 1.3.23.

25 'Live happily … continue thus and never launch your pensioned boat
… learn free of care … go through the years … and precede the
memorials to your long-standing renown.'

26 Statius is recalling the *nigrantem nimbum* promised by Juno in *Aen.*
4.120, and the 'marriage': *pronuba Iuno / dant signum; fulsere ignes
et conscius aether / conubiis, summoque ulularant vertice Nymphae* (167–9).

27 3.1.101: 'You have enclosed your hot nymphs in twinned vaults,'
clausisti calidas gemina testudine Nymphas; cf. 2.2.17–19, 'the
baths steam in twin vaults … and the fresh-water nymph encounters
the bitter sea,' *gemina testudine fumant/ balnea … occurrit dulcis
amaro Nympha mari.*

28 While the reference to the mysterious nocturnal *fistula* shows the
by now usual confusion of Faunus and Fauni with Pan and Panes,
Martial at least is quite fond of Faunus. Cf. 4. 25: in an epicizing

epigram, Sola, the most beautiful of the dryads and nymph of a lake in the Euganean hills, is said to be wedded to Paduan Faunus; in 8.49, celebrating Domitian's Olympian hospitality, Martial talks of the great father reclining at table with the *plebs deorum*, when Faunus was permitted to ask Jove for wine (3–4); besides 9.61, 10.92 calls Martial's holm-oaks the trees of the Fauni.

29 *Comissator* and the verb *comissari* come from Greek *kômazein*, and were introduced in Roman comedy to represent Greek party practices (the verb is not connected with Latin *committere*). For the idea of Bacchus and his retinue carousing unseen by men, compare Lucretius' comments on Italian peasants who imagine Pan and the satyrs, and Pliny *NH* 5.7 on Mount Atlas (in Africa), reported by the locals as flashing with torchlit frolics by night: 'the mountains are filled with the wantonness of Goat-Pans and Satyrs, and noisy with the song of flutes and pipes, and din of tambourines and cymbals,' *Aegipanum Satyrorumque lascivia impleri, tibiarum ac fistulae cantu, tympanorumque et cymbalorum strepitu impleri.* Pliny's record of Greek paintings at Rome shows that there was a genre called *lascivia* featuring Bacchic revels; cf. 35.110: '[Philoxenos] also painted a wanton scene in which three Silenuses are partying,' *pinxit et lasciviam in qua tres Sileni commissantur.* Compare also Nicomachus' 'notorious Maenads with Satyrs creeping up on them,' *nobiles Bacchas obreptantibus Satyris,* and Ariston's 'garlanded Satyr with a cup,' *Satyrus cum scypho coronatus,* in 35.109 and 111.

30 Cf. Nauta 2002, 226–7 and 313 f., and also n35 below.

31 Scholars have made much of this scene's verbal affinities with Alpheus' pursuit of Arethusa (discussed in chap. 4), but various details show that Statius was drawing on Apollo's pursuit of Daphne (*Met.* 1.452–567), Pan's pursuit of Syrinx (1.689–712), Priapus' assault on Lotis (9.346–8), and the more detailed tree-transformations of Dryope (by Lotis, 9.326–93) and Byblis (caused by divine pity, 10.489–502).

32 The tree is not identified as a plane until 2.3.39.

33 Statius surely did not refer to this grassy bank as *nivea*, whether 'snow-white' or as cool/chilly as snow, as Shackleton Bailey suggests, since the poet is about to use the same epithet more conventionally for Pholoë's *niveos ... artus*, in line 32. The text of line 17 is probably corrupt, as Van Dam (1984) suggests.

34 Compare Vessey 1981, 46–52, and the more cautious approach of Billerbeck 1986, 528–36, especially 533–5.

35 See the pioneering studies White 1975, especially 272–5, and Hardie 1983, 66–7 and 216n66. For Junius Blaesus, the wealthy governor of Gaul, who supported Vitellius but was later denounced to him and forced to commit suicide, see Tac. *Hist.* 2.59 and 3.38. But he was not the only contemporary with the cognomen Blaesus: there is a later figure, Velleius Blaesus, in Pliny's correspondence. See Nauta 2002, 313–14.

36 See the plan of the fora in Coleman 1988 and in Shackleton Bailey.

37 Again, see Coleman 1988 and 1999.

38 This is most apparent in poem 3.1, which begins with the designing (117) of Hercules' new temple, then depicts the production of its many building materials (118–38).

39 *Elicere* has a long history, notably from its use in the same enjambed position of the irrigating farmer at *Georg.* 1.109.

40 I am not convinced by Shackleton Bailey's *tepidae* – the word is too undramatic.

41 A note on *fractae* (trans. as 'lamented'): it is not the satyrs' reeds but the plangent note of their lament which calls for this epithet, a common term of rhetoric for unmanly lament or affectation.

42 While Faunus (as an alias of Pan) returns to the background story of book 9, it is more surprising to find Silvanus and Pales, who have no Greek equivalents. They are found only here in the *Thebaid*.

43 This text is now available with the elegant and charming translation of Charles Fantazzi in the complete edition (introduction, text, and translation) of Politian's *Silvae*, vol. 14 of the I Tatti Renaissance Library (Cambridge, MA, 2004).

Bibliography

Abbreviations

CLASSICAL WORKS

AP	*Anthologia Palatina*
Apoll. *Arg.*	Apollonius Rhodius, *Argonautica*
Apollodorus *Bibl.*	*Bibliotheca*
Calp. Sic.	Calpurnius Siculus
Cato *Agr.*	*De Agricultura*
Cic. *Att.*	Cicero, *Letters to Atticus*
– *De Div.*	*De Divinatione*
– *De Or.*	*De Oratore*
– *Fam.*	*Epistulae ad Familiares*
– *Leg.*	*De Legibus*
– *ND*	*De Natura Deorum*
– *Off.*	*De Officiis*
Col.	Columella
Cons.	Pseudo-Ovid, *Consolatio ad Liviam de Morte Drusi*
D.H.	Dionysius of Halicarnassus
Enn. *Ann.*	Ennius, *Annales*
Hom. Hymn Aph.	*Homeric Hymn to Aphrodite*
Hor. *Ep.*	Horace, *Epistles*
– *Sat.*	*Satires*
Lucan *BC*	*Bellum Civile*
Lucr.	Lucretius
Macr. *Sat.*	Macrobius, *Satires*

Ovid *ex Ponto*	*Epistulae ex Ponto*
– *Met.*	*Metamorphoses*
Plautus *Aul.*	*Aulularia*
– *Cist.*	*Cistellaria*
Pliny *NH*	*Historia Naturalis*
Plutarch *Qu.*	*Roman Questions*
Prop.	Propertius
Pseudo-Virgil *Cul.*	*Culex*
Sallust *Cat.*	*Catiline*
Seneca *Ep. Mor.*	*Epistulae Morales*
Suetonius *Gramm.*	*De Grammaticis et Rhetoribus*
Tac. *Ann.*	Tacitus, *Annales*
– *Hist.*	*Historiae*
Theoc. *Epigr.*	Theocritus, *Epigrams*
Tib.	Tibullus
Val. Max.	Valerius Maximus
Varro *LL*	*De Lingua Latina*
– *RR*	*Res Rusticae*
Virgil *Aen.*	*Aeneid*
– *Ecl.*	*Eclogues*
– *Georg.*	*Georgics*

REFERENCE WORKS

AE	*Année Epigraphique*. 1888– . (annual publication of newly discovered inscriptions)
CIL	*Corpus Inscriptionum Latinarum*. Berlin, 1963– .
Enc. Virg.	*Enciclopedia Virgiliana*. Turin, 1984–90.
GL	*Grammatici Latini*. Ed. H. Keil. 8 vols. Hildesheim; repr. 1961.
HRR	*Historicum Romanorum Reliquiae*. Ed. H. Peter. Berlin, 1912.
ILS	*Inscriptiones Latinae Selectae*. 3 vols. Ed. H. Dessau. Berlin, 1892–1926.
Inscr. Ital.	*Inscriptiones Italiae*. Vol. 13.2, *Fasti*. Ed. A. Degrassi. Rome, 1931–2.
LTUR	*Lexicon Topographicum Urbis Romae*. Ed. E. Steinby. Oxford, 1993– .

Kleine-Pauly.	5 vols. 1964–75. (modern concise version of *Pauly RE*; see below)
RE	*Pauly Real Encyclopedia.* Ed. A. Pauly, G. Wissowa, W. Kroll. Real Encyklopädie der Klassichen Alterumtumswissenschaften, 1893– .
RGVV	*Religionsgeschichtliche Versuchen und Vorarbeitungen.* Multiple eds. 1903– .
RKR	*Religion und Kultus des Römer.* By G. Wissowa. Munich, 1912.
RRG	*Römische Religionsgeschichte.* By K. Latte. Munich, 1960.

JOURNALS

AJA	*American Journal of Archaeology*
AJAH	*American Journal of Ancient History*
AJP	*American Journal of Philology*
CA	*Classical Antiquity*
CJ	*Classical Journal*
CP	*Classical Philology*
CQ	*Classical Quarterly*
JRS	*Journal of Roman Studies*
HSCP	*Harvard Studies in Classical Philology*
MD	*Materiali e discussioni per l'analisi dei testi classici*
PBSR	*Papers of the British School at Rome*
PCPS	*Proceedings of the Cambridge Philological Society*
RFIC	*Rivista di filologia e di istruzione classica*
TAPA	*Transactions of the American Philological Association*
ZPE	*Zeitschrift für Papyrologie und Epigraphie*

Principal Editions Cited

Accius, *Oeuvres.* Ed. J. Dangel. Collection Budé. Paris, 2002.
Ennius, *The Annals of Quintus Ennius.* Ed. O. Skutsch. Oxford, 1985.
Festus, Sextus Pompeius, *De significatu verborum.* Ed. W.M. Lindsay. Teubner. Stuttgart, 1913; repr. 1965.
Horace. Ed. F. Klingner. Teubner. Stuttgart, 1970.
– Ed. D.R. Shackleton Bailey. Teubner. Stuttgart, 1995.

– *Odes*, bks 1 and 2. Ed. R.G.M. Nisbet and M. Hubbard. Oxford, 1970.

Martial. Ed. M. Citroni. 2 vols. Biblioteca Universale Rizzoli. Turin, 1996.

Ovid, *Fasti*. Ed. and trans. Sir George Frazer. Loeb Classical Library. Cambridge, MA, 1929.

– Ed. E.H. Alton, D.E.W. Wormell, and E. Courtney. Teubner. Stuttgart, 1988.

– *Metamorfosi*. Vol. 1 (bks 1–2), ed. A. Barchiesi; vol. 2 (bks 3–4), ed. A. Barchiesi and G.P. Rosati; vol. 3 (bks 5–6), ed. G.P. Rosati. Edizione Valla, Mondadori. Turin, 2005. (in process of being published in English by Cambridge University Press)

– *Metamorphoses*. Ed. W.S. Anderson. Bks 6–10, Norman, OK, 1978. Bks 1–5, Norman, OK, 1996.

– Ed. R.J. Tarrant. Oxford Classical Texts. Oxford, 2004.

Propertius. Ed. P. Fedeli. Teubner. Stuttgart, 1984.

– Ed. G. Goold. Loeb Classical Library. Cambridge, MA, 1999.

Statius, *Silvae*. Ed. D.R. Shackleton Bailey. Loeb Classical Library. Cambridge, MA, 2003.

– *Thebaid*. Ed. D.E. Hill. Leiden, 1996.

– Ed. D.R. Shackleton Bailey. 2 vols. Loeb Classical Library. Cambridge, MA, 2003.

Theocritus. Ed. A.S.F. Gow. 2 vols. Cambridge, 1952.

Tibullus, *Elegies*, bk 2. Ed. P. Murgatroyd. Oxford, 1996.

Virgil, *Eclogues*. Ed. W.O. Clausen. Oxford, 1995.

– *Georgics*. Vol. 1 (bks 1–2), vol. 2 (bks 3–4). Ed. R.F. Thomas. Cambridge, 1988.

– Ed. R.A.B. Mynors. Oxford, 1990.

– *Aeneid*, bk 7. Ed. N.M. Horsfall. Brill. Leiden, 2000.

– *Aeneid*, bk 8. Ed. P.T. Eden. Brill. Leiden, 1975.

Alföldi, A. 1960. 'Diana Nemorensis,' *AJA* 64: 137–44. Repr. in his *Early Rome and the Latins* (pp. 37–44). Ann Arbor, 1964.

– 1967. *Les Origines de la République Romaine*. Entretiens de la Fondation Hardt 13 (pp. 223–90). Geneva.

Ampolo, C. 1993. 'Boschi sacri e culti federali: L'esempio di Lazio.' In Cazenove and Scheid 1993 (pp. 171–80).

Audollent, A. 1904. *Defixionum Tabellae quotquot innotuerunt* ... Paris.

Bailey, C.E. 1907. *The Religion of Ancient Rome*. London.
- 1932. *Phases in the Religion of Ancient Rome*. Berkeley, CA.
- 1935. *The Religion of Virgil*. Oxford.
Barchiesi, A. 1989/2000. *Speaking Volumes*. London.
- 1992. *Il poeta e il principe*. Trans. as *The Poet and the Prince* (1997). Berkeley, CA.
Barker, G. 1981. *Landscape and Society: Prehistoric Central Italy*. Cambridge.
Barker, G., J. Lloyd, and D. Webley. 1978. 'A Classical Landscape in Molise.' *PBSR* 46: 35–51.
Billerbeck, M. 1986. 'The Tree of Atedius Melior.' In *Studies in Latin Literature and Roman History, IV*, ed. C. Deroux (pp. 528–36). Brussels.
Bodel, J. 1986/1994. 'Graveyards and Groves.' *AJAH* 9 (for 1986; published in 1994): 1–133.
Bömer, F. 1977. *Ovid: Metamorphoses*. Vol. 4. Heidelberg.
Borgeaud, P. 1988. *The Cult of Pan in Ancient Greece*. Trans. K. Atlass and J. Redfield. Chicago, 1988. Originally pub. as *Recherches sur le dieu Pan*. Geneva, 1979.
Boyd, B.W., ed. 2002. *Brill's Companion to Ovid*. Leiden.
Boyle, A.J. 2003. *Ovid and the Monuments: A Poet's Rome*. Victoria, Australia.
Buchheit, V. 1962. *Studien zum* Corpus Priapeorum. Zetemata 28. Munich.
Burkert, W. 1985. *Greek Religion*. Trans. J. Raffan. Oxford.
Cairns, F. 1983. 'Propertius 1.4, 1.5, and the Gallus of the Monobiblos.' *Papers of the Liverpool Latin Seminar* 4: 61–102.
- 2006a. 'The Nomenclature of the Tiber in Virgil's *Aeneid*.' In *What's in a Name*, ed. J. Booth and R. Maltby (pp. 65–82). Swansea.
- 2006b. 'Propertius and the Origins of Latin Love-Elegy.' In Gunther 2006 (pp. 69–95).
- 2006c. *Sextus Propertius, the Roman Elegist*. Cambridge.
Camps, W.A. 1966. *Propertius. Elegies, Book I*. Cambridge.
Cancik, H. 1965. *Untersuchungen zur Lyrischen Kunst des P. Papinius Statius*. Hildesheim.
Capelli, R. 1999/2001. Report in *National Archaeological Museum of Naples* (pp. 85–8). Naples. (Publication of Museo Nazionale).
Cazenove, O., and J. Scheid. 1993. *Les Bois sacrées*. Naples.

Coarelli, F. 1987. *I santuari del Lazio.* Rome.

– 1993. *Guida archaeologica da Roma.* Turin.

Coleman, K.M. 1988. *Statius,* Silvae IV: *A Commentary.* Oxford.

– 1999. 'Mythological Spokespersons in Statius' *Silvae.*' In *Im Spiegel der Muthos: Bilderwelt und Lebenswelt,* ed. Coleman (pp. 67–80). Wiesbaden.

Connor, W.R. 1988. 'Seized by the Nymphs.' *CA* 7: 155–89.

Courtney, E.J. 1995. *Musa Lapidaria: A Selection of Latin Verse Inscriptions.* Atlanta.

Dorcey, P. 1992. *The Cult of Silvanus: A Study in Roman Folk Religion.* London and New York.

Dumézil, G. 1966/1970. *Archaic Roman Religion.* Vols 1 and 2. Trans. 1970. Chicago.

– 1969. *Idées romaines.* Paris.

Fantazzi, C., ed. and trans. 2004. *Politian:* Silvae. I Tatti Renaissance Library 14. Cambridge, MA.

Fantham, E. 1983. 'Sexual Comedy in Ovid's *Fasti.*' *HSCP* 87: 185–216.

– 1992. 'Ceres, Liber, and Flora: Georgic and Anti-Georgic Elements in Ovid's *Fasti.*' *PCPS* 38: 39–56.

– 1997. 'Images of the City: Propertius' New-Old Rome.' In *The Roman Cultural Revolution,* ed. T. Habinek and A. Schiesaro (pp. 121–35). Cambridge.

– ed. 1998. *Ovid:* Fasti Book 4. Cambridge.

– 2002. 'Ovid's *Fasti*: Politics, History, and Religion.' In Boyd 2002 (pp. 197–233).

Feeney, D. 1998. *Literature and Religion at Rome.* Cambridge.

Forbes Irving, P.C. 1990. *Metamorphosis in Greek Myths.* Oxford.

Fowler, W.W. 1899. *The Roman Festivals of the Period of the Republic.* London.

– 1911. *The Religious Experence of the Roman People.* Oxford.

Fraenkel, E.D.M. 1957. *Horace.* Oxford.

Frayn, J.M. 1979. *Subsistence Farming in Roman Italy.* Liverpool.

– 1984. *Sheep-rearing and the Wool Trade in Italy.* Liverpool.

Fucecchi, M. 2004. *'Nunc teritur nostris area maior equis': Riflessioni sull'intertestualità ovidiana – I Fasti.* Palermo.

Gagné, R. 2006. 'What Is the Pride of Halicarnassus?' *CA* 25.1: 1–33.

Gantz, T. 1993. *Early Greek Myth: A Guide to Literary and Artistic Sources.* 2 vols. Baltimore.

George, E.V. 1974. *Aeneid 8 and the Aitia of Callimachus*. Leiden.

Gleason, K. 1994. '*Porticus Pompeiana*: A New Perspective on the First Public Park of Ancient Rome.' *Journal of Garden History* 14: 13–27.

Goldberg, C. 1992. *Carmina Priapea*. Heidelberg.

Gow, A.S.F., and D.L. Page, eds. 1965. *The Greek Anthology: Hellenistic Epigrams*. 2 vols. Cambridge.

Gransden , K.W. 1976. *Virgil: Aeneid VIII*. Cambridge.

Green, C.M.C. 2007. *Roman Religion and the Cult of Diana at Aricia*. Cambridge.

Green, S.J., ed. 2004. *Ovid*, Fasti I: *A Commentary*. Leiden.

Grimal, P. 1943. *Les Jardins romains*. Paris.

Gunther, H.C., ed. 2006. *Brill's Companion to Propertius*. Leiden.

Habinek, T. 2005. *The World of Roman Song*. Baltimore.

Hardie, A. 1983. *Statius and the Silvae: Poets, Patrons, and Epideixis in the Graeco-Roman World*. Liverpool.

Hardie, P.R. 1991. 'The Janus Episode in Ovid's *Fasti*.' *MD* 26: 47–64.

Herbert-Brown, G. 1992. *Ovid and the* Fasti. Oxford.

– 2002. *Ovid's* Fasti: *Historical Readings at the Bimillenium*. Oxford.

Herter, H. 1932. *De Priapo. RGVV* 23. Giessen.

Hollis, A.C. 1970. *Ovid: Metamorphoses 8*. Oxford.

– 2006. 'Propertius and Hellenistic Poetry.' In Gunther 2006 (pp. 97–126).

Horsfall, N.M. 1989. *Cornelius Nepos: A Selection Including the Lives of Cato and Atticus*. Oxford.

– 1997. 'Criteria for the Dating of Calpurnius Siculus.' *RFIC* 125: 166–96.

Howell, P. 1980. *A Commentary on Book One of the* Epigrams *of Martial*. London.

Hubbard, M. 1974. *Propertius*. London.

Hutchinson, G. 2006. *Propertius:* Elegies, Book IV: *A Commentary*. Cambridge.

Isager, S., and P. Pedersen. 2004. *The Salmakis Inscription and Hellenistic Halicarnassus*. Halicarnassian Studies 4. Odense.

Jenkyns, R. 1998. *Virgil's Experience*. Oxford.

Johns, C. 1986. 'Faunus at Thetford: An Early Latian Deity in Late Roman Britain'. In *Pagan Gods and Shrines of the Roman Empire*, ed. M. Henig and A. King (pp. 93–103). Oxford.

Jones, P. 2005. *Rivers in Roman Literature and Culture*. Lanham, MD.

Kaster, R., ed. 1992. *Suetonius De Grammaticis*. Oxford.

Kuttner, A.L. 1999a. 'Culture and History at Pompey's Museum.' *TAPA* 129: 343–73.

– 1999b. 'Looking Outside Inside: Ancient Roman Garden Rooms.' *Studies in the History of Gardens and Designed Landscape* 1: 7–35.

Labate, M. 2005. 'Tempo del origini e tempo della storia in Ovidio.' In *La Représentation du temps dans la poésie augustéenne*, ed. P. Schwindt (pp. 177–201). Heidelberg.

Larson, J.L. 2001. *Greek Nymphs: Myth, Cult, Lore.* Oxford.

Littlewood, R.J. 2002. '*Imperii pignora certa*: The Role of Numa in Ovid's *Fasti*.' In Herbert-Brown 2002 (pp. 177–98).

– 2006. *A Commentary on Ovid*, Fasti, Book 6. Oxford.

McDonough, C.J. 1997. 'Carna, Proca, and the *Strix* on the *Kalendae Fabariae*.' *TAPA* 127: 315–44.

– 2002. 'Hercules and the Ciminian Lake Legend' *CJ* 98: 9–19.

McKeown, J.C. 1979. 'Augustan Elegy and Mime.' *PCPS* 25: 71–84.

Maltby R. 1991. *Lexicon of Ancient Latin Etymologies.* Liverpool.

Momigliano, A. 1966. *Terzo Contributo alla storia degli studi classici e del mondo antico.* Rome.

Moorton, R. 1988. 'The Genealogy of Latinus in Vergil's Aeneid.' *TAPA* 118: 53–60.

Murgatroyd, P. 2005. *Mythical and Legendary Narratives in Ovid's Fasti.*Leiden.

Murgia, C. 1984. 'Ovid *Met.* 1.544–547 and the Theory of Double Recension.' *CA* 3: 207–35.

Myers, K.S. 1994. '*Ultimus ardor*, Pomona, and Vertumnus in Ovid *Met.* 14.623–771.' *CJ* 89: 225–50.

– 2000. '*Miranda fides*: Poet and Patrons in Paradoxographical Landscape in Statius' *Silvae*.' *MD* 44: 103–38.

– 2005. '*Docta otia*: Garden Ownership and Configurations of Leisure in Statius and Pliny the Younger.' *Arethusa* 38: 103–29.

Nagle, B.R. 2004. *Statius:* Silvae. Bloomington, IN.

Nauta, R. 2002. *Poetry for Patrons: Literary Communication in the Age of Domitian.* Leiden.

Nelis, D. 2001. *Virgil's Aeneid and the Argonautica of Apollonius.* Liverpool.

Newlands, C.E. 2002. *Statius's* Silvae *and the Poetics of Empire.* Cambridge.

Nisbet, R.G.M. 1978. '*Felicitas* at Surrentum.' *JRS* 68: 1–11.

Nock, A.D. 1972. *Essays on Religion and the Ancient World.* Ed. Z. Stewart. Cambridge, MA.

O'Connor, E. 1989. Symbolum salacitatis: *A Study of the God Priapus as a Literary Character.* Studien Zur Klassichen Philologie 40. Frankfurt.

O'Hara, J.J. 1993. *True Names: Vergil and the Alexandrian Tradition of Etymological Wordplay.* Ann Arbor.

– 1996. 'Vergil's Best Reader: Ovidian Commentary on Vergilian Etymological Wordplay.' *CJ* 91: 255–76.

Palmer, R.E.A. 1970. *The Archaic Community of the Romans.* Cambridge.

Parker, H. 1997. *Greek Gods in Italy in Ovid's* Fasti: *A Greater Greece.* Lampeter, UK.

Parker, W.H. 1988. Priapea: *Poems for a Phallic God.* London.

Parry, H. 1964. 'Ovid's *Metamorphoses*: Violence in a Pastoral Landscape.' *TAPA* 95: 268–82.

Potter, T.W. 1979. *The Changing Landscape of South Etruria.* London.

Pouthier, P., and P. Rouillard. 1986. 'Faunus, ou l'iconographie impossible.' In *Iconographie classique et identités régionales*, ed. L. Kahil, C. Augé, and P. Linant de Bellefonds (pp. 105–10). Paris.

Purcell, N. 1995. 'The Roman Villa and the Landscape of Production.' In *Urban Society in Roman Italy*, ed. T. Cornell and K. Lomas (pp. 151–80). Oxford and New York.

– 1996. 'The Roman Garden as a Domestic Building.' In *Roman Domestic Buildings*, ed. I. Barton (chap. 5). Exeter.

Purcell, N., and P. Hordern. 2000. *The Corrupting Sea.* Oxford.

Rackham, H. 1938–52. *Pliny: Natural History.* Vols 1–19, 33–5. Loeb Classical Library. Cambridge, MA.

Radke, G. 1965. *Die Götter Alitaliens.* Münster.

Rehm B. 1932. *Das Geographische Bild des alten Italien in Vergils Aeneis.* Philologus Supplbd. 24.2. Leipzig.

Rice, E.E. 1989. *The Grand Procession of Ptolemy Philadelphus.* Oxford.

Richardson, L., Jr. 1992. *New Topographical Dictionary of Ancient Rome.* Baltimore.

Richlin, A. 1992. *The Garden of Priapus.* 2nd ed. New Haven.

Rieu, E.V., trans. 1946/1961. *Homer: The Odyssey.* Harmondsworth.

– 1950/1968. *Homer: The Iliad.* Harmondsworth.

Rutledge, E.S. 1980. 'Virgil and Ovid on the Tiber.' *CJ* 75: 301–4.

Scheid, J. 1992. 'Myth, Cult, and Reality in Ovid's Fasti.' *PCPS* 38: 118–31.

– 1998/2003. *Introduction to Roman Religion.* Edinburgh. Originally pub. as *La Religion des romains,* Paris, 1998.

Schiebe, M.W. 1986. 'The Saturn of the Aeneid – Tradition or Innovation.' *Vergilius* 32: 43–60.

Schilling, R. 1955. *La Religion romaine de Vénus, du commencement de la république au règne d'Auguste.* Paris.

Schoonhoven, H., ed. 1992. *The Pseudo-Ovidian* Ad Liviam de morte Drusi. Groningen.

Segal, C. 1969. *Landscape in Ovid's Metamorphoses.* Wiesbaden.

Shackleton Bailey, D.R., ed. 2003. *Martial.* Loeb Classical Library. Cambridge, MA.

Sourvinou-Inwood, C. 2004. 'Hermaphroditus and Salmacis.' In Isager and Pedersen 2004 (pp. 59–84).

Thomas, R.F. 1988. 'Tree Violation and Ambivalence in Virgil.' *TAPA* 118: 261–74.

– 1999. *Rereading Virgil's Texts.* Ann Arbor.

Thomas, R., and R. Scodel. 1984. 'Virgil and the Euphrates.' *AJP* 105: 339. Repr. in Thomas 1999 (p. 320).

Trypanis, C.A., trans. 1958. *Callimachus:* Aitia, Iambi, Hecale. Cambridge.

Van Dam, H.-J. 1984. *Statius,* Silvae book 2: *A Commentary.* Leiden.

Vessey, D.W.T.C. 1981. 'Atedius Melior's Tree: Statius *Silvae* 2.3.' *CP* 76: 46–52.

Ward-Perkins, B. 1964. *Landscape and History in Central Italy.* J.L. Myres Lecture. Oxford, 1964.

West, M., ed. 1966. *Hesiod: Theogony.* Oxford.

– 1985. *The Hesiodic Catalogue of Women.* Oxford.

White, P. 1975. 'The Friends of Martial, Statius, and Pliny.' *HSCP* 79: 265–300.

Willenberg, K. 1973. 'Die Priapeen Martials.' *Hermes* 101: 320–49.

Wiseman T.P. 1988/1994. 'Satyrs in Rome.' *JRS* 78 (1988): 1–13. Repr. in *Historiography and Imagination,* ed. Wiseman (pp. 68–85). Exeter.

– 1995a. 'The God of the Lupercal.' *JRS* 85: 1–23.

– 1995b. *Remus.* Cambridge.

– 1998. *Roman Drama and Roman History*. Exeter.
– 2002. 'Ovid and the Stage.' In Herbert-Brown 2002 (pp. 275–99).
– 2004. *The Myths of Rome*. Exeter.

General Index

Index of Principal
Passages Discussed